# Michel Henry's Practical Philosophy

Also Available from Bloomsbury

*Marx: An Introduction*, Michel Henry
*From Communism to Capitalism: Theory of a Catastrophe*, Michel Henry
*The New Phenomenology: A Philosophical Introduction*, J. Aaron Simmons and Bruce Ellis Benson
*Early Phenomenology: Metaphysics, Ethics, and the Philosophy of Religion*, ed. Brian Harding and Michael R. Kelly
*Michel Henry: The Affects of Thought*, ed. Jeffrey Hanson and Michael R. Kelly

# Michel Henry's Practical Philosophy

Edited by
Jeffrey Hanson, Brian Harding,
and Michael R. Kelly

BLOOMSBURY ACADEMIC
LONDON • NEW YORK • OXFORD • NEW DELHI • SYDNEY

BLOOMSBURY ACADEMIC
Bloomsbury Publishing Plc
50 Bedford Square, London, WC1B 3DP, UK
1385 Broadway, New York, NY 10018, USA
29 Earlsfort Terrace, Dublin 2, Ireland

BLOOMSBURY, BLOOMSBURY ACADEMIC and the Diana logo are trademarks
of Bloomsbury Publishing Plc

First published in Great Britain 2022
This paperback edition published 2023

Copyright © Jeffrey Hanson, Brian Harding, Michael R. Kelly, and Contributors 2022

Jeffrey Hanson, Brian Harding, and Michael R. Kelly have asserted their right under the
Copyright, Designs and Patents Act, 1988, to be identified as Editors of this work.

Cover design by Charlotte Daniels
Cover image: Tree of Life © Timothy Neill

All rights reserved. No part of this publication may be reproduced or transmitted in
any form or by any means, electronic or mechanical, including photocopying, recording,
or any information storage or retrieval system, without prior permission in writing from
the publishers.

Bloomsbury Publishing Plc does not have any control over, or responsibility for, any
third-party websites referred to or in this book. All internet addresses given in this
book were correct at the time of going to press. The author and publisher regret any
inconvenience caused if addresses have changed or sites have ceased to exist, but can
accept no responsibility for any such changes.

A catalogue record for this book is available from the British Library.

Library of Congress Cataloging-in-Publication Data
Names: Hanson, Jeffrey, editor. | Harding, Brian, 1933- editor. |
Kelly, Michael R., 1974- editor.
Title: Michel Henry's practical philosophy / edited by Jeffrey Hanson,
Brian Harding, and Michael R. Kelly.
Other titles: Practical philosophy
Description: London ; New York : Bloomsbury Academic, 2022. |
Includes bibliographical references and index.
Identifiers: LCCN 2021030304 (print) | LCCN 2021030305 (ebook) | ISBN 9781350202764
(hb) | ISBN 9781350202771 (epdf) | ISBN 9781350202788 (ebook)
Subjects: LCSH: Henry, Michel, 1922-2002.
Classification: LCC B2430.H454 M56 2022 (print) | LCC B2430.H454 (ebook) |
DDC 194–dc23
LC record available at https://lccn.loc.gov/2021030304
LC ebook record available at https://lccn.loc.gov/2021030305

ISBN: HB: 978-1-3502-0276-4
PB: 978-1-3502-0280-1
ePDF: 978-1-3502-0277-1
eBook: 978-1-3502-0278-8

Typeset by Deanta Global Publishing Services, Chennai, India

To find out more about our authors and books visit www.bloomsbury.com and
sign up for our newsletters.

# Contents

Notes on contributors     vi

1  Introduction     1

Part I  Interpretations

2  From Affect to Action to Interpretation: On Michel Henry's *Theoria* of Immanent Praxis  *F. Seyler*     9
3  Affective Labor and the Henry-Ricoeur Debate over Marx  *S. Davidson*     27
4  Spiritual Life and Cultural Discernment: Renewing Spirituality through Henry  *N. DeRoo*     45
5  Working in the "World of Life": Michel Henry's Philosophy of Subjective Labor  *J. Hanson*     66
6  Freud after Henry  *R. Welten*     88
7  The World or Life's Fragility: A New Critical Reading of Henry's Phenomenology of Life  *P. Lorelle*     110

Part II  Applications

8  The Liberal Subject: The Politics of Life in Michel Henry  *J. Rivera*     125
9  Michel Henry's *Barbarism* and the Practices of Education  *B. Harding*     142
10 Abstract Color and Esthetic Experience: Michel Henry Reading Kandinsky  *I. Podoroga*     159
11 Affectivity and Its Effects: Social Prospects for the Pathetic Community  *J. A. Simmons and M. Wellborn*     180

Index     201

# Contributors

**S. Davidson** is professor of philosophy at West Virginia University. The translator of numerous works by Michel Henry, he edited (w. F. Seyler) *The Michel Henry Reader* (Northwestern UP) five volumes of essays on Paul Ricoeur. He also edits *The Journal of French and Francophone Philosophy*.

**N. DeRoo** is the Canada Research Chair in Phenomenology and Philosophy of Religion at The King's University. He is the author of *Futurity in Phenomenology: Promise and Method in Husserl, Levinas and Derrida* (Fordham UP) and the editor of four volumes on phenomenology and religion.

**J. Hanson** is senior philosophy at the Human Flourishing Program at Harvard's Institute for Quantitative Social Science. He is the editor of *Kierkegaard as Phenomenologist: An Experiment* (Northwester UP) and *Michel Henry: The Affects of Thought* (Bloomsbury). He published *Kierkegaard and the Life of Faith: The Aesthetic, the Ethical and the Religious in "Fear and Trembling"* (Indiana UP) in 2017.

**B. Harding** is professor of philosophy at Texas Woman's University. He is the author of *Not Even a God can Save us Now: Reading Machiavelli after Heidegger* (McGill) and editor (with M. Kelly) of *Early Phenomenology: Metaphysics, Ethics and the Philosophy of Religion* (Bloomsbury).

**M. Kelly** is associate professor of philosophy at the University of San Diego. He is author of *Phenomenology and the Problem of Time* (Palgrave) and editor of *Bergson and Phenomenology* (Palgrave), (with B. Harding) *Early Phenomenology: Metaphysics, Ethics and the Philosophy of Religion* (Bloomsbury) and (with J. Hanson) *Michel Henry: The Affects of Thought*.

**P. Lorelle** is a member of the Institut Supérieur de Philosophie - Fonds Michel Henry at Université Catholique de Louvain. She is the author of *La sensibilisation du sens. De Husserl à la phénoménologie française* (Hermann) and *Le sensible ou l'épreuve de la raison. Une étude phénoménologique* (Mimésis).

**I. Podoroga** is Senior Research Fellow at the Institute of Philosophy of the Russian Academy of Science. She is the author of *Penser en Durée: Bergson au fil de ses images* (L'Age d'homme) and *Le langage des images. Bergson et la question de l'immédiat*.

**J. Rivera** is associate professor of philosophy at Dublin City University. He is the author *The Contemplative Self after Michel Henry: A Phenomenological Theology* (Notre Dame UP), *Political Theology and Pluralism: Renewing Public Dialogue* (Palgrave) and *Phenomenology and the Horizon of Experience: Spiritual Themes in Henry, Marion and Lacoste* (Routledge).

**F. Seyler** is associate professor of philosophy at DePaul University. He is the author of *Barbarie ou culture': L'éthique de l'affectivité dans la phénomenologie de Michel Henry* (Kimé), *Eine Ethik der Affektivität: Die Lebensphänomenologie Michel Henrys* (Alber) and *Fichtes 'Anweisung zum seligen Leben'. Ein Kommentar zur Religionslehre von 1806* (Alber). He is co-editor (with S. Grätzel) *Sein, Existenz, Leben: Michel Henry und Martin Heidegger* (Alber).

**J.A. Simmons** is Professor of Philosophy at Furman University. He is the author of *God and the Other: Ethics and Politics after the Theological Turn* (Indiana) and (with B. Benson) *New Phenomenology: A Philosophical Introduction* (Bloomsbury). He has edited, among other volumes, Phenomenology *for the Twenty-First Century* (Palgrave) and *Re-examining Deconstruction and Determinate Religion: Towards a Religion with Religion* (Duquesne).

**M. Wellborn** a member of the department of philosophy at the University of Oregon. She earned a MA from Fordham University with a thesis on *Excorporation as an Embodied Phenomenological Attitude: Expanding the Concept for Critical Phenomenology*.

# 1

# Introduction

The chapters in this volume concern Michel Henry's practical philosophy. The phrasing of the preceding sentence is purposefully amphibolous and meant to contain at least two distinct ideas. First, the phrasing means that Henry's well-known work in phenomenology has relevance for philosophers not concerned directly or solely with phenomenological method or phenomenological theology. Henry himself has indicated that his phenomenology has practical relevance in his writings on politics and culture, which he based on his phenomenological investigations. Second, this phrasing means that Henry's work in practical philosophy is an essential part of his project, rooted in phenomenology, of returning our attention to the central importance of Life—as opposed to consciousness or being—for understanding the human experience. Indeed, even Henry's most theoretical works can be seen as contributing to a practical philosophy insofar as they attempt to motivate a renewed appreciation of the affective tonalities of Life, an appreciation that, as works like *Barbarism* make clear, inevitably has practical significance.

That Henry's work has a practical significance is not at all a groundbreaking, or even interesting, insight into Henry's thought. But it is one which is sometimes lost in the Anglophone reception of Henry, which has focused mainly on others aspects of his work. While this book is not about the Anglophone reception of Henry per se, it is being published in English; it seems useful, therefore, to pause for a moment to discuss Henry's reception in English. At the very least, it will clarify the remark in this paragraph's opening sentences. Michel Henry's work was first translated into English by Girard Etzkorn in the early 1970s. Etzkorn was perhaps an unexpected translator of Henry, since the bulk of his work before and after has focused on the Franciscan school in medieval scholasticism. But, as Henry notes in his introduction to *Material Phenomenology*, a case could be made that phenomenology is the scholasticism of our times. In any case, Etzkorn published translations of two volumes by Henry: *The Essence of Manifestation* (1973) and

*Philosophy and Phenomenology of the Body* (1975). Despite the enormity of the undertaking, Anglophone phenomenology did not recognize the importance of Etzkorn's achievement immediately; one can only speculate as to why, but it is certainly relevant that both texts were published by Martinus Nijhoff (now Brill) with a high sticker price and as such, had limited circulation outside of highly endowed research libraries. Eight years later, Kathleen McLaughlin published an abridged translation of Henry's book on Marx in 1983, and his *Genealogy of Psychoanalysis* was translated by Douglas Brick in 1993. Some of his essays were also published in translation in the *Graduate Faculty Philosophy Journal* in 1985 ("The Concept of Being as Production") and in 1991 ("On Nietzsche's 'We Good, Beautiful Happy Ones!'"). Despite these efforts and his stay at the University of Washington, Henry's work failed to find the kind of eager reception that other French thinkers found in the United States. Think of the rapid, and roughly contemporaneous, reception of the work of Derrida or Foucault, for example.

Indeed, through the 1970s, 1980s, and well into the late 1990s, even specialists in phenomenology could proceed happily unaware of his work; until recently Henry's thought had little impact on phenomenology, or continental philosophy more generally, in the Anglophone community. The sense that there was a very slow reception of Henry's work is confirmed when one searches for panels devoted to his work at meetings of the Society for Phenomenology and Existential Philosophy (SPEP). The first panel devoted to his work at SPEP was held in 1998—twenty-five years after Etzkorn published his translation of *The Essence of Manifestation*!—with Dan Zahavi, James G. Hart, and Anthony Steinbock presenting on his work. The following year, *Continental Philosophy Review* published a special issue devoted to Henry's thought. The next panel devoted to Henry at SPEP was not until 2007 with Jeffrey Hanson, Antonio Calcagno, and Christina Gschwandtner. The same crew reappeared in 2010 to present on Henry again. In 2012 SPEP again devoted a special session to Henry, with an address by Frédéric Seyler and response by Jeffrey Hanson; by then Henry's work had become much more central to phenomenology as practiced in the Anglophone community. This is why, despite the fact that over three decades had passed since *The Essence of Manifestation* was published in English, and, of course, even longer since Henry began publishing in France, he could be described as a "new phenomenologist." While certainly not "new" *simpliciter*, Henry was new to the vast majority of philosophers working in English.[1]

As one can see, the pace of Henry's reception in Anglophone philosophy began to increase in the late twentieth century and early twenty-first century, and the change came from two places. On the one hand, Dan Zahavi's *Self-Awareness and Alterity* (1999) offered a careful discussion of Henry's theory of subjectivity and made a confrontation with his work essential for philosophers working on these problems. On the other hand, Derrida's later work—beginning, let's say for convenience's sake, with *Adieu: For Emmanuel Levinas*—began to highlight religious themes in his work, which perhaps unintentionally provided a *nihil obstat* for American philosophers wishing to explore similar themes. Jean-Luc Marion's presence in North America at the University of Chicago (starting in 1994) and John Caputo's annual conference on Religion and Post-Modernism at Villanova (running from 1997 until roughly 2002, when it was repackaged and moved to Syracuse University) sparked a new philosophical "scene" in the United States sometimes called "continental philosophy of religion." When Dominique Janicaud intervened against a purported "theological turn" in French philosophy—and fingered Henry as part of the problem—his polemic dovetailed nicely with this scene and was quickly translated into English, with responses from his targets (including Michel Henry) as *Phenomenology and the Theological Turn* (2001). Janicaud's intervention and the subsequent debate had the perhaps unintended consequence of making many previously unaware scholars acquainted with Henry's work and its importance. Prior to then, arguably, the agenda for debate in continental philosophy of religion in the United States was set by Marion, Derrida, and the shadow of Heidegger. While it would be impossible to find data to back this up, one could forgive the strong suspicion that for the many American scholars of a certain generation—that is, those whose intellectual salad days correspond with the late 1990s and early twenty-first century—their first reading of Henry was his essay in the Janicaud book.

A second spring for Henry in English quickly followed; Stanford published Susan Emanuel's *I am the Truth* (2002); Fordham University Press and Bloomsbury both began publishing his major works in translation. Scott Davidson worked indefatigably, translating *Material Phenomenology* (2008), *Seeing the Invisible* (2009), *Barbarism* (2012), and *From Capitalism to Communism* (2012); Christina Gschwandtner translated *Words of Christ* (2012); and Karl Hefty translated *Incarnation* (2015); work continues apace and no doubt by the time this book is published, more of Henry's work will have been translated into English. Special issues of journals were devoted to his work and, as already recounted, sessions at major conferences were organized; edited collections, including Michael R. Kelly and Hanson's *Michel Henry: The Affects of Thought* (2012) were produced. This reception never strayed far from its proximate causes, such that the focus was typically on Henry's articulation of a unique phenomenological method, a theory of subjectivity, or as a contributor to the theological turn. To be sure,

Henry engages with these issues in all his major works, and it is not to the point of this introduction to deny or qualify that in any way. But this emphasis on reading Henry as a theologian or as a speculative phenomenologist can lead to a distortion: Life, the center of Henry's thought, runs the risk of being seen as an *entia rationis*, or less charitably a will-o-the-wisp, rather than, as it really is for Henry, an intimate and intense reality. Life is expressed, Henry argues, in the quotidian tasks of laboring, eating and drinking, and in other practical affairs such as psychoanalysis, education, social, political, and spiritual life, and so on. To the extent that Anglophone scholarship has not paid adequate attention to his practical philosophy, Henry's vision of Life—and therefore his philosophy more generally—is distorted and hobbled. If, as many would argue, Henry's contributions to phenomenology are among the most radical and important in the last generation, then this lacuna is a problem not only for Anglophone students of Henry but also for Anglophone phenomenology more generally. Therefore, our goal in this volume is to widen the aperture of the lenses through which Henry is viewed and pay more attention to the "practical" dimension of his writings—his reflections on economics, politics, culture, and so on. This is not to say that we wish to artificially separate the practical from the theological or speculative elements. Henry is one of Archilochus' hedgehogs; his work is devoted to thinking only one thought and developing all its implications, and it would be misleading to demand radical separation between the theological, speculative, and practical elements of Henry's work.

The volume is divided into two broad sections (Part I and Part II): Interpretations and Applications. The former concerns general interpretations of Henry's practical philosophy, his phenomenological method as it informs and is informed by his practical philosophy, or the interpretation of Henry's relationship with other figures insofar as such engagements bear on issues in practical philosophy. The chapters in Part II analyze how Henry's phenomenology of Life applies to specific issues or philosophical areas. To be sure, the line between the two sections is porous, as would be expected when discussing a hedgehog like Henry. Nevertheless, some organization and division has to be brought to bear, however arbitrary these demarcations may appear.

Part I begins with Frédéric Seyler's "From Affect to Action to Interpretation: On Michel Henry's *Theoria* of Immanent Praxis" (Chapter 2). Seyler develops a careful reading of Henry that demonstrates the continuity between his reflections on phenomenological method, his reading of Marx, and his critique of modern society in *Barbarism* and related works. Developing further Henry's reflections on Marx and his critique of modern society, Scott Davidson's "Affective Labor and the Henry-Ricoeur Debate over Marx" (Chapter 3) examines, comparatively, the evaluations of Marx in the works of Henry and Ricoeur in light of "affective labor"—that is, the requirement that employees provide not only a good or service, but positive feelings as well. While Henry doesn't directly address affective labor in his work, Davidson shows that he provides the resources for a thoughtful and critical analysis of affective labor. Neil DeRoo follows with "Spiritual Life and Cultural Discernment: Renewing Spirituality through Henry" (Chapter 4), which addresses the relevance of Henry's work for spirituality. While the importance of Henry for theology is widely acknowledged, it is less clear how his work applies to the practical living out of theological positions, that is, spirituality; DeRoo's Chapter 4 endeavors to show the applicability of material phenomenology to spiritual life. Henry's analysis of Life, DeRoo argues, is a concrete task of spiritual and cultural discernment, seeking to return our practices to their roots in Life by showing where and how those roots have been cut. Jeffrey Hanson's "Working in the 'World of Life': Michel Henry's Philosophy of Subjective Labor" (Chapter 5) focuses our attention on work and analyzes Henry's philosophy of work; Hanson uses Henry's focus on work to further refine our understanding of Henry's conception of Life and the world. Work is where the immanence of life butts against the difficulty and resistance put up by the world. Ruud Welten's "Freud after Henry" (Chapter 6) closely examines the relationship between Freud (and psychoanalysis more generally) and Henry; more specifically and provocatively, Welten attends to the possibilities for rereading psychoanalytic theory in the light of Henry's work, including especially (but by no means limited to) his *Genealogy of Psychoanalysis*. For Welten, as for Henry, it is not a question of "refuting" Freud, but of radicalizing Freud in light of a phenomenology of Life. Welten endorses psychoanalysis, but a Henrian psychoanalysis, that is, one where Freudian doctrines are deepened and transformed. Finally, Paula Lorelle's contribution, "The World or Life's Fragility: A New Critical Reading of Henry's Phenomenology of Life" (Chapter 7), argues that the sensibility of the world is rooted in the fragility of life, rather than the autonomy of life. Developing hints and suggestions in Henry's writings, Lorelle argues that while self-affection cannot account for the appearance of the world, Life's self-negation, when thought more radically, can provide just such an account.

The chapters in Part II of the book, "Applications," insert Henry's work into other, ongoing areas of philosophical inquiry, showing the wide-ranging relevance of his thought to practical life. The opening chapter in this section, Joseph Rivera's "The Liberal Subject: The Politics of Life in Michel Henry" (Chapter 8), weaves Henry's work into the debate between communitarians and modern liberal democracy; phenomenology and political theory do not make two (to adapt a phrase from Janicaud) since both concern human nature. Rivera argues that despite his criticisms of modern society, Henry's work resists being absorbed into the communitarian critique insofar as he maintains a robust sense of the importance of individual subjectivity. Deftly weaving his reading of Henry with the work of Deneen, Nozick, and Marcuse, Rivera argues that Henry's phenomenology of Life can provide the foundations for the social-democratic project. Following Rivera, Brian Harding's "Michel Henry's *Barbarism* and the Practices of Education" (Chapter 9) focuses on the critique of university life in *Barbarism*, placing Henry's reflections in dialogue with modern educational theorists, especially Paulo Friere. Harding argues that, while stirring, Henry's account is not entirely consistent and needs adjustment both historically and conceptually: the barbarian conquest of the university happened much earlier than Henry thinks it did. In "Abstract Color and Esthetic Experience: Michel Henry reading Kandinsky" (Chapter 10), Ioulia Podoroga expands on Henry's interpretation of Kandinsky and applies it to Russian formalism. She shows both that Henry's phenomenology sheds useful light on these difficult works of art and that these artworks reveal the ineffable nature of Life (thought by some readers of Henry to escape coherent expression). Finally, J. Aaron Simmons and Maia Wellborn's "Affectivity and Its Effects: Social Prospects for the Pathetic Community" (Chapter 11) applies Henry's work to modern cultural and critical theory, in particular the work of Sara Ahmed, and argues that cultural theorists would be well advised to incorporate Henry's work into their analyses, particularly those parts of it that have undergone a self-described "affective turn."

The chapters gathered in this volume represent only the first sustained inquiry into the practical philosophy of Michel Henry in English. And discerning readers will likely (and this is one of our hopes) note lacunae in topics and figures addressed and move to address them. Indeed, this volume should be taken as an opening to contribute to the developing studies of Henry's phenomenology—and the infinite task of phenomenological reflection overall—in all its guises and facets.

# Note

1 See J. Aaron Simmon and Bruce Benson, *The New Phenomenology: A Philosophical Introduction* (London: Bloomsbury, 2013) and the review in *Notre-Dame Philosophical Reviews* by Frédéric Seyler (February 5, 2014): https://ndpr.nd.edu/reviews/the-new-phenomenology-a-philosophical-introduction/ (accessed May 2021).

Part I

# Interpretations

# 2

# From Affect to Action to Interpretation
## On Michel Henry's *Theoria* of Immanent Praxis

F. Seyler

Henry's critique of Husserl's transcendental phenomenology, as well as his substitution of certainty for evidence as the ultimate criterion for truth, lead to a transformation of phenomenological praxis from the practice of the reduction to that of a *counter*-reduction. The latter consists in "bracketing" the visibility proper to intentionality in order to access the self-appearing pertaining to life.[1] From the point of view of material phenomenology, life as appearing cannot be accessed through intentional sight or the visibility of the world, but reveals itself through a phenomenality of its own.[2] This original phenomenality is also thematized by Henry as immanent experience or auto-affection, that is, as transcendental affectivity that is the condition not only of the possibility of particular affects such as fear or joy but also of intentionality itself. Auto-affection is therefore synonymous with the impressional flesh (*chair impressionnelle*) in which intentionality plays, perhaps paradoxically, no part.[3]

More importantly, with regard to the field of practical philosophy in material phenomenology, this radicalized reduction or counter-reduction seems to be necessarily connected to ethics and to ethos. *Ethos* is understood by Henry as original ethics (*éthique originelle*), that is, the "set of continually renewed processes in which life carries out its essence,"[4] but it still has to be distinguished from a discursive-normative ethics that depends on representation. What can thus be termed the ethics of affectivity[5] should be understood as a praxis of self-growth that comports the following aspects. Primarily, the essence of subjectivity is conceived as a dynamic process of life's "arrival into itself" (*parvenir en soi*)—a sort of "effort without effort"[6] through which life's original experience of itself (*épreuve de soi*) is constituted in the form of a primary pathos. "Pathos" refers here to both an element of passivity and the inescapable self-adherence that characterizes life. Life's continuous self-experience is "the irrepressible experience of what grows by itself and deals with itself up to excess,"[7] that is, the emergence of a force that, through need and desire, requires action. This is precisely the point where Henry distinguishes between, on the one hand, cultural practices that are capable of using that force insofar as they rely on and deploy subjective potentialities, and, on the other hand, "practices of barbarism" in which life flees from its own excess by anesthetizing this same force. Thus, for Henry, action and activity are in general brought back to the immanent level of transcendental life. This move can already be observed in Henry's interpretation of Marx, as well as in his critique of the concept of action in Hegel and Feuerbach. Scrutinizing Henry's reading of Marx is thus the first step that must be undertaken in order to understand the concept of immanent action.

## Henry's Reading of Marx: A Prelude to the Concept of Action in Material Phenomenology

While emphasizing that Hegel's oeuvre celebrates the primacy of praxis over *theoria*, and affirms the necessity of action and considers action to be constitutive of being, Henry must logically conclude that the opposition between Hegel and Marx can reside only in the way each conceives of "the being of action," as well as being itself.[8] In other words, what separates Marx from Hegel cannot be the emphasis on action as such but, rather, the ontological status ascribed to it. For Henry, this difference lies in the opposition between subjectivity and objectivity. Whereas for Hegel the being of action is objective in virtue of its essence, it belongs for Marx to the order of subjective-immanent praxis, an order that as such escapes objectification. Hegel's insistence on the movement of self-objectification and its products is, presumably, what Marx has in mind when he affirms in his first thesis on Feuerbach that idealism does not take into account actual sensuous activity (*sinnliche Tätigkeit*) as such[9]—for instance, the one operating in work. If we follow Henry's assessment, it is Marx who will be focusing on the individual and subjective dimension of action, a dimension that Hegel sacrifices in favor of objective universality.[10]

As a reader of Feuerbach, however, Marx still interprets human sensuous activity as productive activity, thus as the production of something that is accessible to sense perception and is, as such, objective. This can be seen, for instance, in the third Manuscript from 1844 in which Marx writes that the human is a "physical being" (*gegenständliches Wesen*) that must express its life through the transformation of "real physical things" (*wirkliche sinnliche Gegenstände*).[11] Here, it becomes clear that, by critiquing Hegel through Feuerbach, Marx is actually in close proximity to an Hegelian position: when Marx claims that Hegel reduces sensuous action or activity to the empty form of self-objectification and thus forgets to account for its real aspect, it now seems that it is Marx himself who is defining human activity through this very form of objectification.[12] A closer look at the concept of sensuous activity reveals that it contains a reference to that of a produced objectivity, and that it is, therefore, inaccurate to describe the phenomenologically real content of action that material phenomenology seeks to highlight. In short, the concept of "sensuous activity" has to be abandoned since it shares with the concept of sensible intuition the same reference to objectivity and externality that is unable to account for the subjective essence of action. In order to provide such an account it is necessary to put objectivity and objectification out of play.

But then how should we conceive of such a *purely* subjective praxis? This question, which arises in the course of his Marx reading, provides Henry with the opportunity to develop a material (or "hyletic") phenomenology of action:

> Let us imagine a runner on the track of a stadium. As an object for intuition, as an empirical, objective, sensuous and natural phenomenon his action is perceptible to everyone. The spectators, however, are only looking at him, they do not engage in any action themselves. Thus, it is not the empirical intuition of this action, its objective appearance that can define it or constitute its reality. The reality of the action of running resides in the subjectivity of the runner, in the lived experience that is given to him only and that constitutes him as an individual, as this individual in the process of running, as this "specific" (*déterminé*) individual, to speak with Marx. *This is what the decisive affirmation of the first thesis means when it claims that praxis is subjective.*[13]

Since sensibility always refers to an object, it can define action only as objective. When we say that an action is real insofar as it refers to an objective "state of affairs" which we can observe and perceive—in other words, an action accessible to intuition—we are limiting ourselves to the third-person perspective of a spectator, for example, we see the runner and claim that the action is real because we perceive it as unfolding in front of us. Our perception, however, is only possible inasmuch as

> that which is represented, that which one is able to see being done and happening, is done and happens elsewhere, namely in the subjectivity of the one who is really performing the action (*agir réellement*). Without such reference

to an individual subjectivity actually engaged in action (*subjectivité agissante*), there is no action, but only a process in the third person, the wind moving the leaves on a tree, the water falling in a cascade.[14]

Access to the reality of action is therefore given by means of a rupture from externality. In this sense, also, there is no such thing as a "real objective action" but only a real action that is, in addition, objectively represented. The real character of the action is independent of objectivity and representation insofar as the "essence and possibility [of action], as well as its being effectively actualized, lies in the immanence of radical subjectivity alone."[15]

Moreover, the life of radical subjectivity is nothing but the continuous self-experience of a life that adheres to itself and to its activity, an activity that is "blind as well as opaque, and that accomplishes itself without any possibility for a contemplative gaze to free it from the weight that it is for itself."[16] Subjectivity, after having been thematized through this reading of Marx, is now conceived in a radically phenomenological fashion as immanence and auto-affection. Such a radicalization of subjectivity makes action—as far as it is real, that is, immanent—completely independent from intuition. It is in this sense that action can be described as both "blind and opaque."

Since subjective praxis is conceived of as immanent and, hence, as both ontologically and phenomenologically heterogeneous to representation, it is easy to see why praxis is deemed to remain opaque and impenetrable to the objectification inherent to (the) intentional gaze. From this standpoint, representations are unable to seize the reality of action and one must, somewhat paradoxically, admit that the spectator cannot actually see the action, that is, the running, if by action we understand the immanent effort accomplished by the athlete. The only thing the spectator perceives is the action's indication in the realm of externality. The fact that such an indication remains dubitable (with regard to the reality of that of which it is indicative) supports the thesis of the heterogeneity of the two modes of appearing: obviously, as a spectator, I can only speculate about what the runner actually experiences. This also means that indication is, as such, unable to surpass its own essence in order to signify that which is absent from the third-person perspective, that is, that which can only be lived through (or *éprouvé*) in the "first person." As Henry writes in the same passage:

> Since praxis is subjective, theory, which is always the theory of an object, cannot access the reality of praxis, of that which it is in and for itself, namely its subjectivity. It can only represent praxis in such a way that these representations

remain necessarily external to the real being of praxis as well as to the effective character of doing (*faire*).[17]

That praxis is not only opaque but "blind" also seems, at first glance, much more problematic, since such a thesis can only signify that sensuous intuition plays, strictly speaking, no part in the reality of action. But how could a real action be independent from any intentional act directed toward world-contents if we grant that even the simplest of actions is possible only to the extent that we perceive our environment, the instrument that we use, or, in the aforementioned example, the running track that we are facing?

Henry's claim that "in intuition we do not act and, conversely, in action we do not intuit"[18] appears at first to be problematic in light of his own concept of praxis since, if being is founded in praxis, this should also be the case for intuition. Intuition, of course, does not engender beings, but it is nonetheless a form of activity, namely the activity of intuiting as it is exemplified in perception. Thus, like running, perceiving belongs to subjective praxis as well, and this is also why, in the intentional act of perceiving, there is something that escapes perception, namely the very action of perception as it unfolds in immanent auto-affection. More generally, this means that the distinction between *theoria* and praxis is subverted by the praxis inherent to *theoria*, which is, indeed, fully real in the sense of Henry's phenomenology as can also be seen in his discussion concerning scientific activity.

Henry seems to have taken into account this kind of objection when he writes in "The Concept of Being as Production":

> Does not such a statement provoke objections? One will object that praxis takes place in the world, that, from the world, it borrows its raw materials, its instruments, its laws, the forms it creates and thereby its ends. But the discourse emitting these objections is precisely the discourse of theory, the one receiving its formulation in Aristotle's theory of the four causes, the one pretending to reduce praxis to *theoria* and to a mode of realization belonging to *theoria*. We shall, on the contrary, accomplish the overturning announced by the theses on Feuerbach: at issue, then, is no longer the beholding of praxis in the gaze of theory, but the founding of theory in praxis. To found theory in praxis is to recognize firstly that theory itself, gazing, is not autonomous and that the very modalities of its realization, its categories, are prescribed to it by praxis [. . .] To found theory in praxis is to affirm, secondly, that the content of seeing, the object of theory, is no more explained by theory than its forms. Intuition does not explain sensible reality. I quote Marx: "Even when the sensuous world is reduced to a minimum, to a stick, as with Saint Bruno, it presupposes the action of producing this stick."

> [. . .] One will object: is it not precisely intuition which yields this activity and the entirety of social phenomena? At this point, we must reaffirm our thesis: intuition is incapable of giving us the real being of action, it can only represent it, reproduce it in the way a photograph represents a real event.[19]

But, again, if theory is founded in praxis, then how can they still be opposed and radically separated? In other words: How can that which is founded in praxis be considered as radically alien to it? Must not, on the contrary, theoretical activity be seen as what it is, namely as a mode of fulfillment of subjectivity, in which case claims regarding the "structural ontological heterogeneity of action and of intuition" and the "reciprocal exclusion of the essence of *theoria* and of the essence of praxis" seem to become even more problematic?[20]

## Real Action, Object-Relation, and Their Interpretation

A closer look at the argument shows that it is the object-relation that Henry aims at excluding from the domain of real action when he writes that

> to Feuerbach's objective intuition [. . .] *objective in the sense in which Man is an objective being insofar as he has outside himself an object with which he is in relation through intuition, in the sense in which "objective" signifies the relation to the object—is radically opposed subjective action, in which subjectivity designates, on the contrary, the absence of this relation, of any intentional relation in general, precisely, the absence and the exclusion from it of intuition.*[21]

Thus, the affirmation of the foundation of objectivity in praxis, on the one hand, and that of the exclusion of the object-relation from immanent-subjective action, on the other hand, allows for only one conclusion: that which is real in the object-relation is not itself objective, that is, not of the order of a relating-to-an-object, but lies "where the potentialities of organic subjectivity suddenly actualize themselves, where the fundamental 'I can' that constitutes our existence unfolds itself, where we are one with ourselves in the originary unity which is bereft of transcendence and of world"[22]—that is, it lies in immanent auto-affection. According to Henry's solution to the problem, seeing is, indeed, a real and subjective action in the sense of material phenomenology insofar as it actualizes certain potentialities inherent to the "I can." The object-relation—as an intentional act directed toward that which is placed in front of us—is, however, external to the real components of action despite the fact that the intentional act in question is founded on those real components. For example, seeing a desk is an act that possesses reality for the perceiver to the extent that the perceiver affects himself as seeing that desk, whereas the object given through perception is merely a sensuous-intentional, and thus irreal, component of the act as a whole. Following this line of thinking, complex actions find their reality in the continuous auto-affective experience that accompanies our every move and without which there would be no desk or other objects, as there would be no representations of them. In short, to say that the reality of action resides in the "abyssal night of absolute subjectivity"[23] and "remains with the internal experience of itself"[24] seems to indicate that the intentional (and sensuous) act of being directed toward an object is not part of this reality.

Assuming that this is the concept of subjectivity that Marx is already promoting while distancing himself from both Feuerbach and Hegel, it would explain why terminology referring to "sensuous activity" is progressively replaced in *The German Ideology* by that of "acting individuals" (*handelnde Individuen*), "living and active individuals" (*lebendige und tätige Individuen*), and it would explain why, in Marx, "'Individual' replaces 'Man' at the same time that action is substituted for intuition."[25] Given this, at least two sorts of questions arise. First, what is the relation of real action to ends and norms, as well as to ethics, if action is to be considered independently of any object-relation? And second, how are the irreal, that is, the objective and intentional, components of action to be assessed?

With regard to the first question, the exclusion of the object-relation from the reality of action also affects the "relation to" the world as the horizon of intentional acts. From the point of view of the phenomenology of life, the world itself cannot be the milieu in which the real causes of actions, as well as their ends, are to be found. According to the thesis of the ontological and phenomenological primacy of immanent subjectivity, determinations such as "causes" and "ends" (assuming such concepts can be transposed to the sphere of immanence) must be found in the sphere of immanence itself since, as Henry writes,

> we always follow paths that are already laid out. Those are not only the paths laid out by human beings before us. The paths which we tread are outlined within us. They are the paths of our body and those paths do not lead astray. They delineate the field of our possibilities and assign its destiny to our life. The whole of social activity, which seems to take place outside us, in reality finds in us and in our subjectivity [. . .] its rootedness, its reality, its predetermination, and its laws.[26]

Work, for example, is understood by Henry as an expression of organic subjectivity and an actualization of its "structures." This, in turn, leads to a renewed assessment concerning ethical norms. Norms and ends still belong to the ethical dimension of action, but they cannot determine life from a standpoint that would be external to life, that is, they must be engendered by life itself in order to be able to "determine" it:

> If one defines ethics as a relation of action to ends, norms, or values, one has already abandoned the site in which it stands, that is, life itself. In life, there are neither goals nor ends, because the relation to them as an intentional relation does not exist in what does not have in itself any ek-stasis [. . .]. In truth, if ends and norms can be prescribed to life—ends and norms make up the entirety of what might be called theoretical or normative ethics—these ends, norms, or values can only come from life itself. Through their help, life seeks to represent what it wants. But such a representation is only a chance occurrence, marking a pause or hesitation in action. It unfolds in the immediacy of its essential spontaneity, without objective possibilities rising before it and taken into the framework of a world. (B 96)

The formation of ethical norms is conceived of here as a product of subjective life, a form of self-objectification and self-affirmation through axiological discourse. Compared to the sphere of immanence from which they derive, however, such objectifications remain secondary in the sense that, as intentionally seized norms, values, or ends, they do not appear immanently. On the contrary, they must be seen as engendered by immanent auto-affection though they stand out as objects of intentionality.

This is certainly consistent with Henry's phenomenology of life, which places immanent auto-affection at the foundation of appearing while radically separating auto-affection from intentional givenness, but it nonetheless raises further questions. If, for instance, life knows "at each instant what must be done and what is suited to it," (B 96) how are we to account for hesitation, and what would such hesitation mean in the realm of action?

As far as the irreal components of action are concerned—that is, the intentional object-relations accompanying action—they are, as we recall, to be distinguished from the reality of action characterized as both "opaque" (for the intentional gaze, including that of the person executing the action) and "blind" (as devoid of intentional or intuitive elements). Applied to the action of running, Henry's aforementioned example in *Marx*, this seems to mean that partial acts like those of *looking* at the running track, *observing* competitors, *judging* the situation, and so on, have to be considered as irreal components of the overall action simply because they are intentional acts. But are these partial acts themselves not both real and subjective, since, although intentional, they are also *necessarily* affective (made of immanently given impressions), that is, they are possible only to the extent that they are founded in the reality of auto-affection? Furthermore, must not these partial acts be *included* in the total act (e.g., of running), insofar as the total action is *necessarily* composed of at least some of them (i.e., the action of running *also* consists of the partial actions of "looking at," "observing," "judging," etc.)? From the point of view of Henry's phenomenology of life, the only consistent position, it seems, is again to distinguish real and irreal components within the total act while maintaining that the latter are founded on the former. It is the same ipseity that accomplishes all the partial intentional acts, yet their reality does not lie *in that which is* seen, observed, judged, and so on, but *in the immanent experience* of seeing, observing, and judging. Intentional acts do possess reality, but this reality is independent of the intentional object; it stems only from the immanent foundation of these acts in life as auto-affection. Thus, indeed, the reality of action is, in Henry's sense, not tied in any way to its actual unfolding in the world.

Which brings us to a decisive point: when we consider actions as they unfold in the world, we must therefore distinguish, on the one hand, between impressions and their immanent experience, and, on the other hand, their "interpretation" in thought and intentionality. If, for instance, it appears to me that I am running, such appearing is both certain *and* dubitable. As self-experience (*épreuve de soi*), it is absolutely real and indubitable, whereas the action's "interpretation" consists of a (dubitable) thematization of these impressions in the realm of representation—for example, when I *think/believe* that I am actually running on this track, in this stadium, and so on.[27] Such "interpretations" or "translations" are not identical with a living certitude, and therefore they do not keep its indubitable character, although they transpose affective givenness into the realm of intentional thought. In a sense, and because of the eidetic difference between the two modes of appearing that are affectivity and intentionality, thought *must* fail to provide an adequate translation of affect: it can, at best, be a copy or representation of life, but never life itself, which is why it is never adequate. Moreover, Henry's position with regard to the fundamentally dubitable character of the intentional object and its worldly horizon may now be seen to account for the problem of hesitation mentioned earlier: to the extent that ethics and ethos are not purely immanent and affective, they require an *orientation* in the world through thought. If, therefore, life "always knows what must be done and what is suited to it," it may nonetheless very well become hesitant as to how such knowledge is to be applied to that which is intentionally given.

## The Relation to Others as Immanent Praxis: The Invisible Community in Life

Henry's substitution of life as immanent auto-affection for that which appears within the horizon of the world must in addition and, as it were, "naturally" lead to the idea that the experience of the other is, at its core, equally affective and invisible. However, one may ask in what sense there is a specific experience of the other that is distinguishable from other forms of *épreuve* or experience, and how it is possible for the other to be part of an experience that is, ultimately and as the concept of auto-affection stresses, always the experience of a self. Or, if the other does not have to *become* a part of that experience, one may ask why the self is always already in an affective community with the other.

The invisibility of the community of the living (*communauté des vivants*), which includes each ipseity, mine as well that of the other, follows directly from the principle of life as invisible auto-affection since it is life that constitutes the essence of this community: Life characterizes not only the members of the community (*les vivants*) but also that which they are sharing (*la vie*) as well as the non-ekstatic milieu and mode of givenness through which they access what is common. It is therefore not the world that is communal in the most original sense, but the way we are given to ourselves, that is, "the internal experience of itself that belongs to everything that is alive and that is alive through this experience and through it alone." (MP 120, translation modified). As such, the experience of itself that characterizes life is invisible, a trait that is transposed to the community and relations with others:

> Inasmuch as life is immediately auto-affected without the separation of any distance, outside of representation and the world [. . .], then everything that has to do with the community, its members and their relations, is from the outset taken outside of the world, even though the world would seem to be the place in which human beings are together. Must we then say that, in spite of all appearances, every community is invisible? Let us take this risk. (MP 123–4)

The experience of the other as mediated through intentionality is possible only to the extent that the other is perceived *as* an other, but this is precisely what "never really happens in the original experiences that we have of others, as long as we are really with them" (MP 127). The ego—mine as well as that of the other—is affected by the irreality pertaining to representation as soon as it is reduced to an intentional correlate and thus its noematic sense. The experienced ego is, at the level of perception, rather more of a "quasi-ego" than a real ego, a "quasi-other" rather than a real other, inasmuch as the affective relation is replaced by its representation. What are, then, the original experiences of the other in which subjectivity is affected without the other or the transcendent ego being thematized as such? In a sense, each experience of the other is originally affective, that is, its phenomenological matter is always an affect. This must be the case if we admit with Henry that every experience is necessarily and continually affective. It further means that the immanent process, here that of experiencing the other, is not brought to an end when the other is thematized and given through intentionality as an other. Rather, it is a constantly present and active process that underlies intentional sense-formation. There are, however, cases through which this affective principle underlying the relation to the other can be demonstrated more easily. For Henry, the first relations between a newborn and its mother are such experiences "at the limit" because they do not comport a perceptive differentiation of self and other, but are, on the contrary, marked by a subjectivity that is "driven back to itself" (*acculée à soi*) (MP 127). Further examples given by Henry include hypnosis and psychoanalytical transference.

With regard to the phenomenon of transference, it is worth recalling that it takes place in a setting that does not allow the analysand to see the analyst, and this setting is usually seen as a *conditio* sine qua non for psychoanalytical practice. Transference, in turn, is possible only as a repetition of affect: "Life is repetition inasmuch as it does not occur in a world. In the absence of every act of putting at a distance and in the impossibility of introducing a distance between itself, life is forever what it is" (MP 129, translation modified). Driven back to itself, life is caught in the repetition of an obstinate *Agieren* (MP 129). Having arrived at a point where it has become unbearable to itself, it attempts to change itself as drive—that is, as force and affect, as desire and need. That which repeats itself through transference is thus essentially affect, "consciousness in itself, which, unlike every represented being, cannot cease to be present, such is the affect, about which Freud says that it is never unconscious" (MP 129–30).

Each community—not only those that are artificially created through a psychoanalytical setting—is therefore deeply marked by its affective or "drive" character. From this standpoint, the relation with the other is real only in virtue of the affect that it triggers, and it is real only to the extent that it brings immanent and affective forces into movement. The requirement for such a relation is not that the other be represented as other, but the possibility of a change in affect within the shared realm of auto-affection. If the origin of community is not situated in the world but in life, it follows that such a community exists, as it were, "prior" to the world, that it is "a priori" (MP 131). In Henry, Life, as absolute, that is, as surpassing the singular living being, is this *a priori* and acosmic community of the living in which the relation to others "takes place." Paradoxically, perhaps, absolute life is not strictly speaking the other for the singular living being. As Henry writes, this

> is the mystery of life: the living being is coextensive with all of the life within it, everything within it is its own life. The living being is not founded on itself, it has its basis (*Fond*) which is life. This basis, however, is not different from itself; it is the auto-affection in which it auto-affects itself and thus with which it is identical. (MP 132, translation modified)[28]

But, here, also, there is a need for interpretation (in the sense described earlier), a point that remains unacknowledged in Henry's analyses. This seems obvious if we recall the example of psychoanalytical transference. Interpretation, understood as intentional orientation toward that which is external to pure affect, is here unavoidable, not mainly because the psychoanalytical setting sooner or later leads to the task of interpreting associative material (a hermeneutical task that Henry rejects as a mere playing with representations), but because speech is the *necessary mediation* through which transference is engendered. If, with regard to Henry's two other examples, such orientation is admittedly absent in the early stages of infancy, as well as in hypnosis (thus conveying the idea of an original layer of pure affectivity persisting in all relations), it is undeniably present in *most* types of relations to others. Here also, it seems that the conclusions drawn with regard to action in general apply to the problem of intersubjectivity. With regard to the other, life may know "what must be done and what is suited to it," and yet it will also hesitate as to what must be done *in the world*, with *this* other, and so on. It will hesitate as to the sense to be given to this relation. It will require orientation through a process of self-representation and self-objectification that is intentional by nature.

From the point of view of immanent praxis, Henry's approach to community as an *a priori* community in absolute life suggests further implications regarding societal organization. For instance, societal functions and roles can now be conceived of as a superficial layer covering a deeper communal layer. A community or subgroup cannot be thought of only in reference to the functionality of observable behavior since the acceptance of social roles engages the individual and the group at a prefunctional and affective level. This means, more generally, that cooperative action in the world at the same time engages a common being-in-life that is thus being put at stake.[29] By the same token, it means that societal norms have to take into account the invisible and affective foundation of communal life.

In accordance with the thesis of the duality of appearing, the experience of the other comports the same dual nature. Yet, the requirements of this experience, like those of praxis in general, lead to the necessity (and difficulty) of articulating both affectivity and intentionality. This is also demonstrated by Henry's reference to the concept of mediation.

## The Mediations of Praxis

As the actualization of a subjective potentiality, each form of praxis unfolds in immanence. Yet, the immanence of praxis does not preclude the importance of "objective" conditions for its deployment. Such conditions can be found in the environment and include, more specifically, the various aspects of societal organization. Several passages from *Barbarism* suggest that these conditions must be taken into account as necessary mediations for praxis despite their apparent belonging to the realm of externality. As Henry writes:

> Imagine a world where there are no longer any churches or temples, where even the most modest and utilitarian edifice is no longer topped by a pediment or flanked or preceded by a colonnade (as in Ephesus). Imagine a world where the organization of work is no longer rooted in organic subjectivity, where work is no longer the actualization of one's powers through the immanent play of their inner disposition, their coming to themselves and thus the "liberation of their energy." Then, instead of this feeling of liberation, a profound malaise comes to affect existence and numb it. (B 103).

The status of such conditions appears, however, to be problematic. If they are considered to be purely "objective circumstances," then it is difficult to see how such external circumstances could have any impact on subjectivity. In addition, their objective-noematic character makes them irreal. If, on the contrary, they are seen as an integral part of subjective life—as Henry's analyses concerning Marx suggest to a certain extent—their real character is secured; but it is then hard to see why they would still have to be considered as "conditions," that is, as facts that are imposed on individual life such that, at least in part, they provide a general "framework" or environment that determines individual life. With regard to the inheritance of societal structures—a question that relates immediately to that of worldly environment—Henry emphasizes that such an inheritance is not simply passive. Instead, "every generation finds itself in the same situation as all the others, and so does every individual: *each is the creator of social relations to the very extent to which he suffers them, to the extent to which he performs the activity that is his own.*"[30] This means that societal structures and traditions are real only to the extent that they are "incorporated" into immanence, an incorporation that is achieved through subjective activity. This does not completely solve the problem, however, since making such "subjectification" of social determinations does not in itself clarify the origin of these determinations. Even if it is granted that there is no hetero-affection without auto-affection, that is, no transcendence without its incorporation into immanence, one still has to admit that societal determinations are essentially alien to the individual insofar as it is forced merely to reproduce them.

In his Marxian critique of economy, Henry considers alienation to be real precisely when such a forced reproduction happens in the workplace. The worker experiences the work as determined from the outside to the extent that it does not correspond to his subjective potentialities, or to the movement through which life would deploy such potentialities, were it not coerced by external determinations.[31] The debate between Henry and Ricœur further illustrates this issue. For Henry, socioeconomical structures are able to determine the *reality* of individual existence because it is individual existence that gives these structures their reality. They are thus "inseparable from our being."[32] Against what could be seen as a reduction of objectivity to subjectivity, Ricœur holds that subjectivity is, on the contrary, *originally determined* by objectivity, which means that the individual is constituted through determinations that are not produced by it.[33] Whereas for Henry the question is to know how the individual can experience the conditions that it produces as an "external destiny" (*destin extérieur*), Ricœur argues that, far from producing these conditions, the individual only produces within them.

On the one hand, it seems undeniable that societal determinations can determine individual existence only under the condition that they are not entirely alien to it, that is, if they do not remain purely external to subjective life. This is to say that objective determinations remain powerless if they are not individually enacted. But, on the other hand, it seems equally undeniable to note that such enactment *re*produces, rather than actually producing societal determinations. The concept of mediation, which Henry mentions but does not elaborate, puts this debate a step further. The experience of an activity as "external destiny" must be connected to Henry's idea of alienation as intrasubjective, that is, as immanent conflict between accidental and essential determinations of subjectivity. Obviously, mediations of praxis can vary and carry with them variations on a strictly immanent level, as shown for instance in the analysis of the division of labor that Henry makes in the context of his interpretation of Marx.[34] The factory is thus a mediation that conditions subjective praxis; it allows for certain actions while making others impossible. This illustrates how subjective differences in praxis are, in fact, determined by mediations that are not themselves products of the individual on which they are imposed.

Moreover, the concept of mediation is useful with regard to social praxis. From Henry's standpoint, praxis is essentially individual and intrinsically subjective; therefore "collective" or "social" praxis can refer only to the interaction and to the resulting sum of the praxis carried out by singular individuals. Such social praxis can be apprehended only from an external point of view, namely that of representation. The externality of social praxis and of its products ceases, however, once such products are considered as mediations for *individual* praxis. Our societal world is the result of social praxis, but this world provides—very much like the factory in Marx—the "framework" in which subjective praxis will have to unfold. This is the reason why, within Henry's strict meaning of "reality," the world of mediations must be fully real. The building of a city, for example, is obviously a collective achievement. Considered as a whole, the city is a representation and, as such, irreal. And, yet, it is still a "place," that is, a mediation for individual life and action in the sense of subjective immanence.[35] In analogy to the incorporation of the earth and the instrument into the subjective body,[36] mediations are incorporated into subjective praxis and can be said to be real only to the extent that they are experienced in the immgediacy of immanent pathos:

> There is indeed an objectification, namely that of the world that presents itself as empirical individuals and actions, whose connections form what we call social praxis and that thus appears as an objective process. But this objectification is only a re-presentation: That which appears in its light is never the reality of life as lived through and internally experienced in the immediacy of its radical subjectivity. It is not the real work, not the active and suffering bodies that appear there, but only their outward appearance, their representation precisely, something that stands in lieu of them, an indication or a trace of them.[37]

*Barbarism*, therefore, does not originate in the fact that there are mediations for praxis—how could this not be the case?—but, rather, lies in the tendency to consider objectifications as ultimately real, thus obscuring their transcendental origin. Yet, as the need for orientation in the world is a need for the living being, objectifications are necessary to such a life that is not purely acosmic, but that is also an *existence*. To existence, the perhaps endless and repetitive task of interpretation remains assigned. While existence remains grounded in absolute transcendental life, the always provisional answers to its desire are communal, aesthetic, and intellectual.

*Frédéric Seyler*
*DePaul University*

## Notes

1. See for instance: "Descartes's Counter-Reduction," in Michel Henry, *Incarnation*. Engl. trans. K. Hefty. Evanston: 2015, 103–5.
2. Michel Henry, "Phénoménologie non-intentionnelle: une tâche de la phénoménologie à venir," originally published in *L'intentionnalité en question. Entre phénoménologie et sciences cognitives*, ed. D. Janicaud (Paris: Vrin 1995), 383–97. Reprint in Michel Henry, *Phénoménologie de la vie*. Vol. I (Paris: PUF, 2004), 105–22, here page 115.
3. Ibid., 117. See also: Michel Henry, *Material Phenomenology*. Engl. trans. S. Davidson (New York: Fordham University Press, 2008), 7–42.
4. Michel Henry, *Barbarism*. Engl. trans. S. Davidson (London and New York: Continuum, 2012), 97.
5. See Frédéric Seyler, *Barbarie ou culture. L'éthique de l'affectivité dans la phénoménologie de Michel Henry* (Paris: Kimé, 2010) and more recently: "The Ethics of Affectivity and the Problem of Personhood: An Overview," *Analecta Hermeneutica*, 8 (2016): 218–34.
6. Henry, *Barbarism*, 98.
7. Ibid., 100.
8. Michel Henry, *Marx. Tome I: Une philosophie de la réalité* (Paris: Gallimard, 1976), 333. Engl. trans. by K. McLaughlin, *Marx* (Bloomington: Indiana University Press, 1983), 148: "If Hegel and Marx both conceive of being, in an original manner, as production and action, can the opposition of the second to the first signify anything other than an opposition in the way of conceiving of the being of action, than a radical and final opposition in the way of conceiving of being itself?."
9. K. Marx and F. Engels, *Werke. Vol. 3: 1845–1846* (Berlin: Dietz, 1969), 533.
10. For a detailed account on this point, see Henry, *Marx*, 327 sq. / 146 sq. (for the Engl. trans.)
11. K. Marx and F. Engels, *Werke. Vol. 40: Schriften und Briefe 1837–1844* (Berlin: Dietz, 1985), 578.
12. Henry, *Marx*, 346/ (page not translated for the Engl. edition).

13 Ibid., 353 (Translation original).
14 Ibid., 348 (Translation original).
15 Ibid., 348.
16 Ibid.
17 Ibid., 353.
18 Michel Henry, "Le concept de l'être comme production," *Revue philosophique de Louvain* 73 (1975): 79–107. Engl. trans. by P. Adler in *Graduate Faculty Philosophy Journal*, 10, no. 2 (1985): 3–28, reprint in S. Davidson and F. Seyler, *The Michel Henry Reader* (Evanston: Northwestern University Press, 2019), 143–67, here 158.
19 Henry, *Marx*, 161–2.
20 Ibid., 324/143.
21 Ibid.
22 Henry, "Le concept de l'être comme production," 160.
23 Ibid.
24 Ibid.
25 Henry, *Marx*, 349 (Translation original).
26 Henry, "Le concept de l'être comme production," 162.
27 Unsurprisingly, this is directly opposed to Merleau-Ponty's position in the *Phenomenology of Perception* for which perceiving (an ashtray, for example), in the real sense of perceiving, is the same as to be assured that there is an ashtray.
28 This concept of life as absolute announces Henry's analyses in *I am the Truth* (1990).
29 This point has been made clear by R. Gély, *Rôles, action sociale et vie subjective. Recherches à partir de la phénoménologie de Michel Henry* (Brussels: P.I.E Peter Lang, 2007). A presentation in English can be found in R. Gély, "Towards a Radical Phenomenology of Social Life: Reflections from the Work of Michel Henry," in *Michel Henry: The Affects of Thought*, eds. J. Hanson and M. R. Kelly (New York and London: Continuum, 2012), 154–77.
30 Henry, *Marx*, 252/108. In a different context, this point seems also to be made by Gadamer with regard to tradition: "Even the most genuine and pure tradition does not persist because of the inertia of what once existed. It needs to be affirmed, embraced, cultivated. It is, essentially, préservation, and it is active in all historical change" (H.-G. Gadamer, *Truth and Method* (London: Sheed & Ward, 1989, 277).
31 This raises the following question: if that which is objective becomes real only through subjectification, how are we to distinguish between that which is accidental—a given set of societal determinations—and that which belongs to the essence of subjectivity, namely the spontaneous movement of life as oscillating between needs and satisfaction of needs? And would such differentiation still be in accordance with Marx' position which claims that one individual's development is conditioned by the development of all others (Marx and Engels, *Werke*. Vol. 3, 423)?

32  Michel Henry, "La rationalité selon Marx," in *Rationality Today*, ed. T. Geraets (Ottawa: Ottawa University Press, 1979), 116–29. Reprint in Michel Henry, *Phénoménologie de la vie*. Vol. III (Paris: PUF, 2004), 77–104, here 101.
33  Henry, "La rationalité selon Marx," 101.
34  See Henry, *Marx*, 255–79/109–17.
35  To stay with the example of urban planning, the difference between a place surrounded by public parks or one surrounded by highways is on this account both real and subjective.
36  See Henry's concept of bodily-ownness in *Barbarism*, 50–2.
37  Michel Henry, "La vie et la république," *Enseignement philosophique* 3 (1989): 148–60. Reprint in Henry, *Phénoménologie de la vie*. Vol. III, 147–66, here 152 (Translation original).

# 3

# Affective Labor and the Henry-Ricoeur Debate over Marx

## S. Davidson

For Karl Marx, the prototype of work is the manufacture of goods that occurred within the context of a nineteenth-century industrialized factory. But much of today's work has moved outside the confines of the factory and is no longer defined primarily by the production of material goods. As Hardt and Negri observe, contemporary work has shifted toward the production of immaterial goods, or, what is often called the service economy.[1] In her sociological study of work in the service sector, Arlie Russell Hochschild observes that service employment—such as the work performed by the nanny, the nurse, the teacher, or the flight attendant—has increasingly become a matter of dedicating one's own energies to the social transmission of immaterial goods in the form of feelings.[2] Consequently, service sector workers are expected to act out a role: the display of a warm smile, the enthusiastic recitation of a company script, the carrying out of an empathetic conversation, and so on. In playing this role, they are expected to either evoke or suppress their own feelings in order to display a feeling and produce a corresponding feeling in customers. Flight attendants, for instance, might be expected to manage fear on the airplane during turbulence by suppressing their own feelings of fear, displaying poise, and calming the fears of passengers. Throughout the service sector, work comes to be centered on an interpersonal performance that involves the production or manipulation of affects.[3]

In his article "In Defense of Soviet Waiters," Peter Frase contrasts the contemporary form of affective labor with the often-maligned service economy that prevailed in the former Soviet Union, most notoriously, the dismissive attitudes of restaurant waiters of the time.[4] There are many humorous stories of the rude behavior of Soviet waiters who often imposed long delays in order to discipline customers who happened to displease them. Clearly, one contributing factor to this difference is that Soviet workers, unlike their American counterparts, were guaranteed jobs. So the fear that motivates fake smiles in workers today was inoperative in the Soviet Union. With the collapse of the Soviet Union, Western employers discovered a workforce that had not yet been enculturated in the concept of customer service. Along these lines, a business school professor recounts the experience of opening the first Russian McDonald's and the challenges of instilling a customer-focused workplace: After several days of training about customer service at McDonald's, a young Soviet teenager asked the McDonald's trainer a very serious question: "Why do we have to be so nice to the customers? After all, we have the hamburgers, and they don't!" This response pinpoints the source of the difference between fake American smiles and authentic Soviet rudeness: whereas the Soviet system required customers to make workers feel good, the affective labor of customer service calls for workers to make customers feel good.

A more extreme example of the commodification of affective labor can be found in the treatment of employees at the British restaurant chain Pret a Manger.[5] Above all else, their workers aren't supposed to be unhappy. They are recruited and selected precisely for their positive personality in the first place. Among the desired traits of a Pret employee is someone who can "work at pace," "create a sense of fun," and be "genuinely friendly." Co-workers also evaluate other employees' job performance in terms of their ability to display these desired characteristics in the workplace. And this affective display has to be real: managers believe that authenticity matters, because customers can tell if someone is faking it. The job of a Pret employee, accordingly, requires not simply the actual transmission of affect but also that the employee actually feels this positive affect in carrying out his/her work.

These examples highlight the extent to which affective labor has become a highly valued commodity in today's economy and has come to define the successful performance of one's job. But if there is a good deal of money to be made from "affective labor," this chapter poses the question "what are the costs of this 'forced happiness'?" By examining the psychic toll and emotional strain resulting from affective labor,[6] the primary focus will involve the expectation placed on workers not simply *to conceal* their own unhappiness but also *to be authentic* in their transmission of positive affect. *Being* happy in carrying out one's job comes to be a measure of job performance. But does this expectation go too far? Does the commodification of affective labor signify an alienation from one's own affective life? Does it ultimately alienate workers from their own alienation by forcing them to renounce even their own feelings of alienation?

In pursuit of these questions, the starting point for this chapter will be to analyze the commodification of affect from an Henryan perspective. Even though this topic is not taken up directly by Henry, his work is well suited for an analysis of affective labor. The topic of affectivity itself is central to his phenomenology of life in general, and the affective dimension of labor is emphasized in particular by his interpretation of Marx. Accordingly, the Henryan analysis of affective labor will begin with a review of his reading of the Marxian critique of the commodification of labor. Wage labor, according to Henry, is not simply alienating due to insufficient compensation for work; more profoundly, it produces alienation on an ontological level: an alienation from one's own being. To be precise, it seeks to replace the affective experience of labor—"living labor"—with an entirely different type of reality: the wage paid to the worker. From this vantage point, Henry's critique of wage labor can be extended seamlessly to the commodification of affective labor. The commodification of affective labor, likewise, produces an ontological alienation, albeit in a manner that is perhaps even more extreme and insidious. It seizes hold of and lays claim to one's own affective life and turns it into a commodity for the benefit and consumption of others.

Yet, Henry's reading of Marx is not without its critics. Shortly after the publication of Henry's book *Marx*, Paul Ricoeur published an important review essay which identifies a blending of Marx's voice with Henry's own philosophy. This results in a subjective interpretation of Marx that minimizes the various ways in which living individuals are receptive to involuntary circumstances. Even if Ricoeur does not address affective labor explicitly either, his critique of Henry can also be extended to this topic and help us to evaluate the extent to which the affective life of the individual comes under the influence of external factors like education, socialization, and training. From the Ricoeurian perspective, it becomes plausible to say that one's own affective life emerges in response to the external world as much as it comes from within oneself. By acknowledging the significance of these external influences, the Ricoeurian reading of Marx opens up the possibility for a different interpretation of affective labor according to which external influences over affects are not inherently exploitative or alienating. Indeed, external factors can also help individuals to calibrate an appropriate balance between themselves and the circumstances of life with others. In so doing, they open up the possibility for social coordination through which the individual is guided to respond appropriately to life circumstances and a life with others. The pursuit of the Henry-Ricoeur debate over Marx, accordingly, brings into view an important conflict of interpretations with regard to affective labor.

## Henry's Marx

Henry's careful two-volume study *Marx* sets out to provide both an interpretation and a surpassing of Marx's thought.[7] In this sense, his book is not simply an account of "what Marx meant"; it also serves as a gateway to Henry's own philosophy of life.[8] This explains why Ricoeur is not mistaken in identifying "two voices" in Henry's book, a point which Henry himself willingly concedes.[9] Indeed, it is possible to say the same thing about each of Henry's studies of individual thinkers, whether it is Descartes, Freud, Husserl, or even Kandinsky. In each case, Henry offers an interpretation of the thinker that likewise serves as a point of entry into his own phenomenology of life. But if Henry's reading of Marx is not innocent, the simultaneous presence of these two voices is what accounts for the originality of Henry's reading as well as its possible interpretive violence against Marx.[10]

With this context in mind, Henry asserts that the primary aim of his book is to restore "the voice of Marx" against Marxism, which he defines as "the interrelated set of misinterpretations that have been given concerning Marx."[11] In his view, Marxism commits the mistake of standing Marx's thought on its head. The fundamental flaw of Marxism is that it has been constructed out of secondary notions—such as the concepts of productive forces, social classes, and so on—that are actually rooted in more fundamental concepts whose reality is either ignored or denied by Marxism.[12] The Marxist emphasis on abstract, secondary notions thus misses what is truly fundamental for Marx: the concrete reality of the living individual. And this oversight might also explain the failure of regimes that have been constructed on the basis of Marxism: they have promoted abstract notions that turn against and destroy the living individuals who are the genuine basis of society. In order to restore the true voice of Marx, it is therefore necessary to perform a sort of *epoche* of the Marxist legacy of misinterpretation and return to the philosophy of living reality that emerges in the writings of the young Marx. Accordingly, the first volume of Henry's work focuses on Marx's theory of reality developed prior to *Capital*, whereas the second volume utilizes these founding concepts to reconstitute the philosophical meaning of the economy. This way of organizing Marx's thought provides a direct counter to Marxist readings that dismiss Marx's early writings and see *Capital* as the true culmination of Marx's thought.

Henry contends that Marx's great discovery is the development of a new philosophical conception of the human being. Before Marx, Western philosophy promotes an abstract conception that defines humanity in terms of its intellectual activity; the human being is thus defined in terms of thought or the activity of representation. Marx's account of praxis marks an unprecedented development of a radical and radically new sense of subjectivity.[13] In Marx's own words, "it is not consciousness that determines life, but life that determines consciousness."[14] Marx defines the human being primarily in terms of its practical activities and ability. To be clear, the point is not that life provides the content or the material for conscious representations. Instead, to say that life "determines consciousness" means that the reality of living individuals is the ground, the origin, of consciousness. Henry writes:

> This reality is what Marx calls "praxis," "subjective" praxis in 1845—"non-organic subjectivity," 'the subjective force of labor,' 'the force of labor,' 'subjective labor,' 'living labor,' "the living present," "the body of the worker," etc. in the manuscripts and so-called economic texts which compose the essence of the prior work. In the context of the analyses in which they are inscribed, these expressions disclose an essential connection: *Force = Subjectivity = Life*. The fact that subjectivity is life challenges the classical concept of subjectivity which identifies it with "consciousness" in the sense of a "consciousness of something," a consciousness of the object, of a representation.[15]

According to Henry, then, Marx's philosophical discovery of the living individual as the original ground of representation shapes the whole trajectory of his thought. It entails that the living individual and its praxis is the first and necessary premise for any understanding of society, history, and economics whatsoever.[16]

Henry sheds additional light on the meaning of praxis through a distinction between two basic aspects of human action: inner and outer. The outer aspect of praxis could be described as the "what" of the action; in other words, it refers to what is done, the *pragma*. Consider the activity of moving some object from one place to another. Defined in terms of what is done, this action can be represented as an object, and as a result of this objectification, it can be observed, measured, and quantified. This would allow for a determination of where it was moved, how far it was moved, how fast it was moved, and so on. But this representation of the movement of the object does not exhaust the scope of its meaning, insofar as every action is also accompanied by an inner aspect that excludes any external measure or objectification. The inner aspect of action, in the words of Pierre Adler, is neither consciousness nor matter, but living bodily activity.[17] In describing praxis as a living bodily activity, the Henryan account identifies praxis with the subjective experience of the one who performs an action:

> Praxis designates the internal structure of action as it excludes from itself the objectification process, all distancing, all transcendence in general. What is held to be real, consequently, will be whatever excludes from itself this distancing, whatever is subjective in a radically immanent sense, whatever experiences itself immediately without being able to separate itself from itself, to take the slightest distance with regard to itself, in short, whatever cannot be represented or understood in any way at all. What is real, therefore, is need, hunger, suffering, labor too—everything that consists in this inner and insurmountable experience of the self. To the radical immanence of this subjectivity, which now constitutes reality for him, Marx gave the name appropriate to it: life.[18]

The internal aspect of praxis is revealed by the agent's auto-affective experience of its own activity. In the process of moving an object, for instance, I am not only aware of the object that is moved. I am also conscious of my own movement itself, of making the effort to move the object, and of this effort being easy or difficult, and so on. This internal aspect of action is self-revelatory: I know it simply by doing and feeling it. And to the extent that this living reality of praxis is disclosed in the affective experience of one's own living activity, Henry is able to read Marx's work as an anticipation of his own phenomenology of life, which likewise discloses the auto-affective dimension of subjective experience.

This distinction between the outer and inner aspects of praxis, according to Henry, serves as the basis for Marx's critique of wage labor. The outer dimension of labor—the work done—can be measured objectively in terms of the time spent or the amount of work completed. This external representation of labor becomes the basis for the determination of the wage, which is based on the amount of time spent laboring or the amount of work accomplished. But, as Henry goes on to show, wage labor is not alienating due to the fact that one's work is underpaid or undervalued. If that were the case, alienation could be overcome by an increase in wages, a change in a job description, or by some other form of recognition. Instead, the alienation resulting from wage labor is ontological, because it tries to impose something that can be exchanged—money—on to something that fundamentally cannot be exchanged—real labor.[19] For this reason, alienation is "the fundamental concept of the economy" and the underlying principle behind what Henry calls "the transcendental genesis of the economy" (ibid.). How exactly is this the case? Again, economic value—measured in terms of money—provides an external measure of a living labor. In wage labor, this external equivalent—the wage—takes the place of the inner essence of labor as living work. But these two realities are not interchangeable, because they are wholly different from one another. The wage, as an external reality, forever remains different from the inner essence of praxis, understood in terms of the living experience of labor. This inner aspect of praxis is the basis for the genuine determination of the value of labor: it allows specific tasks to be qualified as hard or easy, skilled or unskilled. Wage labor is thus inherently alienating, because it inserts an unbridgeable divide between the worker's own determination of labor's value and its cash value which is determined without reference to the living experience of labor.[20]

To the extent that Henry's analysis of the commodification of labor applies to all forms of wage labor in general, it can be extended to the commodification of affective labor. But the Henryan account suggests that the rise of affective labor turns out to be an even more extreme encroachment on the inner life than wage labor.

A first degree of alienation might be exemplified by the gap between the public display of affects and the actual affective life that it conceals. The fake smile of the worker, for example, displays a certain disposition—a positive attitude toward customers—that is required but not actually felt. This type of alienation is associated with playing a role, putting on a display, that is not an authentic self-expression. But the commodification of affective labor takes this form of alienation to a further extreme. This alienation to the second degree is illustrated by the earlier example of the Pret a Manger employee, who is expected not only to behave in a certain way or to act out a specific role but also to feel this affect genuinely.[21] In such cases, one's own affective experience is expected to fuse with a pre-scripted external semblance of it. The worker is supposed to be genuine and thus to conjure up the desired affect: not simply to display the smile but to be happy genuinely, not simply to display interest but to be interested genuinely, etc. The employee's genuine affect is then commodified as a product that is transmitted and sold to another for the sake of profit. What makes this form of commodification so insidious is that it seeks to take hold of what is most intimately one's own—the inner, affective experience of one's own labor—and then it delivers this inner life as a commodity to be sold by the employer to the customer.

The Henryan analysis distills the profound level of alienation produced by the commodification of affect. It signifies an ontological form of alienation that is even more extreme than that of wage labor, because it encroaches on the authenticity of one's own affective life. In stark contrast with the unskilled labor that dehumanizes by calling for too little of oneself, it might be said that affective labor dehumanizes by requiring too much of the self.[22]

In spite of the clarity and precision of the Henryan analysis, there are several different lines of criticism that deserve some consideration. In the first place, some critics might doubt whether the commodification of affective labor is intrinsically alienating.[23] From their point of view, it might be the case that non-alienating forms of affective labor are also possible, given that many people do voluntarily engage in activities of care and find such activities to be deeply fulfilling. Such individuals might welcome the fact that their positive disposition and interest in displaying concern for others is now a valued asset and not simply taken for granted. The commodification of affect would not be alienating to them, because the transmission of positive affect is an authentic form of self-expression for them and suited to who they are. Additionally, some other critics might question the broader account of affectivity on which the Henryan critique of affective labor is based, specifically, the sharp division that is established between the inner and the outer aspects of praxis.[24] They would call into question whether the living individual is, indeed, the source of its own subjective affective experiences, given that rival theories of affectivity consider affective life to be produced, to varying degrees, through social interaction. The affective life of the individual, accordingly, is not simply a self-contained reality; it is shaped by the emotional atmosphere or climate of the individual's surrounding environment. A pathway for both of these two criticisms, as it turns out, is opened up by Ricoeur's critique of the Henryan reading of Marx.

## Ricoeur's Review of Henry's Marx

Henry summed up the key elements of his Marx book in a presentation entitled "La Rationalité selon Marx," to which a panel that comprised Ricoeur, Mikkel Dufrenne, and R. P. Dubarle offered their responses.[25] In the exchange following Henry's presentation, an interesting dispute between Henry and Ricoeur comes to the surface.[26] While Ricoeur expresses his immense esteem for Henry's accomplishment, he nonetheless accuses Henry's reading of Marx of committing an interpretive violence. To be precise, he contends that the book steers Marx's thought toward Henry's own philosophy, which was articulated in his earlier work. This is the source of the sharp wedge that Henry drives between a praxis that is rooted wholly in the subjective experience of one's own body and an economic realm that is entirely objective. Henry goes too far, according to Ricoeur, by advancing the claim that one side of this division—namely, the subjective dimension of praxis—is the ultimate foundation for all of Marx's thought. As a result of this one-sided emphasis, Ricoeur believes that the involuntary influence on praxis—which situates action in a set of unchosen circumstances [*Umstände*]—is unduly diminished by Henry's reading. As an alternative, Ricoeur proposes that for Marx praxis fundamentally involves an interaction between the subject and the world, where the "acting individual is put into situations that it did not posit."[27] In response to this objection, Henry acknowledges that Ricoeur is touching on something "absolutely fundamental";[28] he observes that, in *The German Ideology*, Marx says that living individuals act and also create the circumstances in which they act.[29] For Henry, the social and economic conditions are nothing other than the products of living individuals. Consequently, they can be traced back ultimately to "*a single origin, a single creative principle* [naturans] *that produces the conditions of production, classes and ideas.*"[30]

This brief exchange, in my opinion, involves much more than a mere technical dispute over the proper interpretation of Marx; it touches on a fundamental question concerning the nature of human action. This question is at once methodological and epistemological: Can praxis be understood directly in terms of subjective lived experience alone, without passing through the filter of ideology? Or does praxis always require the mediation through some form of ideology and through the other involuntary circumstances in which one lives and acts? Whereas Henry's reading of Marx traces all action and all circumstances back to their subjective origin in living individuals, the Ricoeurian critique will emphasize the role of involuntary circumstances in shaping the lives of living individuals. For Ricoeur, to act in circumstances implies that all subjective action occurs in response to a prior unchosen situation that is biological, historical, linguistic, and so on. After developing this contrast between their respective readings of Marx, we will then be prepared to locate these differences in relation to the interpretation of affective labor.

Following their brief exchange, Ricoeur went on to develop his remarks in a lengthy book review of *Marx* that was published in 1978 in the journal *Esprit*.[31] Ricoeur's review again raises the central question of whether one hears more of Henry's own voice than Marx's in this book. As we have seen, Henry finds a deep affinity between his own philosophy of life and Marx's philosophy of praxis, insofar as the essence of praxis is identified with its inner aspect as an affective experience of living activity.[32] To be sure, Ricoeur agrees with Henry that the acting individual is the fundamental reality for Marx, but he suggests that there may be a greater distance between Marx's own understanding of practical activity and the suffering of life's pathos than Henry suggests.[33] In tracing the full meaning of praxis back to this single origin in the individual, Ricoeur suggests that Henry "introduces, in his encounter with practical reality in Marx, a philosophy of the pathos of reality, which perhaps secretly differs from it."[34]

In contrast with Henry's emphasis on the subjective aspect of praxis, Ricoeur asserts that "life cannot be radically immanent to itself and be human."[35] This is why, for Marx, praxis can never be purely subjective but, instead, is both determining and determined. Instead of defining praxis either in wholly subjective terms and economy in wholly objective terms, Ricoeur proposes that what matters is *"the acting individual entering into determinations that it has not posited"* (Vol 3.: 101). By defining the fundamental situation of praxis in these terms, Ricoeur's reading will highlight two keywords in Marx—*Voraussetzung* (presupposition) and *Umstände* (circumstance)—that lend greater weight to the influence of nonvoluntary conditions on praxis. Praxis thereby comes to signify a way of responding to a given set of circumstances, such that "the great discovery of Marx here is of the individual under definite conditions."[36]

In his book review, Ricoeur unpacks a variety of ways in which this notion of the individual acting in circumstances challenges the Henryan reading of Marx. Instead of repeating all the details of Ricoeur's book review, I will focus primarily on its final section which is entitled "The Central Equation." This section concerns the role of ideology, which is described in mostly negative terms by Marx as well as Henry. The central equation mentioned in this section heading is the following: reality = praxis; irreality = ideology.[37] Accordingly, ideology would have a distorting function. It refers to the realm of conscious representations that stand in opposition to the realm of real life. The symbolic order of society, as Marx understands it, is the product of the underlying class divisions of a given society; the ideology of a given society is the expression of the interests of its ruling class. The conceptual alternative to ideology for the early Marx, Ricoeur says, "is not science but reality, reality as praxis."[38] The counterweight to ideological distortion is thus a kind of realism of life, a materiality of praxis.[39]

This division between ideological representation and life is heightened by the Henryan interpretation of Marx, which treats praxis as "entirely enclosed in itself, entirely subjective, coinciding with its deeds and exhausting itself in them, it is only what it does; the pathos of its own effort circumscribes the insurmountable limits of its individuality and confers a radical ontological meaning to it."[40] In contrast with the symbolic representations of consciousness, the living reality of praxis is posited as an entirely nonsymbolic and nonideological reality. But, according to Ricoeur, this makes Henry's analysis vulnerable to concerns relating to how any supposedly irreal theory—including his own—could ever grasp the nonrepresentational and nonconceptual reality of praxis. This leads him to wonder: "What is the status of the theory of ideology in a philosophy for which theory is powerless and life alone is operative?."[41]

Here Ricoeur touches on a fundamental problem resulting from Henry's introduction of a sharp contrast between praxis as reality and ideology as irreality. The main concern is whether it would, indeed, be possible to provide a nonsymbolic or nonideological account of the reality of praxis. If, as Henry suggests, this symbolic order is not consubstantial with human action, then why would it ever be added to praxis in the first place? Although one can speak legitimately about the need to remove ideological distortions of reality, it is quite another issue to argue in favor of the elimination of ideology—understood as the symbolic order—altogether. Indeed, Ricoeur does not believe that it is possible to imagine any "modality of action that would not be articulated originally by rules, norms, models or symbols."[42]

In support of the view that there is no nonideological access to praxis, Ricoeur borrows what is known as "Mannheim's paradox." This paradox raises the question of whether it is possible to escape ideology and arrive at an unfiltered view of reality. Even if one is carrying out a critique of ideology as Marx does, Mannheim's paradox suggests that one can do so only from some point of view, that is, from the perspective of some ideology or another. Thus Marx's critique of ideology, like any other attempted critique, is itself developed from the perspective of an ideology. Ricoeur writes:

> The objections that one can make against every genealogy of true thinking on the basis of life seems . . . to be addressed equally to the Marx of *German Ideology* and to Michel Henry. These objections concern, ultimately, the possibility of defining praxis itself before or without a symbolic space in which it might be articulated. In short, can one distinguish between individuals "such as they can appear in their own representation or in that of the other" and individuals "such as they are really, that is to say acting and materially producing"?[43]

In addressing this paradox, Ricoeur emphasizes the following point: instead of setting ideology and praxis in opposition with one another, what is "most basic is an inner *connection* between the two terms."[44] In this respect, Ricoeur abandons the view that one can attain an immediate, nonlinguistic, nonsymbolic meaning of praxis and replaces it with a symbolically mediated conception of praxis. Here Ricoeur draws from the work of the anthropologist Clifford Geertz who, along with others, suggests that symbolic systems are inextricable from human action.

From such a perspective, praxis is always filtered through representation in terms of some kind of symbolic structure.[45]

At the core of Ricoeur's reading of Marx, then, is the question of whether it is possible to speak of ideology without reducing it to a purely negative or distorting function. In his later lectures on Marx in *Ideology and Utopia*, Ricoeur seeks to identify a positive function of ideology that links it to praxis in a nondistorting manner. This leads him to the question of "whether there could be a language of real life which would be the first ideology, the most simple ideology."[46] Ricoeur finds that a "language of real life" is fundamental to Marx's analysis:

> The production of ideas, of conceptions, of consciousness, is at first directly interwoven with the material activity and the material intercourse of men, the language of real life. Conceiving, thinking, the mental intercourse of men at this stage still appear as the direct efflux of their material behavior. The same applies to mental production as expressed in the language of the politics, laws, morality, religion, metaphysics, etc., of a people.[47]

This language of real life in Marx opens the possibility for overcoming the sharp opposition between representation and reality, between ideology and the real, that characterized the Henryan account of praxis. The language of real life reveals a nondistorting function of ideology, a "symbolic structure of action that is absolutely primitive and ineluctable."[48] It establishes the key point that our ideas, our conscious representations, are not simply imposed onto praxis and real life. Instead, the language of real life roots praxis in the symbolic dimension from the outset; it is the true expression of living reality itself, emerging from itself and by itself.

Following from the identification of the "language of real life" with the positive function of ideology, there is an unsuspected opportunity for a rapprochement between the seemingly opposed positions of Henry and Ricoeur. But this would be possible only if Henry gives up the two assumptions that were mentioned earlier: that affective life is freed from external influence and that external influences are inherently alienating. The language of life, as Ricoeur develops it, opens up an integrative function in constituting social reality. Without this symbolic expression of life, human action would be unintelligible to others. In its positive role, ideology allows human actions to be situated within a social context and a symbolic order that makes their actions intelligible for other members of society. It is only on the basis of this primary function of the language of life that it can then become meaningful to speak about the distortive function of ideology.

## An Analysis of Affective Labor

To conclude, I want to unfold the implications of the Henry-Ricoeur debate for an evaluation of the commodification of affective labor. In today's workforce, we have observed that employees are expected increasingly not simply to produce goods or services but to also transmit a particular type of affect in so doing: in short, loving the job becomes a part of the job. The Henryan analysis of praxis, as we have seen, locates the value of labor in a prior self-relation, an affective pathos of one's own labor; the reality of living work is separate from the external realm, which measures the value of work in terms of the wage. From this perspective, the commodification of affective labor is perceived as a heightened form of expropriation in which one's very own affective life is appropriated by others (both employers and customers). Echoing this encroachment of capitalism on all facets of life, Hardt and Negri observe that contemporary capitalism ensures that it is "no longer possible to identify a sign, a subject, a value, or a practice that is 'outside.'"[49] The result of the commodification of affect, for Henry, is an ontological alienation in which the affective life of the self is externalized into its false equivalent: a commodity to be exchanged. The Henryan analysis, in my opinion, provides a clear insight into the threat to the inner life posed by this new stage of capitalism.

At the same time, Henry's critics make a compelling case that the affective realm cannot be understood apart from the circumstances of the social world, including its ideology. Affective life, they assert, does not belong only to oneself or originate solely from oneself; it is the product of social processes and influences. In support of this contention, the training and enculturation of Pret a Manger employees is a good example of the social influence over the individual's affective life. These workplace interventions imply that one does not simply have a positive disposition or a particular form of affective life exclusively one's own; instead, one adopts a positive attitude or develops a positive personality through a process of training and the establishment of a workplace culture. While Henry's account offers an important word of caution regarding the potentially coercive and manipulative strategies of such programs, it is an overstatement to claim that these influences are always or necessarily alienating.

This highlights a problematic feature of Henry's account of affective life: the assumption that the influences of others and of ideology are intrinsically alienating. It is quite undeniable that there are countless ways in which others can and do influence one's own affective life in a positive manner. To deny this fact would not only be to deny that we can learn from other people how to respond to circumstances differently or how to find greater meaning and satisfaction in life. Correlatively, it would also be to deny that one's own affective responses can be in error or in need of improvement. Consider, for example, the performance of basic life tasks such as caring for a house or caring for children. These tasks are not intrinsically alienating, nor do they necessarily become alienating when they are commodified. If I do experience these forms of affective labor as alienating, it could very well be the case that I am wrong to judge them that way. My negative assessment might be guided by false assumptions about gender roles or about what a person like me is supposed to be doing.[50] These assumptions may prevent me from seeing the fact that the performance of these tasks is a matter of doing my fair share or that I am not above this type of work. So while it is true that ideology may dupe me into settling for an unfair or unjust reality in which my affective life is commodified, it is equally possible that ideology (such as misogyny, elitism, etc.) can dupe me into a wholesale rejection of affective labor or its commodification.

Ricoeur's critique of Henry offers an important reminder that ideology does not always distort life but can also play a positive role. In its positive function, ideology can help to provide an integration between my affective life and the social circumstances of life. If I happen to feel that all affective labor and all displays of concerns for others are a form of alienation, ideology can recalibrate my relation to the world. It can help me to become more willing to accept the fair distribution of work and to contribute my fair share to the social world. Likewise, the influence of other people, who offer their advice or criticism, can perform a similar function. In this regard, the influence of ideology and the social world can help me to realize a more, not less, authentic version of myself.

In assessing this debate's contribution to the topic of affective labor, it is not necessary to choose sides and declare either Henry or Ricoeur as the winner. What is more productive is to move the dialogue forward by highlighting the important questions that remain unanswered and the work that remains to be done. If living work is anchored in affectivity, does it follow that all work is affective labor? If all affective labor is auto-affective, does it follow that all external influences are alienating? If living work is inextricably tied to others in the social world, must it not involve more than auto-affectivity? And might this open the door to a non-alienating affective relation to the other? These remain open questions, but together they point to the need for a broader account of living work. Building from the existing resources in Henry and Ricoeur, this broader account would define work as an essentially social activity that offers the living expression of care for others and is accomplished through living collaboration with others. In short, to arrive at a fine-tuned assessment of affective labor, we first need to develop an account of living work that is anchored in solidarity: in what Henry calls "the community of the living."

# Notes

1. Hardt and Negri define immaterial goods in the following terms: "Most services indeed are based on the continual exchange of information and knowledges. Since the production of services results in no material and durable good, we define the labor involved in this production as immaterial labor—that is, labor that produces an immaterial good, such as a service, a cultural product, knowledge, or communication [. . .] The other face of immaterial labor is the affective labor of human contact and interaction [. . .] This labor is immaterial, even if it is corporeal and affective, in the sense that its products are intangible: a feeling of ease, well-being, satisfaction, excitement or passion" (Michael Hardt and Antonio Negri, *Empire* (Cambridge, MA: Harvard University Press, 2000), 290–2).
2. Arlie Russell Hochschild, *The Managed Heart: Commercialization of Human Feeling* (Berkeley: University of California Press, 1983). A more theoretical and explicitly Marxian approach to this topic is deployed by Michael Hardt, "Affective Labor," *Boundary* 26, no. 2 (1999): 89–100.
3. It is important to note that here we are perhaps dealing with a broader phenomenon concerns not only the emotions of workers but also those of consumers. Emotions themselves have become commodities that are marketed and then purchased by consumers, for instance, the relaxation that is provided by the vacation resort. As Eva Illouz observes, "Consumer capitalism has increasingly transformed emotions into commodities, and it is this historical process which explains the intensification of emotional life" (Eva Illouz, *Emotions as Commodities: Capitalism, Consumption and Authenticity* [New York: Routledge, 2018], 10).
4. Peter Frase, "In Defense of Soviet Waiters," *Jacobin*, February 6, 2013.
5. Peter Myerscough, "Short Cuts: Review of *Dead Man Working*," *London Review of Books* 35, no. 1 (2013): 25.
6. Timothy Noah, "Labor of Love: The Enforced Happiness of Pret A Manger," *The New Republic*, February 1, 2013. https://newrepublic.com/article/112204/pret-manger-when-corporations-enforce-happiness.
7. As a general observation, discussions of this text have to proceed with caution because there is a large discrepancy between the content of the French original and that of the English translation. The work was largely rewritten and condensed by Henry from two volumes to one for the English translation, as Tom Rockmore

explains in his "Foreword." So one must always assess the English translation against the broader context of the French original.
8 Michel Henry, *Marx* (Bloomington: Indiana University Press 1983), 16.
9 As a minor point of clarification, Ricoeur connects this other voice back to Henry's *The Essence of Manifestation*, but it seems to me that the stronger influence here is Henry's reading of Maine de Biran in his *Philosophy and Phenomenology of the Body* (1975). In an unpublished note, for instance, Henry writes, "this book on Marx is one application of the program sketched out in *Philosophy and Phenomenology of the Body*" (Ms A 17708). Cited by Roberto Formisano, "Vie et représentation: Henry et Ricoeur sur le problème de la praxis," in *Paul Ricoeur et Michel Henry*, 195. It has been said rightly that Henry—with his emphasis on the subjective aspect of praxis—reads Marx from a Biranian perspective, grounded in his interpretation of Biran's "primitive fact." Henry, "La Rationalité selon Marx," in *Phénoménologie de la vie III: De l'art et du politique* (Paris: PUF, 2003), 77–104, p. 104.
10 Paul Ricoeur, "Le *Marx* de Michel Henry," in *Lectures 2: La Contrée des philosophes* (Paris: Seuil, 1999), 265–93, p. 268.
11 Henry, *Marx*, 1.
12 Ibid., 14.
13 Ibid., 145.
14 Ibid., 168.
15 Henry, "La Rationalité selon Marx," 125.
16 Henry, *Marx*, 91.
17 Pierre Adler, "Neither Consciousness, nor Matter, but Living Bodily Activity," *Graduate Faculty Philosophy Journal* 10, no. 2 (1985): 147–61, p. 158.
18 Henry, *Marx*, 160.
19 Ibid., 200.
20 The most extensive application of the Henryan account of work occurs in the work of Christophe Dejours, in particular in his two-volume project *Le Travail vivant* (2009). Dejours cites Freud's remark from *The Ego and Id* that "the ego is first and foremost a bodily ego" and develops a theory of the development of understanding and awareness through the body. Work plays a primary role in this awareness, according to Dejours. It is situated between an imperative, something one must do, and a limit, the way in which the world resists one's imperative or demand. For an explication of how his work is inspired by Henry, see Dejours' 2013 essay "Travail et phénoménologie de la vie."
21 To some extent, the condition of the Pret employee recalls Sartre's famous description of the waiter who, in bad faith, has immersed himself entirely in his role and becomes a waiter in his full being, including even the slightest gesture. In limiting himself to this role, the waiter in the Sartrean view, lives in self-deception; he seeks to avoid his own transcendence of the role and his freedom to become what

he is not. The key difference, however, is that the waiter takes on this role himself, whereas the Pret employee takes on this role as an expectation imposed by others.

22  see Kathi Weeks, "Life Within and Against Work," *Ephemera* 7, no. 1 (2007): 233–49, p. 242.

23  see Hochschild, "Can Emotional Labor Be Fun?" in *So How's the Family?: And Other Essays* (Berkeley: The University of California Press, 2013), 24–31.

24  Renaud Barbaras, *Introduction a la philosophie de la vie* (Paris: J. Vrin, 2008); Margaret Wetherell, *Affect and Emotion: A New Social Science Understanding* (London: Sage, 2012).

25  It is worth noting that, as an acknowledgment of its significance, Ricoeur devoted part of an issue of *La Revue de la métaphysique et de la morale* to a set of critical responses to Henry's book as well.

26  This article, including the responses by Mikel Dufrenne, R. P. Dubarle, and Paul Ricoeur, is published in Henry, *Phénoménologie de la vie III: De L'art et Du Politique*. Paris: PUF, 77–104.

27  For Ricoeur's remark, see Henry, *Phénoménologie de la vie III: De L'art et Du Politique*: Paris: PUF, 101.

28  It is surprising, though, that Henry acquiesces so easily to Ricoeur's criticisms. For it seems that a response is already prepared in his book, which acknowledged precisely that the origin of ideology is most often designated by the pair "the individual and conditions" in *The German Ideology*. Henry notes, however, that these conditions are nothing other than the determinations of individual life. Because individuals define these conditions and determine them, it follows that this creative principle is what makes ideology possible. It is life which constitutes the ground for the representations of consciousness, the origin of their content, while as representations, they are only modalities of consciousness itself.

29  In a letter dated June 14, 1984, Henry responds to a previous letter that Ricoeur had sent concerning his study of Marx. There Henry refers to a "pertinent but difficult" question that Ricoeur had posed about something that Henry admits to not covering. He concedes that the aim of socialism, for Marx, is, indeed, the "development in living subjectivity of its own teleology." Perhaps this is a reference to this particular exchange following Henry's presentation. But it is difficult to determine the precise significance of this claim, due to the fact that the initial question is unknown. See Michel Henry, "Lettre de Michel Henry (June 14, 1984)," 20.

30  Henry, *Marx*, 171. Recently, Grégori Jean and Jean Leclercq have sided with Henry and have argued that Ricoeur's criticism completely misses the point (Grégori Jean and Jean Leclercq, "Sur la situation phénoménologique du *Marx* de Michel Henry," *Journal of French and Francophone Philosophy* 20, no. 2 [2012]: 1–18).

31  Ricoeur's book review—"Le *Marx* de Michel Henry"—is reprinted in Ricoeur, "Le *Marx* de Michel Henry," 265–93.

32 Henry, *Marx*, 142. This affinity can perhaps also be traced to Henry's interpretation of Maine de Biran's notion of the "primitive fact." Indeed, in an unpublished note Henry writes, "this book on Marx is one application of the program sketched out in *Philosophy and Phenomenology of the Body*" (Ms A 17708). Cited by Roberto Formisano, "Vie et représentation: Henry et Ricoeur sur le problème de la praxis," in *Paul Ricoeur et Michel Henry*, 195. It has been said that Henry—with his emphasis on the subjective aspect of praxis—reads Marx from a Biranian perspective.
33 Ricoeur, "Le *Marx* de Michel Henry," 274.
34 Paul Ricoeur, *Oneself as Another*, trans. K Blamey (Chicago: University of Chicago Press, 1992), 274.
35 Ricoeur, "Le *Marx* de Michel Henry," 291.
36 Paul Ricoeur, *Lectures on Ideology and Utopia*, ed. George H. Taylor (New York: Columbia University Press, 1986), 101.
37 Ricoeur, "Le *Marx* de Michel Henry," 285.
38 Ricoeur, *Lectures on Ideology and Utopia*, 5.
39 In later developments of Marxism and especially the structuralist interpretation, this realism of life comes to be replaced by a purported body of scientific knowledge of reality (whence ideology comes to comprise what is nonscientific).
40 cited by Ricoeur, "Le *Marx* de Michel Henry," 287.
41 Ibid., 293.
42 Ibid., 291.
43 Ibid., 293.
44 Ricoeur, *Lectures on Ideology and Utopia*, 10.
45 Ricoeur, "Le *Marx* de Michel Henry," 268.
46 Ricoeur, *Lectures on Ideology and Utopia*, 77.
47 Karl Marx, *The German Ideology*, Parts I and III, ed. R. Pascal (New York: International Publishers, 1963), 42. It bears noting that Ricoeur and Henry are not opposed on this point. Henry also quotes the same passage from Marx, and likewise considers the language of real life to be the origin of ideology (Henry, *Marx*, 168–9).
48 Ricoeur, *Lectures on Ideology and Utopia*, 77.
49 Hardt and Negri, *Empire*, 385.
50 see Sara Ahmed, *The Promise of Happiness* (Durham, NC: Duke University Press, 2010).

# 4

# Spiritual Life and Cultural Discernment
## Renewing Spirituality through Henry
### N. DeRoo

The oeuvre of Michel Henry seems idiosyncratic, as it is not always easy to see the tie that binds reflections on Freud, Marx, Kandinsky, philosophy of language, the person of Christ, materiality, manifestation, and truth (to name a few) into a coherent project. If one tries to unify the *oeuvre* around the notion of "Life," one quickly comes to question how any of these reflections can be useful for us, given the enormous difference between Life as Henry explores the concept and "life" as the everyday practice carried out by billions of people worldwide every day. So, it seems the only way to unite the otherwise eclectic collection of topics is via an abstraction that threatens to become divorced entirely from the concerns of any actual persons living in the world. If Henry's project is coherent, it is so only because it is entirely nonpractical.

This problem is only heightened by the often dismissive comments Henry makes about "the world" and its relation (or lack thereof) to Life. If Life is, indeed, wholly distinct from the world, then it remains immensely difficult to tell what relationship ought to hold between Henry's reflections on Life and our engaged action in the world: Is Life purely a descriptive term, for Henry, in which case, what, precisely, does it describe, insofar as it can, by definition, never appear in the world? Or does it have some normative force, that is, is knowing Life somehow "better" than not knowing it? Do Henry's reflections on Life *improve* things somehow by making Life more available to our understanding?[1]

Inspired by the project of this volume, in what follows I hope to show the essentially practical nature of Henry's work. To do so, I will highlight a notion of spirituality that runs throughout Henry's work, connecting humans inherently to Life, as well as to each other and to the world (Spirituality in Henry). The spiritual connection to the world manifests itself in culture as the growth and development of Life through living beings in the world (Spirituality as Affectivity: The Connection between Life and World). Henry's analyses of Life can therefore be seen to be driven by the "practical" concern of improving our cultural life together: He is concerned with Life as it shapes the spirituality at work in various cultural contexts (such as art, science, and religion), rather than as some abstract concept in need of strictly theoretical clarification (Spirituality and the (Life)World: Culture). A particular task is therefore both revealed in Henry's work and issued as a call for others to take up: the task of diagnosing and critiquing the "spirits" of our contemporary age as they manifest themselves in contemporary culture (The Task of Spiritual-Cultural Discernment).

## Spirituality in Henry

I will begin, then, with an examination of the notion of spirituality at work in Michel Henry. The place to start this examination is not with Henry's religious writings, but, rather, with *Barbarism*. There are two reasons for this: first, beginning with the religious writings might predispose the investigation toward a particular religious account of spirituality (where "spirit" is seen as essentially distinct from, perhaps even in opposition to, the "material" world), an account that would not cover the breadth of what spirituality means for Henry. We might call this the methodological justification for starting with *Barbarism*, and its importance will fully reveal itself only as we go along. The second reason to begin with *Barbarism* is what we might call the historical justification: *Barbarism* was written before the religious texts and is explicitly cast, by Henry himself, as a meditation on a certain kind of spirituality (B, 3).

Such a historical tracing should go back before *Barbarism*, to the Husserlian account of spirituality (in the *Crisis* and texts of that time) from which Henry starts in *Barbarism*.[2] This debt to Husserl is not merely accidental or a case of a few minor references; rather, the Husserlian texts set up the problem of "rational" or objective thinking that Henry will be critiquing throughout the work, and the very use of "barbarism" as the name for the type of culture under consideration is itself drawn (uncited, as near as I can tell) from Husserl. Indeed, it does not seem amiss to read the entirety of Henry's work in *Barbarism*—and perhaps even more broadly than just that work—as arising in response to the concluding paragraph of Husserl's "Vienna Lecture":

> There are only two escapes from the crisis of the European existence: the downfall of Europe in its estrangement from its own rational sense of life, its fall into hostility toward the spirit and *into barbarity*; or the rebirth of Europe from the spirit of philosophy through a heroism of reason that overcomes naturalism once and for all. Europe's greatest danger is weariness. If we struggle against this greatest of all dangers [. . .] then out of the destructive blaze of lack of faith [. . .] will rise up the phoenix of a new life-inwardness and spiritualization as the pledge of a great and distant future for man: for the spirit alone is immortal.[3]

While it is unlikely that Henry would echo Husserl's almost unbridled optimism for the power of reason to save European humanity, there remain significant similarities between *Barbarism* and the project called for in the "Vienna Lecture": not only does Henry describe *Barbarism* as making the case that "the disarray of the present time results from the extreme development of scientific knowledge and the technologies to which it has given rise and from its rejection of the knowledge of life" (B, 21), clearly echoing "The Vienna Lecture," but his insistence on the need to recognize Life as auto-affection seems to be a response to the call for a new "life-inwardness" that Husserl makes in the concluding sentence. Calling this decaying culture that has forgotten about the inwardness of Life "barbarism" seems an obvious nod to the first, *barbarisch* (barbaric or barbaristic), option laid out by Husserl, and seems a sure signal that *Barbarism* arises in direct response to Husserl's *Crisis*, if not to the "Vienna Lecture" itself.

Husserl's claims arise out of a particular conception of spirituality.[4] In the "Vienna Lecture," Husserl uses the concept of "spirit" to refer to the life, accomplishments, and products of human living. Such "spirit" is therefore personal (insofar as it pertains to persons) and communal. For Husserl, "Personal life means living communalized as 'I' and 'we' within a community-horizon" that is part of a "surrounding world" in which we, as humans, always live.[5] Such a surrounding world "is the locus of all our cares and endeavors," and, as such, "is a spiritual structure in us and in our historical life."[6]

Husserl summarizes this account of spirit by referring to it as a "vital presentiment" (Crisis, 275). This highlights two key elements of the account of spirit: first, spirit is essentially living, that is, tied to Life;[7] spirit is a *dynamic force* and not merely a concept, position, or goal. Spirit is affective, not merely effected. It moves people, shaping the very way they engage with the world around them in profound and innumerable ways, while at the same time being constituted in or by the (surrounding) world(s) in which it finds itself. This is the "vital" part of spirit as a "vital presentiment."

Second, in calling spirit a "presentiment," Husserl means much more than just that spirit causes us to feel a certain way. Rather, building on his notion of horizons, Husserl's invocation of "presentiment" here is meant to indicate that spirit provides the very basis of sense itself: functioning pre-objectively (*Gegenstandlich*)[8] as a precondition of rational or theoretical thought, spirit is more felt than thought, more a product of passive than active synthesis. Spirit, then, is an active, dynamic force that shapes how we bring the world to intuition. One could say that it shapes our imagination,[9] our social imaginary,[10] or our plausibility structures[11] in such a way as to make experience possible. This possibility of experience always occurs in a horizon of expectations that is operative in any and all experience. Without such prefigured expectations, experience would simply not be possible.[12]

But its role in our constitution of meaning does not mean spirit is simply a subjective attitude or action: "the attitude [in which spiritual meaning is seen] does not itself constitute the spiritual entity, the material-spiritual is already preconstituted, prethematic, pregiven."[13] Indeed, the invocation of the "material-spiritual" is important here to signal that spirituality is not somehow divorced from material conditions. Husserl's is not a dualistic, supernatural spirituality, but, rather, a notion carrying the preconditions of the very meaningfulness inherent in material things themselves: "spiritual meaning" is "embodied" in the environment of the lifeworld,[14] such that we can see "houses, bridges, tools, works of art, and so on"[15] as "spiritual products"[16] insofar as they have a "spiritual" meaningfulness[17] that is "not externally associated, but internally fused within as a meaning belonging to [the material object] and as expressed in it."[18]

In summary, then, to speak of "spirituality," for Husserl, is to speak of a dynamic, vital force that shapes our pre-theoretical horizons—indeed, shapes the very material makeup of our world—in a way that is necessary for experience itself but of which we may not be consciously aware, even as we are being guided by it.

While there is much that is interesting in Husserl's account of spirituality, not least the way it gives spiritual meaning to the material conditions of the lifeworld itself, it does seem to be inherently Husserlian in ways that Henry might find problematic. By that I mean that it seems to remain tied to subjectivity as "the condition of the object" and to consciousness as the "power of 'showing'" (B, 9), and therefore too tied to hetero-manifestation as the sole and only type of phenomenality. But this typical Henryan criticism is not the only problem with this account of spirituality. That is, Husserlian spirituality—which provides the historical background of Henry's account of spirituality in *Barbarism*—is problematic, not just because it does not offer an account of Life as auto-affection, but also because it leaves unclarified the account of "affective force" by which it operates. As we will see, these may not, in fact, be two different critiques: while Husserl is able to show how spirituality is able to shape and affect the entirety of our relation to the (life) world, he fails to adequately account for the relation to Life at work in that relation. Whether this is simply an omission that can be added back into this account of spirituality, or whether doing so would radically alter this account of spirituality, remains to be seen.

But it should be noted here that, in raising the question of the affectivity of spirituality, we raise again the question of the relation between Life and the world. The seed of an answer to this question lies implicit in *Barbarism*. There, Henry discusses how barbarism—as the forgetting of Life—ultimately arises within Life itself. This reveals itself in the "paradox" of (modern, barbaristic, "objective") science:

> On the one hand, science is a mode of life that belongs to absolute subjectivity. On the other hand, each of the operations of scientific subjectivity is carried out through the putting out of play of this subjectivity [. . .] [Science] does not just misunderstand this essence of Life—it denies it. It is thus a form of life that is turned against life. (B, 63)

This paradox is not accidental to barbarism, but, rather, "is posited as the sole form of culture" within a barbaristic society, such that "the decisive trait of 'modern culture' is thus not only scientific culture; it is the elimination sought and prescribed by it of all other spiritual models" (B, 63).

This final statement is significant for two reasons. First, it clearly establishes the object of Henry's analysis in *Barbarism* to be a "spiritual model"—Henry is talking about spirituality when he is talking about barbarism. Second, the heart of barbarism—the denial of Life—is paradoxical, for only a living being [*vivant*] can deny Life, can create a culture premised on the denial of the very Life that is revealed in and by culture. As such, barbarism arises within Life, even as it denies Life.

This is significant for what it says about the relation between Life (even when it is not adequately thematized, and, indeed, even when it is forgotten or denied) and the (life)world. Insofar as "the self-negation of life does not refer back to an abstract proposition, a general principle of analysis, or a working hypothesis," but "is instead a concrete process, immanent to each phase of scientific activity," "the negation of life is precisely a mode of this life [. . .] It is not a pure forgetting but a deliberate intention, the *scientific intentio*" (B, 64). This intention, Henry shows in *Barbarism*'s third chapter, is essential to modern science itself, and it is characterized, Henry claims, by "a manner of feeling and experiencing oneself" in such a way that "one suffers from the fact of experiencing oneself," a kind of self-experience that leads to a particular kind of desire: "The wish of this suffering is to no longer be oneself" (B, 66), and "the best way to flee oneself is to consider the object exclusively and to consider it as a purified object" (B, 72). Science is therefore rooted in the lives of scientists, and their desire to pursue science is, in some way, rooted in a desire to transcend their own subjective feelings in a knowledge of the universal, the True, that which "really is," which always lies beyond that which is merely felt (B, 60–2).[19]

But this account of objective truth—endemic to modern science and the barbaristic "culture" that arises alongside it[20]—is neither the only, nor even the most basic, account of truth, for Henry. Rather, he argues for a "more original truth" that is "not initially something in front of which one must disappear, in order to allow being to be as it is in itself. Instead, one must give assistance to it, *give the gift of one's own flesh*" (B, 69). This original truth is "identified with absolute subjectivity," "historical in a mind and body as the flesh of the Individual" (B, 69). Before the "objective truth" of modern science, then, there is this deeper truth that is incarnated in the lives of those performing the scientific *intentio*; the fleeing of one's own Life and affectivity by devoting oneself solely to the objective, stripped of all subjectivity, is an activity that is carried out by living beings as the fleshing out, the incarnation, of a deeper truth at work in their lives. The forgetting or denial of Life at work in barbarism and modern science is performed by living beings as a modality of Life, and, as such, remains nothing other than "an auto-affecting praxis" (B, 44). Given Henry's claim that "As long as it overlaps with individual spontaneous praxis, *techne* is simply the expression of life" (B, 46), we can see that science—even "objective" science—can be seen as an expression of Life: even the forgetting or denial of Life remains part of the ongoing activity of Life itself.

## Spirituality as Affectivity: The Connection between Life and World

So far, then, we have seen that, in *Barbarism*, Henry takes up the Husserlian project of spiritual diagnosis. In doing so, he shows that even barbarism—a spirit that denies Life—must be understood as a kind of subjective praxis that is therefore an expression of Life. But the way that spirit operates—the nature of its "affective" force—remains unclear: while *Barbarism* suggests that the world can be an expression of Life, it is not clear how, in part because the role of spirituality is not clearly laid out there.

The role of spirituality in connecting Life to the world is not fully clarified until *Words of Christ*. There, it begins to unfold via Henry's (severely underdeveloped)[21] notion of the heart as that by which "humans experience everything else and also experience themselves" (WC, 12). For Henry, the heart is the condition of human beings as affectivity (WC, 12) and, as such, it inherently connects humans to the essence of Life (WC, 13). This affectivity by which humans "experience themselves" is the "exact reason that humans find themselves at the same time capable of experiencing and sensing all that surrounds them, namely the world and the things which show themselves within it" (WC, 12). So, while there is a distinction (in modes of appearing; cf. WC, 17) between the world of things, on the one hand, and the world of human reality as affectivity, on the other, there is also "a movement . . . which accompanies us from one order of reality to another" (WC, 14). This movement is tied both to human reality as derived from the affectivity of Life itself (WC, 14) and to humans as "[i]ncarnate beings who have flesh, indeed, who are flesh: this moving and unbreakable totality of sensible, affective, and dynamic intuitions which constitutes the concrete reality of the fleshly beings we are" (WC, 14).

This movement that connects Life to the world in the human is spirituality.[22] It does not arise, first and foremost, with humans, but within the human (as) heart(ed), as "the inner movement by which absolute Life engenders itself in generating the First Self in which it experiences itself, without which no life, no living being, no 'me' would be conceivable" (WC, 102). This movement is necessary because "absolute Life is not a concept or an abstraction [. . . but] a real life which experiences itself really in itself" (WC, 83),[23] and therefore Life, as auto-affection—that is, self-affection or a self-revealing movement—must have/be/generate a self to whom it can reveal itself. Via this "inner movement" of Life within the heart, each person "experiences itself in the Self of this Word [*Verbe*][24]" of Life (WC 110). Our experience of ourselves is generated within Life's experience of itself, and this generation happens "in" the heart as the condition of human reality.

This generative relation of Life-with-itself is, for Henry, modeled on the doctrine of the Trinity:[25] if God is Life, we can understand Christ as "the First

Living Self in which absolute Life actually experiences itself and reveals itself to itself" (WC, 83). Christ is, therefore, the first "Son," the first Living [*vivant*] self-generated within Life, rather than created by Life. *Qua* living, the human, too, is generated within Life, and therefore is also a "son" (or daughter)[26] of Life: not the Firstborn Son, eternally equivalent to, and wholly immanent within, absolute Life, but, rather, a finite son or daughter, generated within Life without being itself Life, as the human does not have the power to bring itself forth in life nor to sustain itself (WC, 35). So, while Christ, as Life, remains wholly generated within Life, this is not the case for humans. Since "any process imparting Life is a process of generation" rather than creation (WC, 84), the human, as living [*vivant*], is generated within life, even as the human, as finite "thing" in the world, is also created "in the opening of this horizon of exteriority" (WC, 84) that is the world. And the heart, "the only adequate definition of the human" (WC, 107), the very site where Life speaks (to itself), therefore makes possible that my relation to Life can be expressed in the world (WC, 102): the fundamental relationship to Life within ourselves causes Life to be "more ancient" in us than the "word of the world" (WC, 102), but it also enables us to interact with and experience the world—since Life is (auto-)affectivity, our hetero-affectivity (*qua* affectivity) is rooted in Life. We experience ourselves in, as, and because of Life, and we experience the world as, and because we are, a self.

To return this to the question of spirituality—or, rather, to discover the way in which we have never yet left that question—we must finish our analysis of the Trinity. For if absolute Life engenders a "First Living" within itself eternally so that, and insofar as, it can experience itself, the nature of the relationship between Life and the First Living is one of "reciprocal inwardness" that can be called "an interiority of love, which is their common Life, their Spirit" (WC, 85). Spirit, for Henry, names the relationship, within life, between Life and its experiencing of itself. Spirit is the relationship between experience, the experiencer and what is experienced:[27] it is affectivity. And, given the dual nature of the human as both generated (i.e., inherently related to Life) and created (i.e., external to Life itself and therefore "in the world"), this implies that human spirituality is also dual: our internal connection to Life in its generativity (auto-affectivity) and our inherent "openness" to the world as created (hetero-affectivity).

It is, therefore, precisely in spirituality that we discover the common root of our relationship to Life, to ourselves, and to the world. The "internal connection to Life" that is spirituality-as-affectivity allows, Henry claims, an internal resonance with our own being: we experience Life in and as "our" life, and we experience "our" life within and as an experience of Life. This resonance with Life is not only the principle of our relation with ourselves but also of our relationship with the world (WC, 31) and our "connection with others" (WC, 30) who, *qua* livings [*vivants*], are also generated within, and resonate with, the same Life that generates and resonates within myself (WC, 37). Indeed, it is only this resonance with Life that enables us to truly love other people (WC, 38) because love "is just another name for life" (WC, 38), or, as we can now say more precisely, given our earlier analyses: love is just another name for the relation of Life with Living that is also known as spirit.

## Spirituality and the (Life)World: Culture

From *Words of Christ*, then, we have learned that spirituality is nothing other than the name for our (generative) relationship with Life itself. Insofar as Life is (auto-)affectivity, our relation to Life must be essentially connected to that affectivity. We can therefore say that spirituality is, in some essential sense, affectivity itself—an affectivity that, in humanity's condition as heart-ed beings, is dual insofar as we are both generated within Life (living/*vivant*), but also distinct from Life (i.e., "in the world"). Therefore spirituality, as our relationship with Life and/as affectivity, is the principle of our connection to ourselves, to others, and to the world.

Spirituality helps us see that it is not simply the case that we have two wholly distinct types of affectivity (auto- and hetero-affectivity) that put us in contact with two wholly distinct types of things (myself/Life, and other people and things). For our relationship to others and to the world is not originally a relationship to something outside ourselves, but, rather, something that resonates within our very being as living, heart-ed, spiritual (i.e., affective) beings. It is Life that enables our relationship with others and the world, just as it is affectivity that enables us to have hetero-affective experiences.[28]

This shared connection with Life by which our own internal resonance with Life also allows us to resonate with others is easier to concede in regards to other people than it is to the world: given that other people are clearly living beings [*vivants*] with their own essential inherent connection to Life, our relations to them are more easily understood as "a matter of relations among beings predestined by their interior relationship which each of them maintains" with Life (WC, 41). But can the world also be living, such that our relationship to it must also be premised on a shared connection to Life? This question—central to Henry's account of spirituality—returns us to the Husserlian impetus of *Barbarism*, by returning us again to the question of whether there can be a genuine sense of the lifeworld at work in Henry. If there is such a lifeworld, it is, of course, different in kind from the "word of the world" critiqued in *Words of Christ*, in which other people are removed from their intrinsic relation to Life, and posited merely as things "out there," and in which we even reduce ourselves either to "things in the world" (if we offer merely physiological explanations of the person) or to the condition of the appearing of such things (if we reduce ourselves merely to consciousness, and construe consciousness simply as the "power of showing and displaying, or in other words, phenomenality itself" (B, 10)). Since we know that Henry thinks it is possible to experience other people and ourselves in a more Life-affirming way, it is at least possible that other "things" in the world could also be experienced in and as living. The question of whether there can be a lifeworld (a living world) for Henry, therefore, is not closed down from the outset by his criticisms of "the word of the world."

Instead, the possibility of a lifeworld is opened up by Henry's description of the world as "where we develop our projects and concern ourselves with their realization" (WC, 15). Such a description returns us to Henry's analysis of the relationship between a person and the world/earth in *Barbarism*. Early on in that analysis, it seems impossible for "things" to be living: only "that which experiences itself and reveal[s] itself to oneself in this mute experience of oneself," can be considered alive; all "that which cannot carry out the work of this auto-revelation and lacks it forever [is] nothing more than a 'thing' and nothing other than death" (B, 40). But the production of things need not, inherently, be life-denying, even as we concede that currently the "content of modern technology . . . is made up of a set of devices that are no longer living and are no longer life" (B, 47). Notice here that modern technology is made up of devices that "are *no longer* living" and are "*no longer* life": it's not that they are simply not living or were never connected to Life; they are just "no longer" so connected. Which implies that they once were. And, indeed, Henry does believe that "the world is always initially the lifeworld" insofar as, "before even being a sensible world, the world is the correlate of the movement of a Bodily-ownness (*corps-proprié*)" (B, 46). This is because the human's initial engagement with the world is not that of theoretical knowledge—observation and understanding—but that of "know-how," or praxis: an "original knowledge whose essence is doing," a "knowledge [that] consists in" a particular kind of making "that carries its own knowledge within itself and constitutes itself" (B, 44). The original praxis—the original knowledge that is simultaneously a doing and a self-constituting knowing—"is our Body" (B, 44). This body runs up against "resistance" as it tries to actualize its own doing-as-knowledge: first, the relative resistance of our "organic body," "the primal 'configurations' whose entire being consists in their being-given-to effort and exhausted in it" (B, 44); and second, the "absolute resistance" in which "the use of the powers of the subjective body, runs up against an obstacle that no longer gives way. The Earth" (B, 44). But this Earth is not set over and against me, in opposition to my praxis; rather, "[b]y its essence, nature is available to an original Body" since the "Earth is not conceivable except as that on which we place or can place our feet, as the ground on which we stand" (B, 45). In this way, my manipulations of the Earth are the fulfillment of myself as an embodied "I-Can," a practical agent who simply *is* "the task of making the Earth give way and move back" (B, 45). In exercising this task, "elements of the Earth were taken away from it in order to be turned against it. They were used in order to dig, move and modify the Earth in multiple ways and to give it a new form" (B, 45). We call these things tools, and the "tool is originally nothing but an extension of the immanent subjective Body" (B, 45), and therefore part of living—tied to, and resonating with, Life.

The tool is therefore the beginning of the original lifeworld.[29] This original lifeworld is premised on the co-belonging (*Copropriation*) or co-embodiment (not merely in the sense of being embodied together, but in the sense of sharing the same *corps-propre*, a shared Bodily-ownness) of Body and Earth (B, 45).[30] This, in turn, entails that "[a]s long as it overlaps with individual spontaneous praxis, *techne* is simply the expression of life" (B, 46).

This genuine expression of life in and through the world is embodied in culture, which includes the "higher forms of culture such as art, ethics or religion" that "are also modes of *techne*" (B, 47), but also "cultures of food, shelter, work, erotic relations or relations to the dead" (B, xv). Beyond concrete things and institutions, culture also includes "the moral or religious *habitus*" that are "direct and immediate expressions of living subjectivity" (B, 47) and which, as Husserl's analyses of spirit and the lifeworld have shown us, are deeply constitutive of the whole of the subject's engagement with the world.

But this subjective engagement, Henry reminds us again and again, is not primarily (theoretical) intuition, but praxis: "it is the world as the effect of praxis but, more essentially, as its exercise. It is the world, not as an Object, but as

Action: its Action is the Body" (B, 48). The world, as Lifeworld, is the proper body (*corps-propre*) of the living being (*vivant*) because that world is the cultural expression of the living being's relation to Life. And because the world can be seen as the proper body of the living being (*vivant*), our various ways of relating or engaging with it can be seen as proper (cultural) expressions of, not only the body, but also the Life that resonates within it (cf. WC, 102). In this regard, culture—arising from the impetus of Life in living beings (*vivants*) and enacted in praxis (which "is life itself"; B, 44)—is not simply the expression of Life, but "the auto-revelation of life in its self-growth" (B, xv). Culture simply is the various ways Life grows itself via living beings' relations to themselves, others, and the world.

## Spirituality, Culture and the (Practical) Value of Paying Attention to Life

Culture, then, names our engagements with the world as expressions of the relation to Life that lies at our core as human beings, and spirit—as the name of that relation—is therefore an essential element shaping "culture." Hence, the ubiquitous effects of the "spirit of barbarism" across the spectrum of modern culture that Henry analyzes in *Barbarism*. But, given that barbarism, too, emerges out of Life (as we discussed earlier) and can be seen as an expression of Life, we may wonder why Henry takes such great pains, in *Barbarism*, to point out the forgetting of Life enacted (and expressed) by the spirit of barbarism: if barbarism, too, is an expression of Life, then are we wrong to read *Barbarism* as suggesting that barbarism is a distorted or somehow "bad" "spiritual model"?

The question of the possible normativity of Life is not new.[31] We can say, in an "objective" or theoretical sense, that thinking about Life allows us to offer a better phenomenological description of our situation, insofar as Life, being living, is, in fact, part of our situation. At the least, then, *Barbarism* would posit that it is phenomenologically preferable to account for Life, if we want to stay true to the matters themselves under investigation. But, given Henry's claims of a "more originary truth" beneath and beyond the "objective" truth of modern science, and given the vociferousness of his critique of "objectivity" in *Barbarism*, it seems unlikely that the force of his critique is motivated simply by such a theoretical, "objective" normativity.

Instead, I want to highlight a "practical" benefit that arises from being able to think about, and thereby theoretically account for, Life.[32] This benefit does not lie merely in the description of Life that it offers us, but in how such a description enables us to engage practically with the world (which is, you will recall, our primary mode of engagement with the world, according to Henry). My claim, then, is that being able to describe and recognize Life requires (and reinforces) a form of spirituality that is itself (practically) better in (and for) our current social circumstances. This is not a normative claim *sub specie aeternitatis*, but, rather, a grounded and contextual normativity: it is not "better" in some absolute sense, but in a sense relative to our current cultural situation. Understood this way, the claim of *Barbarism* would be that, in the context of modern science, we need to recover a knowledge of Life if we want to "know" better, and the claim of *Words of Christ* would be that, in the context of contemporary religion (and especially contemporary Christianity), we need to recover a knowledge of Life if we want to "love" better.

But why might the recovery of Life be helpful for us, today, in these domains of culture (science and religion)? Henry's analyses in *Barbarism* suggest that we currently live in a culture that actively seeks, not just to forget Life theoretically, but to *enact* that forgetting again and again. This active forgetting leads to a culture premised on technology rather than on *techne*, a culture in which "things" are produced, rather than tools. While tools, as we saw, grow out of human praxical engagement with the Earth as an extension of the lived body, technology "is nature without the human being" (B, 52). As such, it is premised upon an "objective network that has taken the place of life" (B, 51): exchange value replaces use value (B, 52), action is separated from knowledge (B, 49), and humans cease to be the agents of economic production (B, 47–8), scientific and technological discovery (B, 54), work (B, 103–4), and leisure (B, 112–14). And since it is human praxis that extends Life to the (Life-) world, when humans cease to be the agents (of production, discovery, etc.), Life (and the energy or movement that resonates in it) ceases to be transferred or deployed into the things produced. As more and more things are produced in which that energy[33] of Life is less and less deployed, it is harder and harder for us, as humans, to have experiences in which we resonate with things in the world through the interior resonance of living beings. As a result, the Life resonating within us has nowhere to go, and can only bounce back and forth within us, causing anxiety and malaise, which lead ultimately to violence (B, 104–5) or to a culture of perpetual distraction which "no longer does anything" because it "is content just to look" (B, 113).[34] At stake, then, in a culture that denies Life is not just our ability to resonate with Life and with other things, but also the very creation of things with which resonance may or may not be possible: it is not just our engagement with the world that is affected by our cultural-spiritual expressions, but the very material makeup of the world itself.[35]

Given the role that spirituality plays in and as this resonance, our current (barbaristic) culture constitutes a spiritual problem that poses practical problems for our ability to live in the world: both the types of things that are created in the world and the mode of our engagement with them are altered by our spiritual condition. Henry's objection to the spirit of barbarism is therefore not based on preserving Life (since even barbarism grows out of Life), but on improving culture: a spirituality that allows us to better attune to Life will allow the resonances with Life that shape our experiences with others, the world, and ourselves to resonate more acutely within us, and so attune us better to others, the world, and ourselves. This, in turn, will free the energy of Life to be deployed in ways that "let it grow" (B, 100) rather than stagnate, and this growth of Life "brings about the growth of our own being" (B, 101) and the creation of things-as-tools, that is, of culture as living, praxical engagement with the world. It is, therefore, culture—and the improved state of individuals *qua* living subjectivities within that culture—that is at stake in Henry's critique, not Life itself. Insofar as culture is the self-development of Life, we can say, perhaps, that Life itself is at stake. But since Life remains living even in its denial, it is more accurate to say that the *form* of spirituality (as the relation of Life-with-itself) is what is at stake, and that the form of spirituality is potentially problematic, not primarily on the auto-affective grounds spirituality allows humans to have, but on the hetero-affective ones that it also allows: our relation to Life is the focus of Henry's analysis because the nature of that relation—that is, the nature of our spirituality—is essential to determining how we will relate to ourselves, others, and the world.

It is those relationships to ourselves, others and the world that are the cause of Henry's concern in works like *Barbarism* and *Words of Christ*, and not simply our relation to Life. For while the spirit of barbarism affects how we experience both Life and the world, the effect of those two experiences is not the same: while Life is denied in barbarism, it nonetheless continues on, even in its denial[36]— both joy and suffering are equally "alive," from the perspective of Life. Culture, on the other hand, as the investing of the energy of Life, is greatly affected when that energy, rather than being "invested in the great activities of art or in those of daily life" (B, 104), is denied or repressed. And since the "overpowering Presence of life" that Henry calls "energy" (B, 109) "remains in the repression" (B, 104), when that energy is not properly channeled to building culture, the resulting unused energy builds up, causing anxiety and, ultimately, violence and/

or perpetual distraction. And while anxiety, violence, and perpetual distraction (which manifests as a kind of malaise or boredom) remain the product of Life's energy, this does not mean that they are "good," culturally speaking: while both joy and suffering are equally "alive," we, as living beings, might prefer joy to pain and suffering, and so might prefer cultures that lead more to joy, and less to pain and suffering. So, while violence and healing might both be expressions of spiritual relations to Life, the cultural expressions they lead to may not be equally "good" from the perspective of us, as culturally situated individuals who prefer to be healed than violated.

Hence, Henry's call to recover Life comes not for Life's sake, but for the sake of our (cultural) life together (and also for the sake of the Earth, which loses its place as co-belonging with us, and is reduced to an object, be it of consumption or conservation). And if we want to alter or improve that life together, we must first alter the "spirit of the times" (B, 107) that "affects all the other modalities of individual and social life one after another" (B, 106).

## The Task of Spiritual-Cultural Discernment

Henry's work, I am arguing, is therefore premised on the idea that radical[37] social and cultural change is possible only when there is spiritual change. In our current situation that means altering the barbaristic bent of our culture.[38] To do this, we must be able to see that barbaristic spirit and the ways it affects our culture; and to do *that*, we must, in our current spiritual climate, first recover the possibility and necessity of spirituality itself (as one cannot speak meaningfully of spiritual life in a culture where Life is actively ignored). Spiritual renewal requires an awareness of spirituality, a careful articulation and elaboration of the spirit at work in our current times, and, perhaps, the suggestion of an alternate spirituality, such that we can see that our current spirituality is not necessary, just because it is (currently and culturally) ubiquitous. *Barbarism* provides just such an attempt at spiritual renewal: responding to Husserl's phenomenological call for the spiritual "rebirth of Europe" via "the spirit of philosophy," Henry outlines how the "spirit" that "philosophy" can offer is itself insufficient for this task, if it does not open itself first of all to the possibility and necessity of Life. In exploring the various ways in which this spirit of barbarism manifests itself (in technology, in ideology, in practices such as work and watching television), Henry seeks to show both how culturally pervasive spirituality is (in our case, the spirituality of barbarism), and how the spirit of barbarism is not the only spiritual possibility. This is the first step in the possibility of a spiritual renewal that can lead to real, radical, cultural change.

The task of Henry's philosophy, and the task that he perhaps sets for those who would follow his philosophy, is not, therefore, spiritual renewal itself (which can come only from the work and words of Life), but, rather, the task of spiritual-cultural discernment: the careful articulation of the spirits affective in our cultural expressions, and the weighing of whether or not those spirits are "good" for those cultural expressions. This is no transcendent normative project: the standards of "good" and "bad" spirituality are not established once and for all outside of the ongoing self-revelation, self-development, and self-experience of Life in its "history," "individuality," and "singularity" (B, 69). It is only within Life's ongoing self-development (i.e., within culture) that we can come to discover the ways Life is growing and developing—or is denying and negating itself. Hence, the task of spiritual-cultural discernment laid out by Henry must necessarily take place within various cultural expressions—the arts (Kandinsky), work/labor (Marx), science/the academy (*Barbarism*), religion (the "Christian trilogy"), and so on—and for the sake of those cultural expressions.

To be clear, the call for "cultural-spiritual discernment" in service of "spiritual renewal" is *not* a question of some kind of "religious" revival or the championing of a "return to religion" in the traditional sense. Religion is a mode of culture,[39] one way of expressing the spirituality at work in and as our relation to the Life resonating within our heart. But as Henry makes clear in *Words of Christ*, it is also entirely possible that religion—as a cultural mode—can be bent in such a way that it, too, denies, ignores, and covers over Life.[40] *Words of Christ* shows the need for spiritual transformation rather than simply ethical, moral, or political reform (WC, 23). That it does so explicitly in the language of Christianity is not accidental: Henry purposefully situates this critique within Christianity because he thinks Christianity itself needs to undergo a spiritual transformation—to be renewed, by the power of Life, to resonate with Life anew (WC, 122). Indeed, the book's most explicit theme of the power and efficacy of the "words of Christ" is first and foremost a call for spiritual renewal within Christianity, before it is a call for a spiritual renewal centered on Christianity. *Words of Christ* therefore provides an example (*Barbarism* is another) of Henry situating his spiritual critique within the context of one particular cultural mode, so as to improve how that mode expresses Life for the benefit of those individuals engaging in that mode of culture.

The tie that binds Henry's *oeuvre* together is, therefore, not simply some abstract philosophical concept—"Life"—but a concrete task (spiritual-cultural discernment) taking place within concrete, cultural settings. This task is eminently practical, insofar as it seeks to root our cultural developments again within praxis as the knowledge of Life so that we can live in a way that promotes the growth of (spiritually) healthy individuals who love other living beings. Arising in love—which is to say, arising in the spirit—this preference is practical because it is spiritual, getting to the root of, and therefore inexorably shaping, our entire engagement with ourselves, others, and the world.

## Notes

1 Simon Jarvis explores this question of the descriptive or normative power of Life in "Michel Henry's Concept of Life," *International Journal of Philosophical Studies* 17, no. 3 (2009): 361–75.
2 The first two references in *Barbarism* are both to Husserl's late work: first to the *Crisis* and then to the late unpublished paper "The Arch-Originary Earth does not move"; cf. B, 7–8.
3 Husserl, "The Vienna Lecture," in *The Crisis of European Sciences and Transcendental Phenomenology*, trans. David Carr (Evanston: Northwestern University Press, 1970), 269–99; 299 (emphasis added).
4 I explore the question of spirit in Husserl's philosophy in much greater detail in "Spiritual Expression and the Promise of Phenomenology" (in *The Subject(s) of Phenomenology: Re-Reading Husserl*, ed. Iulian Apostelescu. Dordrecht: Springer, forthcoming 2019); much of what follows in this section is summarized from that longer account.
5 Husserl, "Vienna Lecture," 270.
6 Husserl, "Vienna Lecture," 272. In saying this, Husserl is making manifest at least two claims: first, that spirit is not merely produced by us, but is also in us, constituting us even as it is constituted by us; and second, that spirit is the driving force of our lives, determining both what we care about and what we do. Both of these claims, as we will see, remain central to Henry's account of spirituality.
7 Though the "word *life* here does not have a physiological sense; it signifies purposeful life accomplishing spiritual products: in the broadest sense, creating culture in the unity of a historical development" (Crisis, 270). Henry, of course, will suggest that, despite this caveat, Husserl's notion of Life is not sufficiently radical. Hence, the relationship between Henry's and Husserl's accounts of spirituality begins with this question of Life, as we'll explore in section b below. It is perhaps worth noting that the notion of Life "creating culture in the unity of a historical development" remains (at least structurally) consistent with Henry's account of the relationship between Life and culture.

8  See Edmund Husserl, *Analyses Concerning Passive and Active Synthesis: Lectures on Transcendental Logic,* trans. Anthony Steinbock (Dordrecht: Spring, 2001), § 28 and Edmund Husserl, *Formal and Transcendental Logic,* trans. D. Cairns (Dordrecht: Springer, 1969), 69.

9  Cf. James K. A. Smith, *Desiring the Kingdom: Worship, Worldview and Cultural Formation* (Cultural Liturgies Volume 1, Grand Rapids: Baker, 2009) and James K. A. Smith, *Imagining the Kingdom: How Worship Works* (Cultural Liturgies Volume 2, Grand Rapids: Baker, 2013).

10  Cf. Charles Taylor, *Modern Social Imaginaries* (Durham: Duke University Press, 2003).

11  Charles Taylor, *A Secular Age* (Cambridge and London: Harvard University Press, 2007).

12  I defend this claim at some length in the second chapter of *Futurity in Phenomenology: Promise and Method in Husserl, Levinas and Derrida* (New York: Fordham University Press, 2013).

13  Edmund Husserl, *Ideen zu einer reinen Phänomenologie und Phänomenologischen Philosophie. Zweites Buch: Phänomenologische Untersuchungen zur Konstitution* (Husserliana Band IV, The Hague: Martinus Nijhoff, 1952), 238 n. 1. This text is hereafter cited as Hua IV. See also Pulkinnen, "Lifeworld as an Embodiment of Spiritual Meaning: The Constitutive Dynamics of Activity and Passivity in Husserl" (in Jensen and Moran (eds.), *The Phenomenology of Embodied Subjectivity.* Contributions to Phenomenology 71 (Dordrecht: Springer, 2013), 127.

14  Cf. Edmund Husserl, *Die Lebenswelt. Auslegungen der vorgegebenen Welt und ihrer Konstitution. Texte aus dem Nachlass (1916–1937)* (Husserliana Band XXXIX, Dordrecht: Springer, 2008), 427; hereafter cited as Hua XXXIX. This theme is examined at much greater length than I can do here in Pulkinnen, "Lifeworld as Embodiment." I draw heavily on Pulkinnen's translations of material from Hua XXXIX; unless otherwise cited, all translations from that volume are Pulkinnen's.

15  Edmund Husserl, *Erste Philosophie. Zweiter Teil: Theorie der phänomenologischen Reduktion* (Husserliana Band VIII, The Hague: Martinus Nijhoff, 1959), 151; hereafter cited as Hua VIII.

16  Husserl, "Vienna Lecture," 270.

17  Edmund Husserl, *Phänomenologische Psychologie. Vorlesungen Sommersemester 1925 (*Husserliana Band IX. The Hague: Martinus Nijhoff, 1962), 111; 118; 384f; 408 f.; hereafter cited as Hua IX. See also Hua IV, 236 ff.

18  Cf. Hua IX, 112; Pulkinnen, "Lifeworld," 125.

19  For purposes of time, I will not analyze this pathos of science at length here; the above summary is too quick, and threatens oversimplification, given that "The pathos of science is complex" and "if an analysis of it aims to be exhaustive it must be pursued on multiple levels" (B, 67). Still, the brief summary given earlier should be sufficient for our purposes today.

20  The relationship between barbarism and modern science is not strictly causal, though there is an essential relation between them: "Science thereby serves as a guiding thread for barbarism's intelligence" (B, 73).
21  I begin to develop the notion of the human as "heart-ed" in "Discerning the Spirit: The Task of Christian Philosophy," in *Christian Philosophy, Today and Tomorrow: Conceptions, Continuations and Challenges*, ed. J.A. Simmons (Oxford University Press, 2019), 132–52. This notion of "the heart" draws heavily on the work of Dooyeweerd and his followers; cf. Dooyeweerd, *A New Critique of Theoretical Thought, Volume 1: The Necessary Presuppositions of Philosophy*, trans. David H. Freeman and William S. Young (Philadelphia: The Reformed and Presbyterian Publishing Company, 1953), and *Reformation and Scholasticism in Philosophy, Volume 3: Philosophy of Nature and Philosophical Anthropology*, trans. Magnus Verbrugge and D. F. M. Strauss, ed. D. F. M. Strauss, Harry Van Dyke and William Ouweneel (Grand Rapids: Paideia Press, 2011). Whether Dooyeweerd's account of the heart can be beneficial to understanding Henry's account of the heart depends, in part, on their respective relationships to phenomenology; cf. N. DeRoo, "Meaning, Being and Time: The Phenomenological Significance of Dooyeweerd's Thought" in *Phenomenology for the Twenty-First Century*, ed. J. Aaron Simmons and James E. Hackett (Palgrave Macmillan, 2016), 77–96.
22  If we compare the previous paragraph to our earlier summary of Husserl's account of spirit (a dynamic, vital force that shapes our pre-theoretical horizons—indeed, shapes the very material makeup of our world—in a way that is necessary for experience itself but of which we may not be consciously aware, even as we are being guided by it), it is clear that there are significant resonances between the affective movement in/of the heart in Henry and Husserl's account of spirituality.
23  Compare this to the account, in *Barbarism*, of the forgetting of Life which "does not refer back to an abstract proposition, a general principle of analysis, or a working hypothesis," but "is instead a concrete process" performed by a Living being (B, 64).
24  The transition from the *parole* of Life to the *Verbe* of Life is crucial to the argument Henry is making in *Words of Christ* vis-à-vis the role of Christ in every human life. But, given that, in Life, the *Verbe* and the *parole* are the same (as Henry has established in earlier chapters of *Words of Christ*), we need not make too much of this distinction for our broader purposes today.
25  It is not, I think, necessary to agree with the Christian doctrine of the Trinity to either follow Henry's argument here, nor to agree to it. Here is an example, I think, of Henry trying to explicate his Christianity through his philosophy, rather than vice versa; that is, the philosophical point he makes here does not follow from his Christian commitments, but from his philosophical ones. For a broader argument on why the seeming exclusivity with which Henry treats Christianity might not be quite as exclusive as it first appears, see Christina Gschwandtner, "The Truth of Christianity?: Michel Henry's *Words of Christ*," *The Journal of Scriptural Reasoning*

13, no. 1 (2014), Available online http://jsr.shanti.virginia.edu/back-issues/vol-13-no-1-june-2014-phenomenology-and-scripture/the-truth-of-christianity-michel-henrys-words-of-christ/ (accessed July 5, 2019).

26 On the use of gendered language in Henry, cf. the Translator's Preface to *Words of Christ*, xxxii.

27 There are strong resonances here with Deleuze's account of expression. While we do not have the space and time to pursue those resonances here, they may prove crucial to properly understanding Henry's own account of expression, and therefore of the relationship he posits between Life and world, and the role that spirituality plays in that relationship; cf. Deleuze, *Expressionism in Philosophy: Spinoza*, trans. Martin Joughin (New York: Zone Books, 1992). Audrey Wasser provides an immensely helpful summary and clarification of Deleuze's account of expression in "Deleuze's Expressionism," *Angelaki: Journal of Theoretical Humanities* 12, no. 2. (2007): 49–66; Sean Bowden's account of Deleuzian expression is also helpful; "The Intensive Expression of the Virtual: Revisiting the Relation of Expression in *Difference and Repetition*," *Deleuze Studies* 11, no. 2 (2017): 216–39.

28 I can, after all, have no experience of the world unless I am capable of experiencing.

29 Recall here Husserl's discussion of "spiritual meaning" being "embodied" in the environment of the lifeworld (Husserl, *Die Lebenswelt*, 427), and specifically in "spiritual products" (Crisis, 270) such as "houses, bridges, tools, works of art, and so on" (Husserl, *Erste Philosophie*, 151), discussed earlier.

30 For more on Henry's idiosyncratic use of *corps-propre* and several related neologisms (e.g., *Copropriation* and *corps-proprié*) and their translation into English, cf. the translator's introduction to *Barbarism*, xii.

31 Cf. Jarvis, "Michel Henry's Concept of Life."

32 And we must be clear that, theoretically, all we can really do is "account for" Life, that is, try to give Life a place in the "system" of the world. We cannot define Life theoretically—except as itself—insofar as theoretical definitions, by necessity, separate the *Verbe* from the *parole*, the content from the form. Following Dooyeweerd, we could talk here of the necessity of the *gegenstand*-relation to theoretical thought: theoretical thought must abstract from our naïve experience of the world, pull some element out of that holistic experience, and hold it "up against ourselves" for the purposes of theoretical investigation; cf. Dooyeweerd, *New Critique of Theoretical Thought, Volume I*, 38–45. Henry might talk, instead, of the need to "hold it before our theoretical gaze" in a movement that necessarily requires the opening to exteriority to provide the "place" and "separation" that allows us to hold "it" "before" "ourselves" (cf. his critique of objectivity in the first chapter of *Barbarism*). Either way, theoretical thought requires a distinction between knower and known that is simply not possible for Life, and hence we can never know Life theoretically. Life can only be known practically, that is, in praxis.

33  I am having to move too quickly here, so I cannot adequately explain the connection between the language of liberated or frustrated "energy" at work in chapter 8 of *Barbarism* and the language of resonance at work in *Words of Christ*. Properly explaining this connection would require a rethinking of our conception of materiality itself, in terms not only of Life but also of force (cf. Henry's work on Marx, including a brief reference to Marx on B, 103), and perhaps also of energy (cf. Crockett and Robbins, *Religion, Politics, and the Earth: The New Materialism* [New York: Palgrave Macmillan, 2012]).

34  This "looking" is not a genuine mode of engagement with the world, but is wholly different from "the way that a spectator looks at the work o[f] art" because "it does not deploy any of the inner powers of life" (B, 113).

35  Recall Husserl's earlier claim that "the attitude does not itself constitute the spiritual entity, the material-spiritual is already preconstituted, prethematic, pregiven" (Husserl, *Ideen zu einer reinen Phänomenologie und Phänomenologischen Philosophie*, 238 n. 1; see also Pulkinnen, "Lifeworld as an Embodiment of Spiritual Meaning," 127).

36  Barbarism "is not a mere stoppage of life and its development [but] emerges and is unleashed as its self-negation"; B, 102.

37  "Radical" in the sense of that which gets down to the roots [*radix*] of the problem; cf. Dooyeweerd, *Roots of Western Culture: Pagan, Secular, and Christian Options* trans. John Kraay, ed. Mark Vander Vennen and Bernard Zylstra (Toronto, ON: Wedge Publishing Foundation, 1979).

38  A point that is very much in keeping with Husserl's aim in the *Crisis* and similar texts of that era.

39  And is cited by Henry as such numerous times in *Barbarism*; cf., for example, B, 2, 20, 47, 53, 62, 87, 95, etc.

40  Hence my hesitancy in beginning our analysis of spirituality with the "religious" works—if religion, as we understand it, is infused with a particular type of spirit, then this distinction between spirituality (as relation to Life) and religion (as cultural expression of that spiritual relation) might not emerge clearly within our contemporary "religious" understanding of "spirituality."

# 5

# Working in the "World of Life"
## Michel Henry's Philosophy of Subjective Labor

J. Hanson

## Preliminary Considerations on Henry's Philosophy of Work

Consistent with Michel Henry's singular and overriding vision, there is in his writings a perfect isomorphism between life and labor, on the one hand, and the world and the economy, on the other. The basis of this insight, derived from Henry's reading of Karl Marx as a philosopher of life, comes from a broader articulation of praxis, which according to Henry "designates a real action, that of the craftsman or worker.... But the substantiality of this concrete action, the deed, the acting of action is not contained in the event of the world, in the ekstasis of its horizon."[1] Henry admits that, of course, we can study or observe an action, but in doing so we do not intuit the action itself—the acting of the action—and the action itself gives itself in no way to theoretical inspection; in the same way that to think about suffering is to cease suffering and start thinking—the acting of the action makes itself in no way visible. "One must," therefore, "posit the structural ontological heterogeneity of intuition and action and recognize that in intuition we do not act and that, conversely, in action we do not intuit."[2] It should be obvious that this heterogeneity between action and intuition is precisely analogous to the fundamental and irreducible heterogeneity between life and the world. Like life itself, of which it is an important expression, labor is wholly subjective. Henry's stunning conclusion: "we must say: there is nothing objective about work: It is neither instrument, nor method, nor product."[3]

Work is also subjective inasmuch as it is moved by need and it travels along paths marked out by our own bodies, to use Henry's evocative phrasing. Work is undertaken for subjective "reasons," if we can call it that. Our own needs prompt work as an activity, and we work by means of "structures of organic subjectivity."

These structures are at once inner and inherited, as a function of human beings' irreducible sociality. "We always," he writes poetically,

> follow paths that are already laid out. Those are not only the paths laid out by human beings before us. The paths which we tread are outlined within us. They are the paths of our body and those paths do not lead astray. They delineate the field of our possibilities and assign its destiny to our life. The whole of social activity, which seems to take place outside us, in reality finds in us and in our subjectivity both its rootedness, its reality, its predetermination, and its laws.[4]

Despite Henry's insistence on the wholly subjective character of labor, we are still inclined, it would seem, to attribute to objectivity some kind of contribution to the reality of work. Henry concedes:

> The economic world, however, is constituted by objective determinations, each of which is given to intuition—e.g., the price of a piece of clothing or of a pound of sugar. Moreover, these objective determinations are ideal, quantitative determinations, of which one can form a theory, a science.[5]

So work, even if we do want to call it essentially subjective, does seem to play out in a setting of objectivity, and economics is the science of that objective arena. Yet the kicker from Henry is still to come. He asks rhetorically:

> What relation is there between such determinations and the silent effectuation of organic subjectivity within us? There is no relation. We immediately understand, then, what the economic world is, we understand that the whole economy is nothing but a vast system of substitution, that it is the entirety of the ideal equivalents that we attempt to have correspond to what is most intimate in our personal lives. One speaks of a day's work, of skilled and unskilled labor, where, between sunrise and sunset, there is only the unqualifiable unfolding of a singular life.[6]

Here is the fundamental problem with the interface between work as a subjective, living phenomenon and both the objective world of materials, tools, products, and so on with which work seems nevertheless to interact and economics as the science of that objective world insofar as it bears upon work. For Henry, there is no coordination between these two realms. The world that economics describes is an *ersatz* simulacrum of the living dynamism that is work; it substitutes unreal tokens for the inner reality of work. This is a fatal shortcoming according to Henry. It's not just a matter of there being injustices in any economic arrangement but that the economy, any economy, is in principle incapable of being adequate to the living dynamism that it pretends to capture. This conclusion, though, is perfectly consistent with his philosophy as a whole. For Henry in general, life is not substitutable, and any equivalence between the experience of one living person for another's is necessarily pretended.

## Henry's Philosophy of Work in *From Communism to Capitalism*

In his slim volume published shortly after the collapse of the Soviet Union, *From Communism to Capitalism* (1990), Henry takes as his opening theme the implications of a wholly subjectivized theory of labor. Yet, there are some telling passages in this work that suggest the possibility of labor's playing a stronger role in drawing life and world closer together, as we will see in "Labor and the World of Life: Envisioning a New Possibility", that follows. As should be clear from the subtitle of the book, "Theory of a Catastrophe," Henry greets the demise of communism with tempered enthusiasm, inasmuch as—according to his analysis, grounded as it is, like all else that he writes, in his theory of life—communism and capitalism are simply "two figures of the same death."[7] To be clear, he in no way laments the passing of communism, and, indeed, he never had any love for Marx*ism* in the first place, only for Marx himself. Henry is plain that communism is a species of fascism and that it brought in its train "the negation of human rights, suspicion, arbitrariness, deportation, and even death."[8] However, Henry is equally insistent that capitalism too negates life but in a different way. Communism robs us of all desire for work,[9] but capitalism stays in contact with "the individual and the individual's work which it uses and 'exploits' as much as it can." In this way, at least, capitalism has realized its "most brilliant successes and its unlimited power to change the face of the earth."[10]

Against this background Henry goes on to identify three features about life that he wants to emphasize. In Henry's words, "First, there is the subjectivity of life. This concept means nothing but the fact of feeling oneself, that is to say, of life. All life is subjective."[11] This much is exactly consistent with what Henry has said throughout his career from the very beginning. Less frequently affirmed by Henry, but not inconsistent with his basic positions, is the second feature. "The second feature of life is that it is a force, a productive force. That is to say that it is capable of creating something that would not exist without it." Here we find something of at least a provisional definition of work. For Henry, life is generative;[12] part of what makes the phenomenon of life what it is and so different in kind from mundane phenomena is that it bears its own self-perpetuating power within itself. Life is overflowing of itself; it ceaselessly experiments with itself, overflowing its own limits by a constant inwardly self-renewing energy. This vital force seems to be specified as work when it exercises its "ability to change the natural world around it. By taking some of its elements away and by giving them a particular form, it gives rise to objects that come into existence through it."[13]

A third feature that Henry highlights owes an even more conspicuous and direct debt to Marx, at least as he tells it. For Henry, "life is not a universal entity capable of being realized and of existing as a general reality"; by contrast to "Romantic conceptions," for Henry, and again for Marx as Henry reads him, life is only ever actual as "a living individual," such that in Marx's own texts the word "life" rarely appears on its own, as if to avoid the suggestion that life can be licitly hypostatized. Furthermore, as if to underscore the necessarily individualized instantiation of life, Henry goes on to show how in Marx's vocabulary the living individual is replaced later by "the worker," as if to show that a worker is nothing other than the living individual, empowered by his/her productive, subjective force.[14] Only such an individual—"as living, acting, and moving"—has the power to produce that animates every economy.[15] At the same time, each living individual is by no means strictly autonomous.

For Henry, no living individual gives himself/herself life; every living individual receives his/her life in radical passivity. He/she has the power of living and thus of producing, but this power is not self-conferred. "To be a living being," Henry writes, "is to be precisely that: it is to be born from life, to be carried and given birth by it."[16] Across the entirety of his career, Henry is firmly insistent on this point, which is particularly well developed in his final trilogy on the character of Christian revelation read in accord with his phenomenological principles: only God's life is absolute; individual living humans receive their life from the life of God. We then are generated in a radical and absolute passivity, receiving all our productive power from the supremely productive power of divine life. From the economic point of view, the person's relative position, namely her or his own power to Life bestow upon herself or himself, life puts the human being into a paradoxical position.

On the one hand, it is crucial to note that because life is radically subjective, and because it is radically passive, we experience our own lives primarily by suffering. Experiences of suffering, like pain, hunger, or cold, bring the truth of life home in a striking manner, since it is impossible to "distance" myself from these forms of experience. I can, as Henry admits, "represent my hunger to myself and consider it in various ways, as something 'purely psychological,' as 'bulimia,' or even as an 'injustice' or a 'scandal.' But these ways of envisaging hunger, of interpreting it, understanding it, and 'thinking' about it—do not change anything about the pure impression of hunger."[17] I do not experience hunger as an object of sensation or an impression that comes upon me from without; on the contrary, I am wholly absorbed by my suffering; I am coincident with it; I am consumed by my own suffering and submerged in it. It is no accident that pain, hunger, and cold are also bodily phenomena, for the body, too, is a particularly vivid and potent witness to the truth of life. The body is not an object; I cannot distance myself from my own body; my body is in no way my property—it is inalienable.[18] In Marx's words, I am not capable of "selling off" my own body.

On the other hand, though, and this is the other aspect of the paradoxical position in which the person finds himself/herself when considering his/her economic life, a worker does in a way "come to sell himself, to sell his body, his ability to work, his own life." Fundamentally such a thing is not really possible according to Henry's (and Marx's) phenomenological ontology—I cannot alienate my own life because I am riveted to it. Because I am passive viz-a-viz my own life, I can neither bestow it upon myself nor rid myself of it. Because my life is radically subjective, it can only be mine and no one else's. Yet, there is a sense in which my very life, and precisely in my life's own embodiment, is the cause and occasion for my work, which seems to entail a sort of "selling off" of my own existence. I work because I am obligated to satisfy the needs that "assail life," needs that are material or natural. Yet, Henry cautions here that the nature of needs can be easily mistaken: "Their genuine sense is missed as long as one believes that it is possible to restrict them to a merely empirical enumeration."[19]

The true depth of our subjective need can be plumbed only by refusing enumeration, objectification, and contemplation and plunging ourselves into the turgid reality of fully subjective need sucking us under and crushing us under its weight. The profundity of needs cannot be gauged as long as we rationalize them away by regarding them as "inevitable experiences, for example as natural necessities that have to be accepted, as a curse tied to the 'misfortune of being born,' or as an 'unbearable' burden."[20] These are evasions, born of thought. What is oppressive about subjective need is due to its subjectivity,

> to the fact that one is driven back to oneself without being able to take a distance from it or to get rid of oneself. This immersion of suffering within itself without any outlet or any way to flee it accounts for the ultimate burden of suffering. What is intolerable about it is the pressure of suffering on itself that pushes it, if not to escape—that is impossible and this pressure expresses nothing other than this impossibility—at least to change itself.[21]

Subjective need is insupportable not because of how it is *understood* but because in the experience of need itself—uncolored by any interpretive gloss, every form of which we called advisedly "evasions"—it is in itself inescapable.

Having set, then, any speculation about the nature of work on its proper foundation, Henry goes on in the vital Chapters 5 and 6 of *From Communism to Capitalism* to elevate labor to the status of the foundational principle for all economy. In fact, he goes so far as to say that "force is just another name for labor," a bold assertion when we remember that for Henry life itself is force. So labor is not only an expression of life force but is equivalent to it. "Like force, labor is subjective and living: it is rooted in life and is only produced in life. It is only real in this way. Subjective labor, living labor, and real labor are equivalent terms."[22] Work, then, in truth, lies at the heart of Henry's central philosophical preoccupation and is the cornerstone of his whole edifice of thought; its importance, however, is not yet realized in commentary on Henry, and it is even arguably the case that Henry himself does not develop the full implications of the place of honor in which he puts work.

The key notion of labor is, he claims, at the basis of the economy in two ways. First, the force of life, or labor, is what brings about the transformation of nature in such a way as to make it suitable to redress human needs. This is the production of use values, which includes the totality of all consumable products and all activities undertaken to produce these products, which we need for our survival and development. Human history is nothing other than the history of the transformation of nature according to these techniques and in pursuit of these aims, so "the economic universe is coextensive with this history."[23] That universe, though, is not only concerned with production, but also with exchange. Any economic arrangement produces goods that are required for human life, but every economic arrangement also facilitates the exchange of goods for one another. Indeed, the possibility of exchange Henry calls "surely the first major theoretical problem confronted by humanity," a problem both posed and resolved by life itself. Objects produced in response to human needs are, of course, different (and here Henry mentions wheat, oil, hides, cloth, and artisanal objects in general), but they are all produced by labor, and exchanges among and between them are at bottom exchanges of labor.[24]

At first it seems that equivalent amounts of labor would be the natural basis on which exchange can be founded. Two commodities could be exchanged for one another if they required "the same amount of labor" to produce. The scare quotes here, though, are original to Henry's text, for they flag the obvious problem with this seemingly intuitive thesis. Because labor is only subjective and living, there is no fit measure for it.[25] Any deployment of subjective vital force is fundamentally incommensurable with any other, so there is no basis for comparison between objects produced by what is alleged to be "the same amount of labor." Here, "there is nothing that can be measured. The power of living labor is never revealed in any other way than in the pathos of its effort. But this pathos is no more measurable than the 'taste' in one's mouth or the intensity of love."[26] This is not a local problem that arises within any given economy to bedevil its basic equity; according to Henry, the incommensurability of one person's work with another's is the *"decisive fact that gave birth to this [economic] universe and made its invention necessary."*[27] The economic universe is just the coordinated effort to solve a problem of incommensurability. It does this at the price of inventing its object of concern. "Economic reality," Henry quips, "is an invented reality." Since labor cannot be measured or exchanged, it must be replaced with something that can. This ostensible equivalent must be both (1) objective and thus (2) an *unreal* copy of the real force of lived, subjective labor.[28]

The economic universe, then, is composed of qualitative and quantitative "ideal objective equivalents to labor power." The foremost such innovation on this score is "the measurement of the objective length of labor" by which "objective duration replaces the lived temporality of labor, and it is composed of equal units—hours and minutes—that can be counted."[29] Together these two bases of comparison conspire to make exchange possible between goods produced by the same *amount* (quantitative) of the same *type* (qualitative) of labor. The exchange value that results is just the use value of any object that has been commodified; this exchange value reaches the purest possible expression in money, which is a representation of the amount of social (not real, lived, subjective) labor embodied in any good—an even more rarified form of exchange value. Economic reality, then, is entirely nonmaterial, consisting as it does in merely hypothetical illusory "equivalents" for real living activities, and, indeed, so much so as to constitute a contradiction in terms.[30] This contradiction cuts both ways. Not only does the economy fail to capture anything about life, but life also evades economics entirely:

> As for nature and more profoundly the subjectivity of living individuals, their reality is entirely foreign to economic reality. The deployment of the subjective powers of one's living body—for example, to walk, run, breathe or even to suffer, love, think, imagine—is not economic at all. Likewise, all kinds of things—stones, trees, the air, or the sea—have nothing economic about them either. This

is why it is necessary to delineate unequivocally the relation between life and the economy and to understand them through their complete heterogeneity. Economics stands outside of reality; reality stands outside of economics.[31]

Every process of production is thus twofold, in strict parallelism to Henry's recurrent thesis on the duplicity of appearing. Everything can be manifest as it is in the self-unfolding dynamic of life, or it can be pseudo-manifest in the horizon of the world and its spectral "unrealities." On the one hand, production is the living generation of real things by means of acting subjects, as well as the tools of labor and its raw materials, objective elements drawn from nature and pressed into service by living subjective labor;[32] on the other hand, the unreal aspect of production comprises the bogus so-called equivalents of these elements: the exchange values of the tools, raw materials, and products, and exchange values in the pure form of money, like wages.[33] The latter process is reducible to the former because only labor produces genuine value according to Henry. Capital is not, contrary to some popular theories, capable of supplementing its own value, because an increase in value cannot be injected into a series of exchanges of goods on the market. Any such exchanges are predicated on the equivalency of the values of the exchanged goods. The only good available on the market that is so extraordinary that it can produce value on its own is the living individual himself/herself, who sells his/her own labor because he/she has nothing else to offer. In exchange for a wage, the capitalist "purchases the use of this labor power, through which value will be produced."[34] So now we come to appreciate the resolution of a paradox we saw outlined some time ago. On the one hand, it is impossible to alienate yourself from yourself; we cannot "sell off," as Marx says, our own bodies and the living vital force centered therein—but we can sell our labor power in the sense that we can accept a sort of unreal compensation, a false equivalent or stand-in for the genuine value of our work.[35] Note, too, that this stand-in would be false regardless of the amount of money in which it might consist. No amount could be adequate.[36] On the other hand, we do make available for wages the exertion of our bodies in labor and in that sense apply our living force to the generation of value.

What appears then to be the magic of capital—that value is generated spontaneously out of its own resources—is, in fact, a function of labor.[37] Surplus value comes from the excess of value generated by labor, above and beyond its "cash value" in wages paid out by the workers' employer. This excess is not an economic phenomenon but a result of life's own capacity for the generation of its own self-perpetuation:[38]

> That the created value is higher than the value of the wage is revealed outside of the economic sphere; it is revealed in the sphere of life in the following way: *over this timespan, the living individual is able to create more use value than he or she needs in order to survive.* (Henry's italics.)[39]

Henry frequently speaks of life as its own source of power, constantly crushing itself against itself and issuing in ceaseless experimentation, reiterating its power in new forms of self-expression. This is true, he writes, not just in general but also in the specific sense of laboring for value: "Life is a power of growth. Beyond the vague desire to go beyond itself and surpass itself, it always has the actual ability to do so in virtue of the greater force it always carries within itself."[40] This power is at the basis, then, of every possible society or economic system.

## Labor and the World of Life: Envisioning a New Possibility

Indeed, one can go farther than this. Living labor as the power of life exerting itself on nature for the satisfaction of human need is not just the basis of every possible society or economic system, but also the source of all being, and the domain of the economy, despite its poverty, actually shows us this metaphysical truth in the most immediately compelling fashion available.[41] The reason for this appears at first trivial. Henry observes that in order for living labor to capitalize on its own value, in order for work to generate excess worth, the use value of the elements of that very work have to be conserved, and that means that they have to be maintained and cared for. Without constant maintenance, the raw materials, the tools, and the objective elements of any productive process will break down, lose their use value, and eventually erode to nothing:[42]

> Although this fact may seem trivial, here a general metaphysical law is already revealed to us, namely, that things do not exist or subsist on their own, but only through a mysterious contact with life. It is only to the extent that life holds them in its grasp and keeps them in existence that they are able to escape from nothingness and death.[43]

It is, rather, a sort of primitive animism, Henry contends, that leads us to the false belief that being resides in things and that objects of our regard that seem solid and self-sufficient are in fact so by a power residing within themselves. The truth is that what we sense around us exists only as a correlate of our own sensations, and to think otherwise is a kind of transcendental illusion. "Nothing can exist in the world without life," he boldly affirms, because "Life is the alpha and omega of the sensible as well as the intelligible world: of everything that is given to be experienced, to be understood, to be willed or to be loved. Everything that exists only has its being in life."[44] The reason the economy discloses this sweeping metaphysical drama with special clarity is that the products of labor are even more evidently the correlates of living active labor than the sensible things of our experience are the correlates of our sensation. It is much plainer that life makes things than that sensation sustains perceptible objects (even the examples that Henry gives in the latter case—"like the stones or rock of mountains, like the earth of the plains, like the air in the sky or the water in rivers"[45]—are less obviously persuasive than the argument that artificial objects are sustained by labor). All we have to do is open our eyes to the world around us in order to "see the mark of living labor everywhere within it." The results of living labor are literally all around us, and because labor does not end but keeps being exerted without interruption, we see that

> the world is only the effect of praxis. The relation to the world through which the world is transformed is a practical relation. That is to say that it does not exist outside of this relation and comes to be what it is through it: its substance is living labor, the living individual himself.[46]

In a significant pairing, Henry claims this has been true "as long as the earth and human beings have existed. For the earth itself is nothing other than the ground on which we put our feet, the element resisting their effort."[47] We will come back to this language again, because Henry will, but let us note here that his argument consists in pointing out that economic productivity is a particularly striking exemplar of "an operation that makes being." Real production is an ontological operation, and the economic process is just "a figurative representation of this real process and is only intelligible on the basis of it."[48]

If economic "reality" is not reality at all but a representation that nevertheless gives us some insight into the character of real production, then, according to Henry, this is, in a way, an unusual state of affairs, yet one that discloses an important truth with special clarity. Both communism and capitalism in divergent manners illustrate this truth, but early on in Chapter 6 he argues that the "usual state of affairs [*l'état habituel des choses*]" is different.[49] Because production is a vivid representation for subterranean happenings within the foundational dynamic of life itself, Henry is able to diagnose the shortcomings of both communism and capitalism. Chapter 5 closed with a grim reflection on the dereliction, decline, and decay typical of communist societies, where productivity grinds to a halt, work is totally enervated, and the products of work are neglected to the point that they rust and disintegrate. This outward dilapidation is a sure sign of inner desuetude.[50] The following chapter, to which we now turn our attention, opens with a meditation on the singular effectiveness of capitalism,[51] which results from an, at first, intuitive and then reflective success at grasping the essential truth that the force of living labor is all that matters; capitalism then proceeded to harness this power and exploit it for literally all it is worth.

Yet, neither the communist nor the capitalist arrangement is the "usual [*habituel*]." "It was an opportunity as well as a risk," Henry opines,

> for the nascent capitalism to find this force of living labor available [*disponible*]. This is because the world [*l'univers*] is not separated from it, because the world [*monde*] is a lifeworld [*monde-de-la-vie*] which only exists in and for life, as the correlate [*corrrélat*] of the powers of life's subjective corporeity, as what resists one's effort, and it only exists in this way, as this continual resistance that is the Earth. Life, in turn, cannot be disconnected from what constantly holds it in its grasp: from the air that it breathes, from the ground that it treads, from the tool that it uses, or from the object that it sees. The original co-belonging [*co-appartenance*] of the living individual and the Earth is essentially practical; it has its place in life and rests in it. The force of life is the force through which the Individual and the Earth cohere in this ageless origin (*primitivité sans âge*).[52]

There is much to sort out in this passage. In the usual state of things, apart from the imposition of either communist or capitalist arrangements, living labor is not a disposable force, not available for use in isolation or able to be harnessed in the fashion that capitalist economies require. The reason for this is that living labor is not usually separable from the world because the world is a lifeworld that exists only in and for life. Now, here, we might begin to wonder what Henry is driving at, for no principle is upheld with greater strenuousness in his writings than the absolute heterogeneity of life and world. And yet, here, we find a strange construction, a hybrid formula that seems to blend life and world in a fashion that would appear to be totally inconsistent with the bedrock of his thought.

Henry seems to be saying here that, antecedent to ideological economic constructs, living labor is ordinarily deployed in a world of life that exists in life and for life. This world of life is the correlate of the powers of our subjective corporeity. The last time Henry used the term "correlate" in a significant manner was at the end of Chapter 5, where he said that the objects of sensation, even mountains and rivers, are nothing but the "correlate" of our own sensations; similarly, and more prima facie plausibly, the products of work are nothing but the "correlate" of our bodily labor. It was in that context that Henry claimed "the world is only the effect of praxis." Is the world of life, then, nothing other than this world that correlates to our living powers, both sensuous and laborious? This seems to be a world that is at home in life and rests within it, a tantalizing possibility given the degree to which Henry normally tries to sharply separate the two (i.e., world and life). It is in the same earlier context where Henry first calls the earth the element that resists our effort; here, he returns to the same language, calling the world of life that which resists our effort. Reciprocally, life is not dissociable from the earth (which, again, is nothing other than continuous resistance to life, nothing other than the correlate of life's power, a product of praxis), which entails implication with elemental realities like the ground we tread and the air we breathe, as well as the tools that are used in work and perceived objects (which are overwhelmingly referred to in Henry's writings as the quintessential foil for life, as the paradigmatic *opposite* of what life means). Life is always inner affectivity; the world is first and foremost object consciousness. Yet, here, he says that life is implicated with the world of life even in the perception of transcendent worldly objects.

The apex of this passage is surely Henry's stunning assertion that life and the earth are in a relationship of co-belonging. In this co-belonging, which he also says dates to an ageless primitivity (and recall that earlier he said that what he is now calling the world of life has been one the substance of which is living labor for as long as there have been human beings and an earth for them to tread), we belong to the earth in an essential practical bond. This bond seems to unite the otherwise wildly disparate realms of life and world. The earth and the individual "cohere" together in an ageless unity that rests in life to be sure, but it also seems to bear a constitutive relationship with elemental and objective elements. This pre-economic unity is a hallmark of the world of life, and the world of life seems to be a relaxation of Henry's otherwise consistent militancy against blending life and world in any way.

Should we have any doubts about this possibility, additional textual evidence can be supplied. Henry actually goes on to provide more detail about what he might mean by the world of life. Continuing to speak of the force of life, he calls living labor

> the implementation of this force. It is not an accidental event occurring on the surface of the Earth and affecting the individual from the outside, instead it is the actualization from within of the power through which life holds the universe. Held in this power, things are from the outset what they are shown to be through the action of living labor: they are materials to be informed by its living force, the tools of this force, its ready-made "extensions," and informed by it. Inasmuch as

they are held by life and life maintains them in being, raw materials, and tools are the correlate and extension of life. They belong to it in principle. It is in this way that the human is the proprietor of the Earth. The human is situated in this primal co-belonging of the Universe and Life.[53]

Here, again, it would seem that living labor, the implementation of the force of life itself, is capable of "holding" the universe and relating to the things of experience in a unique way. Rather than being heterogeneous to the world and living in its own invisible self-embrace, life employs materials and tools as "ready-mades" that are seemingly effortlessly informed by life itself, which extends itself as it were into the world, claiming elements of it as its own and belonging to it "in principle." Contrary to his repeated and strident assertions throughout his writings that the human being has nothing to do with the world and never shows up therein, he surprisingly says in these passages that the human being actually finds himself/herself in what Henry once again calls a "primal co-belonging" of universe and life.

The same phrase occurs later, where the associations of the world of life with productivity, the experience of the world as a product of life's living labor, the world of life as a correlate of praxis, and the world of life as a site of resistance to effort are repeated. In the next chapter, Henry writes,

We have identified the creative capacity of this production with living labor, that is to say with the activity of life itself, and, even more profoundly, with the force that makes use of this activity. This creative force of living labor is production considered in terms of its subjectivity. Production, as we have said, also has objective elements: the tools of labor and raw materials. How and why these objective elements belong to the subjective force of living labor is what we have sought to understand on the basis of the original co-belonging of life and the world. In other words, by recusing every external description, we must re-establish ourselves within subjective activity and experience the world only as the correlate of its power, the term that resists or gives way to its effort. Through its resistance or giving way, the world is originally given to the subjective force of life as its "tool" or its "material."[54]

A phrase like "the original co-belonging of life and the world" is quite striking for readers of Henry. The very idea of it opens up a unique possibility, one stated more clearly by Henry himself in this passage than in the other similar ones we have already cited. That possibility is that in an experience of the co-belonging of life and the world we can "re-establish ourselves within subjective activity and experience the world only as the correlate of its power."[55] Thus by a renewed relationship to life would we also open up the way to a renewed relationship with the world, which would be experienced as the correlate of our subjective individual labor power. Entailed with this as we have seen is the experience of the world as, at once, both a site of resistance and one of availability to use by labor power.[56]

Among the many consequences of the world-shattering change brought about by modern technology is one that Henry himself highlights and that belongs at the center of the analyses we are pursuing here:

> The original appropriation of Life and the World [*l'Univers*] is guided by the principle of life. Living labor is its actualization. It is subjectivity that does everything and that holds the world [*l'univers*] in its hands. The elimination of the subjectivity that holds this primitive relation together is the paradox that modern technology accomplishes little by little, to the extent that it replaces this hold on life with insensate objective processes.[57]

Here, again, Henry opens the door to something like an original belonging-together of life and world.[58] Life, of course, as we would expect, is the guiding principle in such a belonging-together, and subjectivity still controls the relation with the world of objectivity, which, we know, is unsurprising. Clearly, though, we are seeing something like a primitive association between life and the world that modern thought has sundered. As Henry anticipated in "The Concept of Being as Production" many years prior, he envisions a future scenario in which such a sundering would be complete, making of production a process that requires absolutely minimal human involvement.[59]

The upshot of this tendency toward less and less actual subjective living labor to be involved in the process of production is a scenario in which capitalism exhausts itself by cutting itself off from its true vital energy. The consequence is twofold: first, the process of production becomes manic, churning out with less and less effort massive quantities of stuff—even when there is no one to purchase it;[60] second, the quality of what is produced becomes more and more removed from influence by living subjectivity and its genuine needs.[61] Henry thus complains:

> The most decisive trait of the real process leading toward complete automation ... *is the fact that it no longer produces use values, or rather, it produces use values of a new and completely strange type.* The use that had always defined them has totally changed. Up to now, "use" meant the use for life. Wheat was grown and bread was baked in order to be eaten, wine to be drunk, clothes to be worn in order to protect from heat or cold, to protect one's modesty or to express beauty.[62]

In short, life, as Henry understands it, the phenomenological life of a living individual, was, prior to the modern upheaval, the one and only purpose of action and the one and only driver for labor.

Now subjectivity is removed "from both ends" of the production process so to speak. Living labor is neither the source of the energy that drives production nor its goal. As he puts it later in the text,

> when technology invades the real process of production to the point of becoming identical with it, there are two results that follow: living labor is eliminated from this process and, along with it, so too is the power of creating value and thus value itself. When the technical-economic universe has reached its goal and the process of production has become purely technological, there will no longer be any workers in the process of production and there will be no way for them to acquire its products, either.[63]

In this limit-scenario, production becomes literally a *"dead process,"*[64] an endgame in which capitalism finally exhausts itself by outrunning its own animating principle: living labor and the bodily needs that resist and stimulate it. In this bizarre, lifeless denouement, *"All that is left is to produce objects that are no longer destined for human beings and to produce objects without them."*[65] If Marx*ism* negates in theory the life of the subjective, laboring individual, issuing in listless decrepitude, then capitalism does so in practice, resulting in frantic, soulless consumption.[66]

For Henry, the avoidance of this Janus-faced death scenario of either communism or capitalism requires something like restoration of the world of life, which does seem to be a way of being that is neither only life's own internal self-development nor a fall into worldliness but something in between, a category that gets little attention in Henry and is rarely even raised as a possibility for living subjects.[67] Work is a particularly promising basis on which to pursue this possibility further. Work, as Simone Weil powerfully argued throughout her writing career, is a sort of pivot point between the spiritual and material worlds. We could look at work as having a similar sort of position for Henry, between life and the world. He, like Weil, calls work a point of resistance, where the materiality of the world pushes back against the immaterial force of will or effort. Work exerts itself *from* the invisible restless need of the spiritualized body *to* make its effects felt in the material world, bringing about results there within the horizon of visible and tangible things. A perennial problem for Henry is exactly why we should honor some sorts of cultural artifacts rather than others as particularly disclosive of life in the world. His own preferences arguably reflect an elitist set of values—high European philosophy and art, particularly Kandinsky, Nietzsche, Marx, classical music—but he never gives us a consistent hermeneutic for why these candidates should be preferred to others. Regarded as products of work, however, these choices can be contextualized in a setting that is both more inclusive and more persuasive.

If we reckon art and thought as sorts of "work" (and even our casual use of language refers to the products of both theory and artistry as "works"), then work can be thought of as a privileged site for the expression of life in the world that encompasses not just works prized by elitist esteem but all manner of labor. "Work" can contain the sorts of artifacts that Henry himself drifts to when he seeks to furnish examples of the possibility he has in mind, as well as a dazzlingly wide range of other sorts of processes and products that ought not to be despised in terms of their potential to disclose the singular, invisible logic of life.[68] In fact, if we keep in mind that work is for Henry born out of need, then this motive would fit work more than artistic or literary production as a corresponding activity. A passage from *Barbarism* would seem to support this supposition. There, Henry writes the following:

> Work or rather spontaneous activity is nothing other than the outgrowth of need and its fulfillment. Yet, subjectivity is entirely need. Higher needs, which result from the nature of need, give rise to the developed forms of culture: art, ethics, and religion. The presence of these "higher" forms in each known civilization is not merely an empirical fact to be acknowledged. Instead, art, ethics, and religion are rooted in the essence of life.[69]

Even if culture in its most developed forms is also a product of need, is anchored in life, and it can be considered work, then this includes a wide range of activities, including those that Henry normally nominates as his preferred examples. Only the very rich don't have to work,[70] which means that in this respect, too, the work of life in the world would be rather more democratic than Henry's customary choice of examples implies. Work is convincingly an activity undertaken out of need, especially bodily need, and it is a nearly universal human undertaking.

Indeed, those who do not work could easily be indicted by Henry on these terms, a potential avenue for polemic that would dovetail nicely with his interest in Christian ethics. The Gospels' constant inveighing against the privileges of wealth, which could easily be aligned with death in Henry's ethical picture, could complement his existing Christian-inspired ethics of life.[71] Aligning work as a privileged category of activity would also complement Henry's theology. In

*I Am the Truth* he draws attention to his revised understanding of action, which we have seen him do in the beginning of this chapter. In *I Am the Truth* Henry now adds that Christianity too teaches the true nature of action as inner invisible dynamism. In that text he writes:

> In tearing action from external Being and from the process of objectification leading to it, Christianity situates action in its rightful place, where to do is to make an effort, take pains, suffer to the point that the suffering of this effort is changed into the joy of satisfaction.[72]

A few pages later, he approvingly cites St. John's report of Christ's declaration that "My Father is always at his work to this very day, and I, too, am working."[73] Henry asserts that this utterance "concentrates within it the cardinal theses of Christianity," according to which, it would therefore seem, God, too, works, as does the Son of God.[74] Since all the attributes of the Christ are, according to this book, transferable to any human being, then the human person is also a worker, and perhaps greater attention to this characteristic activity of humanity would be beneficial for Henry's philosophy.

Remember also that Henry calls the earth the site of labor more than once, and he associates the earth with resistance. Work, then, might include any operation that involves a necessary relationship to resistance, that entails effort to overcome an obstacle or difficulty in the way of the achievement of one's aim. This, too, would make for a more expansive conception and would account for a wide range of possible sorts of human activities "counting" as work and thus as expressions of life in the world.[75] Finally, in *Barbarism* Henry argues that cultures tend to succumb to barbarism, declining from strength into weakness. If cultures are built by labor, and it seems that they are—in fact, we might argue on the basis of *Barbarism*, that what he calls "culture" there is just another word for "world of life"—then life speaks in culture to a wide variety of people. If most people work in any given culture, then that would explain how the word of life is heard across cultures through work (certainly more often than it is heard by looking at works of Abstract Expressionism).[76]

Work, then, for these reasons, is potentially quite a fruitful candidate for a phenomenon of life that would bridge as it were its source and the world, bringing into birth what Henry occasionally refers to as the world of life. It is labor that builds this world. Despite having once echoed the Psalmist's proclamation that the heavens tell of the glory of God,[77] Henry perhaps could more profitably have said that it is the workers that do so.

# Notes

1 Michel Henry, "The Concept of Being as Production," trans. Pierre Adler, in *Graduate Faculty Philosophy Journal* 10, no. 2 (1985): 3–28, p. 19.
2 Ibid., 19–20. In this matter as in others, Henry is actually quite close to Simone Weil, whose philosophy of work is considerably more developed than his. She too argues that at the moment of action thinking has stopped and that thinking precludes action. For her these are the only two human activities, and they mutually exclude one another. An early example of hers is of a runner, who plans to leap over a hurdle and realizes that he has so leapt but in the moment of leaping over the hurdle is precisely not thinking about leaping over the hurdle. See Simone Weil, *Œuvres Complètes I: Premieres écrits philosophiques*, ed. Gilbert Kahn and Rolf Kühn (Paris: Gallimard, 1988), 246. Henry's example is of driving a car, which we know how to do precisely when we stop representing ourselves driving and simply drive. To know how to drive is just to drive. See "The Concept of Being as Production," 20. For Weil, however, the runner is experiencing the spontaneous movement of the living body and is not strictly speaking acting in the way driving is an action. For her, work involves the overcoming of the resistance of matter and the accomplishment of intermediate steps that bridge intention and achievement. For this reason she sometimes speaks of work as overcoming distance (247), language that would certainly not please Henry.
3 Henry, "The Concept of Being as Production," 23.
4 Ibid., 24.
5 Ibid.
6 Ibid.
7 Michel Henry, *From Communism to Capitalism: Theory of a Catastrophe*, trans. Scott Davidson (London: Continuum, 2014), 11.
8 Ibid., 10.
9 Ibid., 2.
10 Ibid., 10.
11 Ibid., 15.
12 Not, it should be noted, creative. Henry rejects the language of creation in favor of the language of generation. There are theological and phenomenological reasons for this. Indeed, for Henry theological and phenomenological rationales are identical.
13 Henry, *From Communism to Capitalism*, 15.
14 Ibid., 16.
15 Ibid., 17.
16 Ibid.
17 Ibid., 23.
18 Ibid., 24.

19 Ibid.
20 Ibid., 24–5. Translation modified.
21 Ibid., 25.
22 Ibid., 57.
23 Ibid.
24 Ibid.
25 Ibid., 58.
26 Ibid.
27 Ibid.
28 Ibid.
29 Ibid., 59.
30 Ibid.
31 Ibid., 60.
32 Ibid.
33 Ibid., 61.
34 Ibid.
35 This is clearly a counterpoint to Marx's famous account of the alienation of labor and its indissoluble bond to the fact of wage slavery. Dissolve the one and the other goes too, according to Marx. The character of alienation though is very different for Marx. See Karl Marx, *Selected Writings*, ed. David McLellan (Oxford: Oxford University Press, 1977), 85–7.
36 Normally we are tempted to think that it is impossible to be paid enough for our work. John Ruskin points out that in many celebrated cases authors and artists never profited at all off their works, which remain inestimably valuable. "How much do you think Homer got for his *Iliad*? or Dante for his *Paradise*? only bitter bread and salt, and going up and down other people's stairs . . . . It is indeed clear that God means all thoroughly good work and talk to be done for nothing." See John Ruskin, *The Crown of Wild Olive*, in *The Complete Works of John Ruskin* XVIII, ed. E. T. Cook and Alexander Wedderburn (London: George Allen, 1905), 423. Ruskin is arguably one of the nineteenth century's more interesting and overlooked philosophers of life, which for him is a fundamental category of artistry and society, his twin great concerns.
37 On this point, John Paul II, following Emmanuel Mounier, agrees. His encyclical on work, *Laborem exercens*, teaches that labor has priority over capital because capital is nothing but the repository of value generated by past labor. In this matter he revises the theory of his predecessor, Leo XIII, who taught that labor and capital were on an equal footing in his *Rerum novarum*. See John Paul II, *Laborem Exercens*, Appendix to Gregory Baum, *The Priority of Labor: A Commentary on* Laborem exercens, *Encyclical Letter of Pope John Paul II* (New York: Paulist Press, 1982), 117. See also Al Gini, "Meaningful Work and the Rights of the Worker:

A Commentary on *Rerum Novarum* and *Laborem Exercens*," *Thought* 67 (1992): 225–39, p. 232.

38  This is in strict parallel to Henry's observation in *I Am the Truth* that life reveals itself in two senses: first, Life (capitalized in the text) reveals itself in that its own self-revelation is attributable to nothing but itself; there is nothing "behind," so to speak, Life that is responsible for Life's own power of self-revelation other than Life—it is its own self-generating force; second, Life reveals itself in that what it reveals is nothing other than itself; it does not reveal something else but only its own ever-effulgent content. See Michel Henry, *I Am the Truth: Toward a Philosophy of Christianity*, trans. Susan Emanuel (Stanford: Stanford University Press, 2003), 24–5; 29–31.

39  Henry, *From Communism to Capitalism*, 63.

40  Hannah Arendt argued that the metaphor of life's own power of self-generation was of irresistible interest to the commentators on early modern economic growth, who beheld unprecedented expansion of wealth and productivity in their day and sought to explain it by analogy to the only other seemingly boundless self-perpetuating energy in the universe: that of life itself. See her *The Human Condition* (Chicago: The University of Chicago Press, 1958), 105–7. For Henry, though, this is no metaphor but rigorous metaphysics.

41  Henry, *From Communism to Capitalism*, 65.

42  Arendt makes a similar observation, and tellingly, links it to the most elemental form of human praxis—what she calls labor, in deliberate distinction to work. For her, labor is the never-ending process of securing what is directly needed to sustain life, and its "products" exist just long enough to be consumed, at which stage labor is again required to provide even more of what is needed, since need is never permanently abated. Work, by contrast, creates comparatively lasting products that often even have the capacity to outlive their makers (tools that are used in the process of labor are an obvious example). Late in her analysis, however, she does seem to include another sort of labor than the main one exposited all too briefly here. This other form of labor is the labor of maintenance, without which the products of work would eventually erode through neglect and in the end pass out of usefulness first and then, at last, existence altogether. See *The Human Condition*, 100.

43  Henry, *From Communism to Capitalism*, 64–5.

44  Ibid., 65.

45  Ibid.

46  Ibid.

47  Ibid., translation modified. Davidson capitalizes "Earth" in the first instance, but both occurrences are lowercase in the French original.

48  Henry, *From Communism to Capitalism*, 65.

49  Ibid., 69.

50 Ibid., 66–8.
51 Here Henry again claims to be closely following Marx, who always considered the secret of capitalism to consist in its remarkable success. See Henry's *Le socialisme selon Marx* (Cabris: Editions Sulliver, 2008), 69.
52 Henry, *From Communism to Capitalism*, 69–70. Translation modified.
53 Ibid., 70.
54 Ibid., 81.
55 Ibid.
56 This way of putting it, once again, draws Henry's thinking on work very close to that of Simone Weil, who also views the world as a site of resistance to human effort; she is clearer that this resistance is not just obstacle but also opportunity, for the resistance to effort is at once what makes work necessary and possible. Imagine a simple example: a pulley will not work without resistance, but if the world afforded no resistance to our efforts, we would not need a pulley. See *Œuvres Complètes I*, 247. See also Simone Weil, "The Pythagorean Doctrine," in *Intimations of Christianity among the Ancient Greeks*, ed. and trans. Elizabeth Chase Geissbuhler (London: Routledge and Kegan Paul, 1957), 178. A thorough comparison between these two thinkers would be most valuable. One point of obvious contrast with respect to the philosophy of work is on the relationship of geometrical thinking and machinery to human labor. Henry despises the mathematization of reality; Weil adores geometry. For her a machine is an active geometrical schema; for Henry a machine is a lifeless automaton and thus does not work at all. See Henry, *From Communism to Capitalism*, 81–4.
57 Ibid., 86. Translation modified.
58 Granted that here he uses the word "univers," where ordinarily he would use the word "monde." Still, we have seen that both are used in these parallel passages, and "univers" still implies the world of objective reality, opened up by the ecstatic horizon.
59 Henry, *From Communism to Capitalism*, 90.
60 Ibid.
61 Ibid., 91. That modern work produces "goods" that answer not to need but to superfluity is a complaint at least as old as Plato and frequently repeated in the literature on philosophy of work.
62 Henry, *From Communism to Capitalism*, 91.
63 Ibid., 114.
64 Ibid., 92.
65 Ibid. This situation was envisioned by Philip K. Dick in his story "Autofac." In his imagined dystopian future, production is carried out entirely by robots no longer under human control who keep delivering undesired goods to the last remaining uninterested consumers. See *Selected Stories of Philip K. Dick* (New York: Pantheon Books, 2002).

66 Henry, *From Communism to Capitalism*, 92.
67 Nowhere, for instance, in "The Concept of Being as Production" does Henry mention the co-belonging of life and world.
68 Again, Weil is rather more democratic (and romantic); she regards the workers as having a close relationship with the divine life by dint of the very difficulty of their work, their exposure to the unforgiving logic of necessity imposed by dealing with unyielding material realities. See her "The First Condition for the Work of a Free Person," in *Simone Weil: Late Philosophical Writings*, ed. Eric O. Springsted and Lawrence E. Schmidt (Notre Dame, IN: University of Notre Dame Press, 2015), 136.
69 *Barbarism*, 19.
70 Stanley Hauerwas once defined work as "that from which rich people are exempt." He did not seem to be altogether joking. See his "Work as Co-Creation: A Critique of a Remarkably Bad Idea," in *Co-Creation and Capitalism: John Paul II's Laborem Exercens*, ed. John W. Houck and Oliver F. Williams (Washington, DC: University Press of America, 1983): 42–58, p. 50.
71 See Chapter 10 of *I Am the Truth* and the whole of *Words of Christ*, trans. Christina M. Gschwandtner (Grand Rapids: William B. Eerdmans Publishing Company, 2012).
72 Henry, *I Am the Truth*, 172.
73 Ibid., 180.
74 Ibid.
75 It might also account for Henry's concern over the potential for the production process to eliminate human involvement altogether. As technology becomes more sophisticated and powerful, the resistance constitutive of work is steadily overcome to a degree that no human capacity is really put to the test by the laboring activity involved in production.
76 I thank my friend and colleague Brian Harding for these insights.
77 See "Material Phenomenology and Language (or, Pathos and Language)," trans. Leonard Lawlor, in *Continental Philosophy Review* 32, no. 3 (1999): 343–65, p. 363. There he writes, "it is still life which speaks in the world, in the world which secretly speaks the language of life to us. *Coeli enarrant gloriam Dei.* The world is the speech of God." I have always found that puzzling on Henry's own stated principles. The emphasis in this article is on the fundamental inability of language, which Henry calls "the universal evil" (See *I Am the Truth*, 9), to provide access to the reality of the absolute. If the world is the speech of God, then we can hear life or God speaking in the world, perhaps only if we are listening correctly, but nevertheless it is still possible to hear the words of God spoken in the world. But this seems to run counter to his main ideas. The world of work rather than of nature seems more fitting a candidate for a "place" where life makes its invisible presence known in the world.

6

# Freud after Henry

R. Welten

Among the numerous rereadings of philosophical texts that Henry undertakes in his work, his rereading of Freud is particularly ambiguous. *Genealogy of Psychoanalysis* (1985) contains one of the sharpest philosophical commentaries on the thought of the father of psychoanalysis. However, this could also be precisely the reason why the book has not received the attention it deserves. His findings are "truly upsetting" for those who rely on Freud as the ultimate master, since Henry's readings reveal serious theoretical difficulties in his master's theory.[1] Yet, Henry's interest in Freud has nothing in common with classical refutations of psychoanalysis, like the ones we know from the debates in the twentieth century. The goal of this chapter is to find out how Henry's readings might contribute to psychoanalysis, rather than to refute psychoanalysis in its entirety. Therefore, I will read Henry along *with*, rather than primarily *against*, Freud. In the second part of the chapter, I will investigate the possibility of a "Henrian" psychoanalytical approach to depression and anxiety. The chapter will conclude with some sketchy suggestions for applications of the approach described.

Before we take a deep dive into a "Henrian reading of Freud," we first have to understand why Henry took all these efforts to critically evaluate Freud's theory in the first place. After all, his interest in Freud might arouse astonishment, since, unlike Maine de Biran, Kandinsky, or Marx, who according to Henry unveil a phenomenology of the self-manifestation of life, Freud does not belong to those exceptional thinkers embraced by Henry. And yet, there is some good reason to suspect the existence of a phenomenology of life in Freud. The problem is that, according to Henry, the master gets lost in a mess of theoretical twists. Still, it is not hard to discover what Henry calls a "radical phenomenology" already present in Freud. Take, for instance, the famous *Outline of Psychoanalysis* (1938), where Freud starts by saying that we know two things about the psyche: "Firstly, we know about the brain (nerve system), the physical organ and scene of the psyche; secondly, we know that there are acts of consciousness that are presented to us in their immediate form and that no description can bring us closer to."[2] Isn't this second "knowledge" not exactly a self-appearing in contrast to the first, which can be understood only through its objectification? Isn't this allusion to the "immediate form" not precisely what Henry denotes as a feeling that feels itself, that is to say, of life? The second one is the experience of being a subject, which Freud has to acknowledge to develop his psychoanalysis.

It goes without saying that the reason for the existence of psychoanalysis is the care of the patient. Fair enough, the practical implications of Freud's thought are the real concern of a practice known as psychoanalysis or psychoanalytic therapy. To Freud, psychoanalysis is not a philosophical theory at all, but, rather, a technique to help the patient who is suffering from neurosis. But what does it imply on a theoretical level? Philosophically speaking, what is a "patient" other than what Henry calls a subject? Not in the empirical or even existential sense that "everybody suffers," but in the sense that subjectivity can be understood only as the immediate, inescapable experience of itself? If the pain is reduced to a concept, it has become an idea, precisely deprived of the feeling of pain. This is why Henry states that the knowledge of the pain is pain itself.[3] Life is the feeling of life itself, which, as a feeling, is always already my life. It is an appearance—hence phenomenology—that cannot be reduced to the appearance "*of* something." When I feel the heat of the stone I'm sitting on, it is not the heat as a property of the stone that appears as an objective fact of science, but it is first and foremost the living subjectivity that appears. Henry famously describes this as life. Life, then, is subjectivity. But to Henry, the term "subjectivity" does not entail an ontological psyche, a monad, or a rational totality. It is far less than that. It is the appearance that is always already mine. To Henry, "subjectivity" is that which experiences itself. And he adds: "Not something that had, moreover, this property of self-experience, but the very fact of self-experience itself in and of itself."[4] There is not first a self, in order to experience itself, but the self-experience is given in one stroke. That is to say, to Henry, the subject is not the "carrier" of experience, it is not a *hypokeimenon* or underlying basis that makes experience possible. It is, to reframe Freud's line quoted earlier, "presented in its immediate form." Let us emphasize how Henry, despite his critical readings of Freud, shares the insight of the second "knowing" in the Freud quote. And so psychoanalysis is not a "science" of the psyche since that would suppose an object of science (cf. the psyche), but an approach to the human subject as its subjectivity. In fact, not only Freud but also Jacques Lacan will emphasize, psychoanalysis is not a science of the unconscious. Nor is it a science of neurosis or other mental "objective" deviation. And so psychoanalysis is not "psychology," like *The Interpretation of Dreams* is not a science of dreams, as the title already makes clear. As Henry states, science is about objectivity, about objective facts. It strives to eliminate the first-person, "subjective" perspective. This is the reason why Henry writes on many occasions that science "knows nothing of life."[5] Rather, it eliminates life as subjectivity. The domain of psychoanalysis is the subject in its subjective experience. Granted, the term "subject" is not a term coined by Freud, nor does it make a frequent appearance in his work.[6]

Freud explicitly states, in the lines that follow after the earlier quote, that there is no direct relationship between these two endpoints of our knowledge.[7] As Henry might put it, there is not something "between" life and science, and this is exactly why science presents itself without any contact with life. When a doctor examines me in order to find the cause of my pain, there is on the one hand just the pain, which is inalienably my pain, and on the other, the objectifying science, that is the knowledge that the doctor has at his disposal. Fortunately for the doctor, my pain is not his. In short, there is nothing between the subjective pain and the pain as an object. Later in the same text, Freud writes: "The starting point of this investigation is the unparalleled fact of consciousness, which defies all explanation and description. Indefinable and inexplicable it may be, but if we speak of consciousness then we nonetheless immediately know from our most personal experience what is meant by it."[8] In a footnote to this passage, Freud calls this the "basic fact" and accuses other "psychologies" of ignoring this basic fact. Yet, isn't this "basic fact" not precisely the kernel of Michel Henry's thought, namely, that consciousness cannot be reduced to its objects and even less be subjected to objectification, but that it appears to itself?

## What Is the Unconscious after All?

And so, says Henry, "a philosophical reading of Freud is possible" and "a new reading of psychoanalysis" is needed.[9] Notwithstanding the bulk of dialectical, even Hegelian (Lacan, Slavoj Žižek) interpretations of Freud, to understand Henry, we need to approach Freud from a phenomenological perspective. That is, we have to go back to the matter itself, the givenness of experience. It is undeniable that Freud is very well aware of the experimental, sensational, or affective layer of life. The least we can say of it is that within

Freud's thought, there always remains something, however vague and often undervalued by the master himself, of an immediate experience that escapes objectification. Jean-Paul Sartre already noted that psychoanalysis must know what it is looking for, otherwise it is impossible to reach its goal.[10] Isn't this goal always there to be found in experience, even if we cannot *start* from experience but only afterward (*nachträglich*)? After all, what would be the meaning of psychoanalysis if the patient at the end of the treatment didn't experience some kind of relief? Moreover, whatever structuralist or language-centered interpretation of psychoanalysis we may choose to follow, any such interpretation must acknowledge that sooner or later the patient feels that the neurosis has decreased. The assumption that the patient tries to conceal this experience only proves that there is something to conceal anyway. The reason for this concealment, escape, or repression, or whatever one might call it, is to be found in experience.

Consider, for example, the patient who suffers from certain memories. Of course, he cannot go "back into time." One cannot restart the experience in order to modify it. From the pragmatic assumption of psychoanalysis, that is, the patient suffering from certain memories, it follows that the therapist and the patient have nothing but language at their disposal. Since Lacan, all attention has been focused on this. However, seen from a phenomenological perspective, this implies that this suffering from memories is primarily suffering that cannot be reduced to the memories themselves. The memories, so to speak, *affect* consciousness. It makes sense to say that this suffering is "unconscious" because it escapes language, symbolization, etc. However, according to Henry the talk about "the unconscious" fails to bring us any further. Henry dismissed the concept of the unconscious as early as his study on Maine de Biran: "The new idol of modern times is no more than another name for an old metaphysical entity."[11] In fact, this is the core of the message of the later *Genealogy of Psychoanalysis*, in which Henry shows how Freud is not quite the Copernican revolutionary people have taken him for, but, rather, a belated heir of modernity.[12] From a phenomenological point of view, the "unconscious" is nothing more than a negation of consciousness and can only "exist" as such.[13] That is why the unconscious was already there when Western philosophy introduced the notion of consciousness. There is no such thing as a pure ontological unconscious. Yet, even for Freud, the unconscious is not *a priori*. That is why the unconscious is always already absolutely conscious, otherwise psychoanalytic therapy would be impossible. Psychoanalysis never works with the unconscious *as* unconscious but by virtue of the ultimate possibility of making the unconscious conscious. If "conscious" means appearing (to be "aware"), it is this appearing as such that to Henry is the kernel. However, what is conscious to our minds, is the representation, the "what," of the memory. To put it in Husserlian jargon, consciousness is consciousness *of* something. This implies that the unconscious is understood as what is not represented. For instance, there are memories I am not thinking of right now but nevertheless have their effects. However, the unconscious remains understood against the horizon of the conscious. Since the unconscious is understood as the domain that is not represented, it is nothing but a function of the conscious. The conscious is the subject that represents, that is mainly an "I represent therefore I am," whereas the unconscious is the acknowledgment that I do not fully represent everything that I am, that my consciousness isn't coextensive with my being.[14] As Henry states: "The philosophy of the unconscious is here a consequence of the metaphysics of representation, it is inextricably bound up with it."[15] Fair enough, if consciousness is narrowed down to a rational idea of "thinking" or "understanding," it makes sense to say that life is "unconscious." In a psychoanalytic stance, we can say that the pathos of life might be suppressed, but it can never be repressed since self-affection is the very manifestation of any kind of suppression anyhow.[16] To put it in popular terms: even when I "feel" something that is unclear to me, I still feel. The feeling cannot be abandoned because it isn't clear. On the contrary, if this bothers me too much, it might be a reason to call on my psychoanalyst. Was this not from the outset the practical idea of what psychoanalysis should do?

Is it right to say that psychoanalysis is concerned with feelings and passions that are unconscious? Well, yes and no. Yes, according to psychoanalysis, the subject primarily suffers from its memories and its being. The subject will try to escape this suffering through the strategies of suppression and will develop a neurosis that is accessible only by its symptoms and the patient's talk. But the answer to the question is at the same time negative: since access to the neurosis is apparently possible only through symptoms and the patient's talk, it is the sphere of representation and imagination, of language and narrative that gets the central attention from Freud and even more in Lacanian psychoanalysis. To Freud, the patient has to talk about his dreams and fears, not to "understand" himself but to get access to the unconscious to undo the neurosis.

And so Henry's reproach to Freudian theory is that it is built on the aberrant, even paradoxical, concept of the "unconscious representation."[17] To Freud, the unconscious representation would be the cause of neurotic behavior, which appears as a problem to be solved by making it conscious. But this leads to an infinite regress, since the unconscious representation is, as the word says, a representation itself that has all the characters of a representation (it is not what it is). Freud affirms this in his text on "screen memories," where representations might be replaced by other representations.[18] Or take the technique of free association, according to which the patient encounters resistance at a certain point. The process of free association reveals resistance sooner or later when words are close to a word that stands for a traumatic event. But this technique can make sense only because there is another side of the representation: a feeling or emotion that in itself cannot be represented. The resistance is exactly not a representation. The representations that pass by in the free association or during the dream are conscious as far as it concerns their appearing. They are the very experience of the self-manifestation of life. Not that there is something "beyond" the representation, but the appearance of the representation *is* its very appearance, notwithstanding its contents. That is to say, the representation is marked by representation, but the representation cannot be reduced to that. There is an "other side" of the representation, in that it appears anyhow. Without this affective layer of the subject, the free association would be infinite and therefore lead to nothing, exactly because it leads to everything.

## The Affect

It is the ambiguity of passions and feelings in Freud's work which is the focus of Henry's attention. Henry applauds Freud for refusing any speculative approach to the unconscious and for leaning on the "incontestable pathological material."[19] But this is also where Freud goes astray: The kernel of Henry's criticism of Freud is that the latter—paradoxically—destroys what he has discovered, namely this incontestable pathological material. The patient suffers from memories, fears, tensions, and so on. Henry calls this an "original pathos" which is "affectivity," a term that comes close to Freud's notion of the "affect." Things become even more complicated because Freud did not devote any full-text treatment about the affect and seems to change his views on it over the several stages in his career. However, this difference between affect and representation, often underestimated in the history of psychoanalysis, is crucial for Freud.

My attention will, therefore, go to the *affect*. What is an affect? We might say that an affect is a feeling, sensation, pathos, or emotion. Whatever it is, the affect is not mediated by representation. To Henry, the affect is the feeling of what is felt: "That which is felt without the intermediary of any sense whatsoever is in its essence affectivity," Henry writes in capital letters.[20] The affect is not just a nonrepresentation by way of a representation that is "not yet": it is not like repressed memories that exist to become conscious. Instead, the affect is the unconscious foundation of psychoanalytic therapy in the first place. From an Henrian viewpoint, it is the "incontestable pathological material" which justifies the notion of the affect: "Why is it incontestable? In that it appears."[21] It is there and cannot be denied. It is clear that, to Henry, affectivity stands for "emotion" as an immediate experience. In a long exposition on the philosopher Jules Lachelier on the nature of pain, Henry concludes that "The truth of pain is its affectivity."[22] Henry elaborates on the self-revelation of pain by arguing that "The truth of pain is pain itself as such." This means first that when we feel pain, there is no possibility to separate ourselves from it. This is what Henry denotes as "truth." We are the pain, instead of our "having" pain. The pain, so to say, is itself and therefore "true." There is no question here that first there is pain and subsequently a representation that is then subjected to a true test in order to receive the label "true." The subject is not the bearer of the pain but the very manifestation of it. Yet, this "ourselves," this "subject," is not so much the psychological ego relating itself to the pain, but the very experience of it, that is, something that cannot be understood in terms of intentionality ("pain is always pain of something")[23]. On the contrary, pain reveals itself, and this self-manifestation is nothing but a revelation of life. This implies that any representation of pain is not the pain itself. The actor on stage can play as if he is in pain without really being in pain. On the other hand, one can suffer pain without anyone noticing. In short, the representation of pain is not pain itself. Pain is invisible. So, it makes sense to say with Henry that nobody has ever seen pain.

Is this the same as the psychoanalytical notion of affect? There has been a large debate within the circles of psychoanalysis on the notion of the affect. It is even hard to define the term unequivocally. Notwithstanding its genealogy in philosophy (Spinoza, Descartes), in French, "affect" is a specifically psychoanalytic term.[24] Let me take a look at the affect insofar as it concerns one of Freud's central areas of interest, the dream. Say, I dream about being afraid. What exactly is fear here? A representation or the affectivity? From a pragmatic perspective, it is clear that psychoanalysis will immediately focus on the representation in the dream. It will systematically ignore the feeling of fear. The interpretation of the dream follows the idea of an ecstatic, transcendental conception of consciousness. If we now take one of Henry's favorite passages in Descartes, it becomes clear that he, unlike Freud, acknowledges the fully immanent status of the contents of the dream. When I dream of being afraid, I *am* afraid. That is to say, fear, like any "emotion," is not mediated by representation first nor is it caused by it. It is what it is. The fear, joy, or whatever "feelings" in the dream are nothing but the self-sensing, original affectivity in general. But to Freud, only representations can be analyzed while analysis of feelings and passions as such is impossible. The dream is a stage of representations to be interpreted. A feeling might give rise to a representation, its modalities—the feature that representations might be replaced by others—are marked by the "seal of the absolute," says Henry.[25] This is the passage of Descartes from *Passions of the Soul*:

> Thus often when we sleep, and sometimes even when we are awake, we imagine certain things so vividly that we think we see them before us or feel them in our body, although they are not there at all. But even if we are asleep and dreaming, we cannot feel sad, or moved by any other passion, unless the soul truly has this passion within it.[26]

It is interesting to note that Freud himself makes a similar remark in the first chapter of *The Interpretation of Dreams*, in which he quotes a certain Stricker: "Dreams do not consist purely and simply of delusions; for example, if one is afraid of robbers in a dream, the robbers indeed are imaginary, but the fear is real." Freud comments:

> Our attention is here called to the fact that the affective development of a dream does not admit of the judgment which one bestows upon the rest of the dream-content, and the problem then arises: What part of the psychic processes in a dream may be real? More specifically, what part of them may claim to be enrolled among the psychic processes of the waking state?[27]

Indeed, what, after all, is the dream? The dream-content or the psychic material of the dream, or the "incontestable pathological material" of the dream which cannot be reduced to its contents? The point of Descartes' quote is that the dream isn't "real" or "imaginary" anyhow. Only representations can be "real" or "false." It is this ruse of the dream that plays such an important role in Descartes' first meditation. I simply cannot step out of the dream to prove that the dream is just a dream because this all might turn out to be a dream itself (this is why Freud says that the dream is a psychosis[28]). "I see so manifestly that there are no certain indications by which we may clearly distinguish wakefulness from sleep that I am lost in astonishment," writes Descartes.[29] So, it is quite defensible that it makes no sense at all trying to interpret feelings. In other words, the affect is not exactly interpretable, as Freud incessantly reminds us. There is no interpretation of self-affection, or of life in the Henrian definition of it.

It's for this reason that during psychoanalytic practice, the psychoanalyst focuses on the representations in the dream the patient talks about, not on the feeling that continues to echo after awakening (although as everybody knows from experience, one might be different from the other. One might dream of a beloved person and wonder why one is feeling so gloomy after awakening, despite the joy that is associated with the beloved person in daily life). A professional psychoanalyst is not interested in the patient's feelings, but in the talk about his/her feelings. This is the pragmatist aspect of psychoanalysis. There is talk, not a feeling as such that is talked about subsequently. What psychoanalysis does *not* do is try to find out whether the patient "really has dreamed" about what he is claiming that he has dreamed. On the one hand, folk wisdom claims that dreams are lies, on the other, surrealist André Breton claimed that only dreams are real. From a radical phenomenological position, it doesn't make any difference: the dream is already there as incontestable pathological material. Henry shows how this alleged difference between "real" and "illusion" keeps returning in the history of metaphysics. In fact, in Descartes' previous quote, the experience of the dream is neither false nor real. It is what it is. It is life.

And here we come to the essence of Henry's thought, namely the immanence of self-appearing. Henry's reading of Descartes' famous 'I think I am' is against the grain of the traditional interpretations of it. To Descartes, the soul is a *res cogitans*. But the soul is not so much "a thing that thinks," as if there is a thing first and thinking is a result of an action of the thing: it is not a mind that is thinking; rather, it is nothing but thinking. Its "thingness" is thinking. The material of the thinking is its *pathos*, that is to say, the phenomenological material of the thinking is one and the same. So, "I think I am" is precisely not a "logical" formulation or a discursive linguistic act. It does not matter what it thinks (even if it thinks false syllogisms) but that the fact of thought is the pathological material. In this respect, Henry shows himself a loyal student of Husserl's "principle of all principles" which states that "every original presentive intuition is a legitimizing source of cognition, that everything originally (so to speak, in its 'personal' actuality) offered to us in 'intuition' is to be accepted simply as what it is presented as being, but also only within the limits in which it is presented there."[30] As soon as I ask the question as to whether this phenomenon is "illusory" or "real," I have gone a step too far: the phenomenon is already incontestably there because it appears.

## Beyond Representation

Western philosophy often turns out to be a philosophy of imagination: Life would be somewhere "over there," something the representations of which we live by, instead of feeling it within us. Life, then, would be something "reflected on" instead of lived. We would always be at a distance from life like Hegel teaches. The history of psychoanalysis fits in very well with this picture. Lacan's "imaginary order" only radicalizes this line of argument in Freud. There would be no such thing as a "pain as pain."[31] Life, then, becomes an image, a representation, something that can be depicted in dreams, hopes, art, or the symbols of religion. Pain becomes the image of pain. As Lacan, without mentioning Henry's name, rejects the line of thought of *L'essence de la manifestation*: "suffering is not suffering," and "suffering has its language."[32] In this "representational" strand of psychoanalysis, love becomes the image of a loving mother, as fear becomes fear of something. In other words, the pathological ground is neglected as soon as we access psychoanalysis. Freud's pragmatic choice and systematic refusal to philosophize leads to an underground metaphysics in which the foundation of passion is systematically ignored, exactly like science ignores life. Representation now will lead a life of its own, cut off from passion. The point of the structuralist interpretations of Freud is precisely that there is nothing beyond the representation. Now, Henry's refusal of any structuralist account is *not* that there is something "beyond" representation, but that the appearance of the representation bears its own appearance. Regarded from the perspective of structuralism, everything that appears (symbols, art, myths, etc.) seems to be lacking something, and in an endless scale of displacement, things are assigned a meaning they don't contain.[33] The pathos gets buried under meanings. Even worse, Freud's initial project of going back to the original pathological material, instead of the-ego talk of the patient, is transferred to talk again. Therefore, Freud remains a traditional Western metaphysical thinker (which is, as indicated earlier, the main claim of *Genealogy of Psychoanalysis*) for whom pathos becomes meaning. And from the moment pathos becomes meaning, it is autonomous. It doesn't need any reference to life anymore. What Freudian psychoanalysis unveils is not precisely the pathos, but an alleged hidden meaning. But life has no meaning or intention. It is itself, like the famous rose of Angelus Silesius.[34] Life needs no answer to the question of meaning. Already in Freud's thought, psychoanalysis is sliding toward "philosophy of reflection." Moreover, Freud, according to Henry, acknowledges just one meaning of meaning, that is, "representational" meaning. The unconscious is replaced by a conscious idealism. The strength of Freudianism is precisely that it is not thinking of the unconscious, but that it departs from representational consciousness. The unconscious appears only as a residue of the conscious. No wonder that Lacan states that "the unconscious is structured like a language" because the unconscious itself is understood as the endless displacement of signs and symbols.[35] But what about the appearance of these signs and symbols?

## The Primitive Suffering of Life and Depression

Freudian psychoanalysis pays attention to the representations from which the patient wants to flee. Yet from a radical phenomenological perspective, it is the pathos itself, the affect, that the patient wants to flee. One can try to escape memories or other representations, but one cannot escape the very experience of the escape itself. Again, Henry appears to be a cartesian thinker par excellence, yet not a dualist. And so the flight encounters an impossibility. The escape reveals itself only to itself, that is to say, it is a flight from life itself. Henry shows how Freud's entire analysis tacitly assumes that it is the pathos from which the patient wants to flee. Suppression is an attempt to flee from the feeling of displeasure. To repeat: the feeling, not the representation of displeasure. To elucidate, Henry quotes Kierkegaard, who describes a man who lives by the catchphrase "Either Caesar or nothing."[36] If he doesn't succeed in becoming Caesar, he is in despair. In fact, Kierkegaard continues, the man's self is apparently absolutely intolerable to him. It is not the not-becoming-Caesar that is unbearable, but the self. In other words, the man wants to flee life by a representation, that of Caesar. "What is intolerable to him is that he cannot get rid of himself," Kierkegaard writes. The true delight for the man, at least in his own eyes, is becoming Caesar, that is, not becoming the self. Without this, it is the self that is in despair. In Kierkegaard's words: "For precisely this it is he despairs of, and to his torment, it is precisely this he cannot do, since by despair fire has entered into something that cannot burn, or cannot burn up, that is, into the self." True, this narrative can be interpreted in different ways: a Lacanian interpretation would stress the fact that the man, in order to be, is precisely not himself. The subject is incurably split. He must attach to something which isn't itself in order to become something. To Henry, such an interpretation misses the point that life as self-manifestation is already undeniably there.

Apparently, life might turn against itself. But all this means is that life makes itself manifest, against one's will, that is, one's representation of life. As Henry quotes Freud: "The motive and purpose of repression is nothing else than the avoidance of unpleasure."[37] And as Freud writes: "With an instinct, flight is of no avail, for the ego cannot escape from itself."[38] This implies that there is a real feeling, a pathos here and now, that is nothing but phenomenological. This is why Henry claims that the pleasure principle belongs to phenomenology. Pleasure and unpleasure are nothing but passions, pathos, that is, the subject that reveals itself to itself, or, life.

Life, therefore, is suffering. This is the kernel of the short text "souffrance et vie" (suffering and life).[39] But the word "suffering" here is not to be understood in a negative, gloomy way. In short, it is not a moral claim. What is at stake here is the meaning of the word suffering (*souffrance*). That life is suffering does not mean that life is something that makes us suffer. Life "does" nothing. Life is nothing other than self-experience, pathos, and hence suffering. It is suffering that reveals suffering. This passive suffering reveals nothing but itself, and this is why it is inescapable. At first glance, this sounds like stating the obvious, but in fact, it is what life is: stones do not suffer, nor do they appear to each other. Life, thus, is subjectivity, since life is nothing but self-manifestation it undergoes itself. Henry speaks here of a "primitive suffering."[40] Without this primitive suffering, there would be the inert and dead being of the stone. Life, thus, primarily suffers from itself as it feels its joy by and through itself. Even every form of joy or happiness is possible only because it is never separated from this suffering. We "suffer from joy" like one can "suffer from pain." They are the same in that both psychological modes reveal life itself. One might think here of Heidegger, who uses the term *Stimmung* (which means both mood and tuning) to describe that every being discloses itself in a diversity of singular ways. Every self-manifestation is tuned, but it can never be reduced to just its psychological mood. From a radical phenomenological perspective, the difference between joy and pain is not fundamental. Both are primitive manifestations of life.[41] To Henry, the word "suffering" is understood as pathos, which is the phenomenological mode of affectivity. Like suffering, pathos is passive. It is not an act of an actor. Subjectivity is understood as this suffering, that is not yet understood as a relation toward itself. Subjectivity is not mirrored or reflective.[42] That is why we say that we suffer against our will. As soon as we reflect on our suffering, we want to escape it.[43] But it is this escape itself that is as unavoidable as is the experience that wants to escape from itself. In other words, it is not possible to describe what pathos is within the framework of transcendental phenomenology, since that would imply that there is "something" that can be escaped. But the pathos is not exactly a pathos of something.

One harrowing manifestation of the inescapability of the self-manifestation of life is *depression*. Someone who suffers from depression suffers not "from something." In depression, the subject is not the spectator of the suffering: the subject is revealed to itself as suffering. So to say, phenomenologically speaking, depression has no cause. Depression is not depression of something, but always already manifested as belonging to someone. Henry here refers to *The Sickness Unto Death*, in which Kierkegaard defends the view that despair is sickness of the spirit.[44] Kierkegaard writes that one form of despair consists of not being conscious of having a self. Although the "self" of self-affection of life is not to be primarily understood as the "identical (psychological) self," every self-affection is always already self-affection. That life is self-affection implies that it is subjectivity, and subjectivity is always my subjectivity. It is, in terms of Heidegger, *Jemeinig*. There is nothing anonymous about depression, on the contrary: the depressed person wants to get rid of this mood that is there without any good reason. The depressed person suffers from life that has turned against itself. Henry criticizes an easy way of speaking about a general "crisis of the subject" as some popular media tend to.[45] The same goes for any media hype on the "epidemic of depression." Taken as such, depression would be something like a sociological phenomenon, which can be described and measured from a distance, as a complex of symptoms. From a radical phenomenological viewpoint, depression is nothing but the particular self-manifestation of the self in its inevitability. To clarify this, Henry contrasts depression with despair. In depression, the "me" is there more than ever, while in despair, the "me" is understood in terms of the world. Whereas depression reveals the self of life in its particularity, despair is always despair of the "me," hunting for an identity to be found in the world, that is to say, outside itself. As will be clear by now, contrary to Sartrian or Lacanian thought, to Henry, the relation of the self with itself is never exterior nor mediated, but understood as the immediate pathos of life. Despair is there exactly when the subject is trying to get hold of itself through the exterior world. But this does not imply that the Henrian self is a self as an identity. It is manifestation, revelation, self-experience. When one tries to suppress it, the failure of the suppression only exacerbates it.

## Barbarism, Anxiety, and Neurosis

As I have stated from the beginning of this chapter, despite all his criticism, Henry's fascination for Freud is ultimately positive. In Freud, Henry recognizes a thinker who acknowledges life as a force that can turn against itself. How is that possible? How can life turn against itself? This question is clearly answered in the book, written in near pamphlet style, *Barbarism* (1987). As indicated earlier, Western philosophy and science tend to make life visible at the expense of its self-experience. This "oblivion" of the theory turns out to be fatal because, on the one hand, life is already there while on the other hand, it cannot recognize itself anymore in the scientific representations of it. This is the experience we all have and that was described earlier, about the abyssal difference between the perspective of the concept-pain belonging to the doctor and the self-manifestation of pain. It happens when representations (images, words, theories, the circulation of money in capitalism) become autonomous. "Life," then, is no longer experience, a revelation, but a theme, an abstract entity that governs life. What remains is the feeling of life as anxiety or depression. This is not exactly a "nothingness" as existential philosophy claims, but a fullness, a *parousia*, an ongoing presence of life that is no longer able to deal with itself.

As living beings, people can have the drive to withdraw from life itself but the impossibility of achieving this is anxiety. Depression, as described in the previous section, is a "mode" of anxiety. Anxiety is something that can, of course, be represented, but it can never be reduced to its representation. Anxiety is an affect par excellence. A scream of anxiety might be feigned or acted, but anxiety itself cannot. It is just there in an inescapable manner. This is exactly the message of the classical definition of the difference between anxiety and fear: fear is fear of something, which implies that you can run away from this something. Fear is intentional, transcendent, whereas anxiety is, according to Sartre "without an object." "The self-negation of life is only the will of life to escape itself," writes Henry.[46] But contrary to the existentialist notions of it, according to Henry, anxiety is precisely not nothing or nothingness. Strangely, Henry is here close to Lacan, who, in criticism of existential thought, states that anxiety is "that which deceives not."[47] Life can be a burden, but it can never be "caused" by something outside subjectivity. According to Henry, "Something is a burden through its subjectivity which is burdened with itself up to the unbearability of this weight."[48] In other words, it is not something external that is to be blamed for the suffering but, rather, the attempt to flee from it, not as an action, but as an experience. It is the pathos of life itself that turns itself against itself instead of a lack or nothingness. "The impossibility of fleeing oneself becomes anxiety," writes Henry.[49] One might suppress the ongoing flow of images, but one can never repress the affectivity of it, that is, life. Isn't this attempted outbreak that is doomed to fail in Freudian terms a neurosis? As Henry writes: "The anxiety that Freud described so well, the common denominator of all affects, is in turn merely the anxiety of life's inability to escape itself."[50] And so he gives the reason for his interest in Freud: "Freudianism holds deep within it what our era lacks most. That is undoubtedly the reason—despite its theoretical uncertainties, contradictions, even absurdities—for its strange success."[51] Psychoanalysis entails an understanding of this alleged flight from life. As the later Freud writes: "Life, as we find it, is too hard for us; it brings us too many pains, disappointments, and impossible tasks."[52] It is important to note that Freud says this in *Civilisation and its Discontents* in which he expresses doubt about all these efforts, doomed to fail, by religion and philosophy to formulate an adequate answer to the question of the purpose of human life. Let me once more emphasize that Freud here preludes Henry's thesis that life is not primarily an object to study. This is, I repeat, why psychoanalysis is anything but a science of life, not even a science of the psyche. The least we can say of Freud is that he does not objectify life, but that life reveals itself on the level of the subject. The psychoanalyst is to be exact, not a doctor who "treats" the patient to cure him scientifically, like the mechanic repairs a machine when it is broken.

That we are living in an era of barbarism means that we are living in a time of collective neurosis. To Henry, it is a fatal illusion to consider the achievements of modern science and its Galilean characteristics as autonomous. The problem of Western culture consists, rather, in the hubris of a knowledge that behaves like an autonomous entity. Here we hear an echo of the thesis of the second volume of *Marx*, namely that the economy acts according to its own rules, without any acknowledgment of life.[53] Henry's point is not so that much that we have "lost" life—since that is impossible—but that science thinks and acts as if there's no life: "Science, (. . .) has no idea of what life is; it is in no way concerned with it; it has no relation to it and never will. There can only be access to life in and through life, if it is the case that only life is related to itself in the affectivity of its auto-affection."[54] Indeed, something is lost, yet it is not life itself but the contact of Western thought with life as the ultimate source. Here, we are not far from Husserl's *Crisis*, where the famous concept of the lifeworld is introduced. Henry is, indeed, an heir to Husserl's *Crisis* in that the task of phenomenology, for him, is to go back to the things themselves. And here I come back to Freud: life is too hard to bear for us and it is for that reason that we surrender ourselves to the domain of death, that is to say of scientific symbolization and objectivation. Rather, it is in Freudian vocabulary, suppressed. Life is there, but science doesn't have any access to it, because the only access to life is life itself: by feeling, pathos, sensation, in short, the affectivity of life's auto-affection. The subject that tries to escape from life because it has become unbearable, experiences the naked fullness of life in anxiety. Anxiety is the impossibility to flee from life.

It is, in fact, in *Barbarism* (not by chance written in the same period of *Genealogy*) that Henry makes some important remarks on anxiety. At the social level, this means that our culture is a culture of anxiety. Where culture is always a culture of life, barbarism is the derivative thereof, a result of a structural suppression of Life. Since life cannot be destroyed, the way we experience it is in anxiety, the leftover of the knowledge of science, which leaves us disquieted as we try to find the way out of this disturbance through the same science that caused it.

Henry describes how our culture has become an imaginary cult of science. To science, a kiss is "only a collision of microphysical particles."[55] Life would be a certain behavior as an object of the social-psychologist, in order to gather questionnaires to make serious research of it, with "objective" results. Didn't Stendhal, when he was trying his "science" of love, write that one must have the experience of love first to make a science of it, adding to it: "But where can we see a passion?"[56] In Henry's terms, the passion is invisible. If any passion whatsoever is reduced to terms of "causality" or "measurability," then life in a culture of science implies nothing but death.[57] Death must not be understood as a decay of biological functions but as the denial or suppression of life. In *Barbarism*, anxiety is a property of our culture which doesn't know what to do with the self-manifestation of life—not because we have succeeded in repressing life (for that is impossible) but because, after all, our experience of life has become an experience of anxiety.

## What We Gain from a Henrian Psychoanalysis

Despite some overlap in basic insights, the gap between Freud and Henry remains enormous. Henry is a philosopher, more specifically a phenomenologist. Following Henry, phenomenology is *not* precisely a philosophy of reflection. Philosophy is not "reflecting on life," as if life is a road on which we encounter all kinds of problems about which we need to think carefully. With Henry, we are miles away from such a Greek idea of any "unexamined life which is not worth living." Moreover, phenomenology is a philosophy that does not invent, construct, derive, or build theories, but, rather, the opposite: it brackets theoretical constructions to describe what appears, that is, what gives itself. Taken as such, phenomenology is not a philosophy that directly intervenes actively in the world; rather, the appearing will lead to another attitude. In that regard, it hardly makes sense to call Henry a "practical" philosopher. There is nothing to "apply" here. The application of radical phenomenology has to be found in the fact that something appears, and that this appearance will change our view of ourselves. More concretely, what is at stake for the phenomenologist is the importance of appearing and the reformulation of any practical philosophy that disregards appearance as such. As soon as we are conscious about what appears to us, this will have practical implications. Plato's myth of the men in the cave—is exactly—has consequences because as soon we are aware of the nature of appearing, the entire framework on which we build our practices will change. There is a change of appearance first, followed by practical implications, not the other way around. The same might be true of any kind of conversion: it is not so much the "what" of the appearance as the "that" of the entire frame of appearing itself that has changed. Isn't this exactly what Husserl called the "phenomenological reduction"? And doesn't the same count for psychoanalysis? Don't the so-called practical consequences of psychoanalysis become clear as soon as something reappears to the patient? Something is revealed that in most cases was there from the start, but that was suppressed. And if so, doesn't this presuppose a phenomenology?[58] Indeed, the point of Freudian psychoanalysis is trying to make people remember and talk about the things remembered, rather than doing things. In this sense, it is precisely an analysis of the psyche, not ethics, a philosophy of "what to do?"

It is in this vein of thought that Henry goes along with Freud. Besides, Freud isn't a "philosopher" in that he does not aim to obtain an objective truth, but to obtain the truth of the subject. The entire project of *The Interpretation of Dreams* makes clear that it doesn't make sense to gain general, objective knowledge of dreams, but on the contrary, to obtain precisely subjective knowledge of the dream. This is exactly why I've stated that *The Interpretation of Dreams* is not a science of dreams, which would imply something like a methodology to denote the objective meaning of dream images. The Freudian approach is an interpretation, that is, the dream images are there to be interpreted by the patient, not to be explained by the doctor-scientist. The dream can only be interpreted if the experiences of the day and the life of the dreamer are known. In this sense, Freud's psychoanalysis implies a theory of the subject—not a theory of subjectivity in general, but a knowledge that is connected with the subject itself. This "knowledge" is not gained by observation or theory-testing, but by a process of anamnesis, or, becoming aware of things that happened in the past.

So, both Freud and Henry understand the subject from an invisible layer, against the so-called top-of-the-iceberg-ego. The critical, scientific, self-conscious subject of enlightenment is, first of all, a living subject that at every moment of its rationality risks passing over life. This implies, as Freud remarks on many occasions in his work, that the subject and consciousness do not coincide. The subject is not what it thinks it is. In this sense, Freud's psychoanalysis is a complaint against the Western philosophical presupposition that the subject coincides with consciousness.

Yet, isn't this exactly what Michel Henry *shares* with Freud? To both, life cannot be reduced to consciousness as the self-aware ego. There is always already something unconscious, as soon we start to think about what consciousness is. It is this unconscious that doesn't appear, that remains invisible, but is nevertheless a phenomenological reality, an experience. At least, it will not focus only on representations, but, rather, on the Freudian frame of concepts that can never become objects to consciousness. These "invisible" affects are nevertheless responsible for the neurotic behavior of the patient.[59]

It is not possible within the scope of this chapter to formulate what a "Henrian psychoanalysis" would possibly entail. Therefore just a few short comments. The first thing we might conclude, with care, is that, if there is such a thing as Henrian psychoanalysis, it does not try to suppress life, not even anxiety or depression, but, rather, to regain the source that springs from life itself, instead of "objectifying" it the way modern psychiatry tends to do (like DSM 5, the "scientific labeling" of deviations). It seems that modern psychiatry does exactly the opposite. Life becomes an object that must meet objective preconditions. Patients are then like cars being called back to the workplace. They must again become well-functioning people, according to scientific standards. It is clear that to Henry, this is what barbarism entails. Secondly, the consequences of a Henrian reformulation of psychoanalysis reach beyond the sofa. The cultural-critical potential of psychoanalysis, which already plays an important role in the late Freud, is also reflected in Henry's work. It touches our very culture as Henry in *Barbarism* describes it.

Allow me, without aiming to be exhaustive, even not concluding, to sketch a last suggestion. A whole new field is opened up when we understand culture as springing from life rather than the other way around. Today, both traditional and Lacanian psychoanalysis have influenced many sections of cultural life, like art, religion, film, and literature. Would Michel Henry—also a novelist himself—not admit that radical phenomenological psychoanalysis is suitable to interpreting art and more specifically literature? Is literature, contrary to science, preeminently able to make the invisible visible? Is there not at least a tradition in literature that unveils the self-affection of life beyond the realm of mere representation and narrativity? As Henry mentions in an interview, the novel is based on imagination, to be sure, but the greatness of literature is that it can describe at the same time the self-revelation of life, including anxiety (which has, after all, no "narrative" structure).[60]

Let me, therefore, end not with a "conclusion" but with an example of such a description. In the short novel *Seize the Day* by Saul Bellow, the main character Wilhelm perishes under the pressure that society and especially his ex-wife and his father exert on him.[61] After many troubles, he is losing control of life and feels that he is unable to deal anymore with the "business of life, the real business," as he calls it. A certain Tamkin, described as a psychiatrist, has the type of conversations with him that could easily be described as the famous talking cure. The reader gets the impression of a clever, well-spoken man, but at the same time someone for whom psychiatry is big business. Tamkin talks about life, "spiritual compensation," and about the "real presence" that Wilhelm seems to lack. Wilhelm must live in the "here and now," and "seize the day" is his motto. Nobody even seems to know exactly whether he is a real psychiatrist or not. But as it turns out, it is nothing but empty talk and Wilhelm remains behind with his feelings that in no way correspond to the so-called reality. Tamkin claims that only facts count, and so, although Wilhelm is certainly in need of help, at the end of the day there is no real contact between them. The talk of Tamkin is exactly the discourse of the self-conscious, developed, and scientific man. In the end, life as pathos is completely neglected. The story ends with an outburst of emotion from Wilhelm when he happens to enter a chapel where a dead man is laid out. He does not know the dead man, and people are wondering about the connection between the dead man and Wilhelm, since he is so emotional. He finds himself "past words, past reason, coherence." If we interpret this in terms of this chapter, we can say that unavoidably nothing but life remains: life that is not governed anymore by language or reason, and that in the face of the dead man endures itself.

# Notes

1 Mikkel Borch-Jacobson, *The Emotional Tie. Psychoanalysis, Mimesis, and Affect* (Stanford, CA: Stanford University Press, 1992), 123.
2 Sigmund Freud, *An Outline of Psychoanalysis*, in *The Penguin Freud Reader* (London: Penguin Books, 2006), 1.
3 Cf. Michel Henry, *The Essence of Manifestation*, trans. G. Etzkorn (The Hague: Martinus Nijhoff, 1973), 541.

4 Michel Henry, "Philosophie et subjectivité," in *De la subjectivité. Tome II. Phénoménologie de la vie* (Paris: PUF, 2003), 25.
5 Cf. Michel Henry, *Barbarism* (London and New York: Continuum, 2012), 17.
6 It was Jacques Lacan who introduced the term into psychoanalysis. Cf. Borch-Jacobson, *The Emotional Tie*.
7 Freud, *An Outline of Psychoanalysis*, 1.
8 Ibid., 12.
9 Which is the purpose of Henry's reading of Freud as he states in an article "Phenomenology and Psychoanalysis," in *Phénoménologie de la vie: Tome V* (Paris: PUF, 2003), 70; Michel Henry, *The Genealogy of Psychoanalysis*, trans. D. Brick (Stanford: University Press, 1993), 6.
10 "Certainly, any psychoanalysis must have its principles *a priori*. In particular, it must know what it is looking for, or how will it be able to find it?" Jean-Paul Sartre, *Being and Nothingness*, trans. H. Barnes (London and New York: Routledge, 1969), 602.
11 Michel Henry, *Philosophy and Phenomenology of the Body*, trans. G. Etzkorn (The Hague: Martinus Nijhoff, 1975), 50.
12 Henry, *The Genealogy of Psychoanalysis*, 1–10.
13 Ibid., 284.
14 Henry, "La critique du sujet," *De la subjectivité*, tome 2, 19.
15 Ibid.
16 Borch-Jacobson, *The Emotional Tie*, 139.
17 Henry, *The Genealogy of Psychoanalysis*, 298.
18 Sigmund Freud, "Screen Memories," in *The Penguin Freud Reader* (London: Penguin Books, 2006), 541–60.
19 Henry, *The Genealogy of Psychoanalysis*, 281–2.
20 Henry, *The Essence of Manifestation*, 462.
21 Henry, *The Genealogy of Psychoanalysis*, 282.
22 Henry, *The Essence of Manifestation*, 541.
23 Cf. Saying to self "I must be strong. It is just this moment but I will survive." The psychological ego might ignore the pain, where the Henrian "subject" cannot.
24 As psychoanalyst André Green, who wrote an important study of the affect in Freud's thought, notes: "Its importation into French is due to Freud, who sometimes uses *Affekt*, sometimes *Empfindung*, sometimes *Gefühl*. *Affekt* has always been translated into French by *affect*, *Empfindung* by *sensation*, and *Gefühl* by *sentiment*." Andre Green, *The Fabric of Affect in the Psychoanalytic Discourse*, trans. Alan Sheridan (London and New York: 1999), 5. It is also Green that makes a reproachful remark to Henry, for whom the affect plays a key role already in *L'essence de la manifestation*, but totally ignores the role of psychoanalysis. Green's book appeared before *Genealogy de la psychanalyse*, in which the lacuna is filled. Green, 278, note 10.
25 Henry, *The Genealogy of Psychoanalysis*, 27–8.

26 Ibid., 28. See Descartes, *Passions of the Soul*, article 26.
27 Sigmund Freud, *Die Traumdeutung*, Studienausgabe, Band II (Frankfurt am Main: Fischer Taschenbug Verlag), 96 (my transl).
28 Freud, *An Outline*, 26.
29 René Descartes, First Meditation.
30 Edmund Husserl, *Ideas Pertaining to a Pure Phenomenology and to a Phenomenological Philosophy*. First Book (The Hague: Martinus Nijhoff, 1982), sec. 24 [p.44]).
31 To Jacques Lacan, the imaginary order stands for the original loss of any stable idea of a subject. To Lacan, there is not a subject first to be represented, rather there is a representation that results eventually in a subject, which is already a misrecognition. On several occasions in his work, Lacan refers to Henry, in order to refuse a phenomenology of life. Take, for instance: "In response, I will start off with something I came across in the work of a philosopher recently awarded full academic honors. According to him, 'The truth of pain is pain itself'" (Jacques Lacan, *Écrits* (New York and London: W.W. Norton & Company, 1999, 739). On another occasion, Lacan is explicitly taking a stance against Henry's "The truth of pain is pain itself" by claiming that pain is simply not itself. The subject, Lacan argues, is always "before" or "after" the pain. In other words, the subject relates to pain, which implies a primordial distance toward itself. It is this distance that, according to Henry, is entirely absent in every modification of pathos. Fair enough, Lacan says that life is a topic to which psychoanalysis has not been able to contribute much (J. Lacan (2017 [1972]), *Conférence de Louvain*, J.-A. Miller (ed.), "La Cause du Désir," no. 96, 7–30; 11). See Dominiek Hoens, "Is Life But A Pascalian Dream? A Commentary On Lacan's Louvain Lecture," *Psychoanalytische Perspectieven*, 36, no. 2 (2018): 169–85). Henry, in his turn, rejects Lacanian psychoanalysis: "In all seriousness, people can now say that the unconscious is structured like a language" (Henry, *The Genealogy of Psychoanalysis*, 292).
32 Jacques Lacan, *Le séminaire, livre XVI. D'un Autre à l'autre* (Paris: Seuil, 2006), 69, 70.
33 Henry, *The Genealogy of Psychoanalysis*, 293.
34 "The rose is without 'why.' It blooms simply because it blooms. It pays no attention to itself, nor does it ask whether anyone sees it." Quoted by Michel Henry in *Incarnation. Une philosophie de la chair* (Paris: Seuil, 2000), 321.
35 Cf. Henry, *The Genealogy of Psychoanalysis*, 292.
36 Sören Kierkegaard, *The Sickness Unto Death* (Princeton, NJ: Princeton University Press, 1941), 16–17.
37 Henry, *The Genealogy of Psychoanalysis*, 309.
38 Ibid., 307.
39 Henry, *De la phénoménologie: Tome I. Phénoménologie de la vie* (Paris: PUF, 2003), 143–56.

40 Henry, "Souffrance et vie," appears in *Phénoménologie de la vie I: De la phénoménologie* (Paris: PUF, 2003), 143–56, 152.
41 Cf. Henry, *Barbarism*, 37. "Primitive," because the judgment comes only after.
42 Henry, *Philosophy and Phenomenology of the Body*, 14.
43 This is described by August Strindberg in his *Inferno* as "an extraordinary expansion of my inner sense; a spiritual power which longed to realize itself." August Strindberg, *The Inferno* (New York: The Knickenbocker Press, 1913), 48.
44 Henry, "Souffrance et vie," 153; S. Kierkegaard, "The Sickness Unto Death," Part I, Chapter 1, 19.
45 Henry, "Souffrance et vie," 153.
46 Henry, *Barbarism*, 92.
47 Jacques Lacan, *Anxiety: The Seminar of Jacques Lacan*, Book X (Cambridge: Polity, 2014), 69–84.
48 Henry, *Barbarism*, 99.
49 Ibid., 104.
50 Henry, *The Genealogy of Psychoanalysis*, 7.
51 Ibid.
52 Sigmund Freud, *Civilization and its Discontents*, trans. James Strachey (New York and London: W.W. Norton & Company, 1961), 23.
53 Michel Henry, *Marx: I. Une philosophie de la réalité; II. Une philosophie de l'économie* (Paris: Gallimard, 1976).
54 Henry, *Barbarism*, 17.
55 Henry, *Barbarism*, xiv (preface to the second edition).
56 Stendhal, *De l'amour* (Paris: Garnier-Flammarion, 1965).
57 Michel Henry, *Du communisme au capitalisme. Théorie d'une catastrophe* (Paris: Odile Jacob, 1990).
58 The same point has been made by Jean-Paul Sartre in *Being and Nothingness*. The moment of the "insight" of the patient remains obscure in Freud.
59 Take, for instance, the role of the drives in Freudianism. To Freud, the drive (*Trieb*) itself is never *experienced*. What is encountered is just its representation or idea in the mind. In the history of psychoanalytic theory, this has led to a dualistic theory: the drive can only be known by its symptoms. In classical psychoanalysis, one never starts by analyzing drives, but, instead, their representations. The concept of "drive" is not a metaphysical or ontological concept. Drives are repressed and might only be guessed by their derivatives: associations, symptoms, anxiety, and other kinds of material derived from a repressed drive.
60 Michel Henry, "Narrer le pathos," in *Phénoménologie de la vie: Tome III. De l'art et du politique* (Paris: PUF), 309–24, 313.
61 Saul Bellow, *Seize the Day* (London: Alison Press/Secker & Warburg, 1985).

# 7

# The World or Life's Fragility

## A New Critical Reading of Henry's Phenomenology of Life

P. Lorelle

From where does the world get its sensibility? This chapter hopes to suggest that the world gets its sensibility from life's very fragility. Life is taken here in Michel Henry's sense as the primordial *"how"* of any phenomenality, the affectivity of that which experiences itself through a self-affection. However, life has precisely not been thought by Henry in its fragility. Life's self-affection is an *indestructible* self-affection. Life's absoluteness, which consists in feeling its own indestructibility, is what Henry thinks as its absolute autonomy. Life would be irreducibly bound to itself and, as such, self-sufficient.

Yet, as this chapter will first try to show through a new critical reading of Henry, one cannot deduce the sensible world from life's absolute autonomy. If life is not sensible in Henry,[1] sensibility is fully alive. And Henry aims at explaining the world's sensibility from life's insensible mode of phenomenality. This deduction takes two different forms in Henry, giving rise to two different concepts of "world": (1) Life's *objectification* or *exteriorization*, elaborated by *The Essence of Manifestation* and never really questioned since;[2] and (2) Life's *inner* development, elaborated by *Seeing the Invisible*, Henry's essay on Kandinsky. (1) If the world first appears in its exteriority to life, as this heterogeneous, objective, and non-affective mode of phenomenality, (2) the world also appears as an affective world, inhabited by life's affectivity—that is, as a *"cosmos"* or a "lifeworld." If both deductions fail to generate the world's sensibility, it is not because of life's "subjectivity": Life is not a subject's mode of phenomenality, as a being that would exclude any worldly being,[3] but an ontological mode of phenomenality. Nor would such a failure be because of life's phenomenological determination and structure as a "self-affection": our point here is precisely to suggest that it would be better if the sensible manifestation of the world were thought about from this primordial mode of phenomenality. According to this contention, whether the concepts of "life" and "world" *only* exclude each other *phenomenologically* (as two different modes of phenomenality) or they do not exclude each other at all, nothing prevents the world from appearing as life, in the mode of self-affection—nothing but the "absoluteness" of this self-affection: an absoluteness that precisely ceases to be phenomenological. If Henry fails to generate sensibility from life's self-affection, it is not because of life's subjectivity, but rather because of life's absoluteness.

In a second moment of this reflection, we will try to sketch the converse possibility of the world's sensibility arising from life's primordial fragility. There remains, in Henry, a vestige of this fragility in the concept of "self-negation" developed by *La barbarie* and conceived as life's very own illness. Self-affection would be essentially subjected to a self-negation. Yet, life's self-negation is not thought radically by Henry, and one needs to radicalize the essential dimension of this negation in order to reveal life's essential fragility. Life's self-affection would originally be exposed to the resistance of otherness, its autonomous character being always already negated. And sensibility would arise only from the fragility of this bond, that is, from the fragility of this bond that precisely links Life to itself. But is it not the very definition of fragility to threaten what it determines? The inherent paradox of this thesis will, then, eventually appear: fragility, as the condition of life's and the world's shared and primordial sensibility, to the same degree threatens them with insensibility.

## From Absolute Life to Sensible Life

### The Objective World

We can distinguish two kinds of "generations" of the sensible in Henry. The first one, developed by *The Essence of Manifestation*, consists in an objectification. If manifestation gives itself originally in a self-manifestation—which is the primordial mode of phenomenality—it departs from itself, opening what Henry calls the "phenomenological distance" of a horizon. This alienation is an *opposition* or an objectification: The essence posits the world before itself as the finite horizon of objectivity. And, according to the Heideggerian-Kantian perspective of *The Essence of Manifestation*, the sensible dimension of the horizon results from this power, that is, in the Schematism, imagination.

The horizon of the world is sensible; it is a horizon of visibility because it results from the sensible transposition of the concepts of the understanding by imagination—which, in Heidegger's reading of the Schematism, consists in the creation of a "pre-vision," of a schematic view prior to any perception.[4] Imagination creates the sensible horizon that it receives. As being both spontaneous and receptive, imagination makes the understanding sensible—as Heidegger claims—and it makes sensibility autonomous as well. This is why sensibility can be defined by Henry as the *power* or the *act* of positing the world that it receives.

> The power of rendering sensible, namely, of sensing [. . .] designates the projection of the horizon through which, by receiving it, the essence affects itself [. . .] as the act wherein the essence presents to itself that which it intuits. *The essence of sensibility is included in the structure of such an act.* [Le pouvoir de rendre sensible, c'est-à-dire de sentir [. . .] désigne la projection de l'horizon par lequel, en le recevant, l'essence s'affecte elle-même [. . .] comme l'acte dans lequel l'essence se propose à elle-même ce qu'elle intuitionne. *Dans la structure d'un tel acte est incluse l'essence de la sensibilité.*[5]

Yet, such a description of the essence of sensibility raises two different kinds of issues: methodological and phenomenological.

From a methodological standpoint, this description of the sensible is only presupposed by Henry, without being grounded at all. In fact, *The Essence of Manifestation* starts from the world so conceived, in order to deduce the necessity of a self-affection. Henry builds its whole demonstration upon this misinterpretation of sensibility, maintaining the ontological relevance of the monist presupposition (that is only condemned for its unilaterality). Henry renders the world autonomous in order to deduce life's absolute autonomy. As soon as the world, indeed, consists in an objectifying creation, one cannot understand how this creation can affect itself—since it precisely implies an abstraction from life's affectivity. Hence the necessity of an affective receptivity, prior to the world itself. Sensibility, understood as an objectification, cannot ensure by itself its own affective dimension.[6] Because the world is conceived as a power of transcendence or objectification—a power that could not appear to itself—it becomes necessary, from a phenomenological standpoint,[7] to posit a primordial and non-objectifying self-manifestation. Or, as Henry puts it clearly: "It is because representation essentially pro-jects before itself that which it represents to itself, that the problem arises of knowing how it can receive the content thus pro-jected" [c'est parce que la représentation pro-jette essentiellement devant elle ce qu'elle se représente que le problème se pose de savoir comment elle peut recevoir le contenu ainsi projeté.][8] But, if on the contrary one stops conceiving the world as a horizon of objectivity, one does not need to wonder anymore how it could be affected by this horizon. This suppresses the necessity of positing the precedence of a self-affection. *The Essence of Manifestation* commits here a *petitio principii* that puts into question its own methodological requirement of transparency or autonomy. The world's mode of manifestation, thus conceived as a power of representation, of transcendence or objectification—and that Henry relies upon in order to demonstrate the necessity of a primordial self-affection—already presupposes the necessity of this self-affection. The world, as a power of objectification, presupposes what it is meant to demonstrate: the necessity of a primordial self-affection.

Now from a phenomenological standpoint, Henry fails to explain both the "affective" and the "sensible" dimensions of the world that he wants to deduce. Indeed, if affectivity constitutes the phenomenological effectivity of any sensibility, it is from this very effectivity that sensibility, conceived as an objectification, abstracts itself. Affectivity is this self-affection of phenomenality, life's way of maintaining itself close to itself, whereas the world is precisely life's abstraction from itself, its being posited in the "in front of," as a non-affective objectivity. The world cannot be affective if its very mode of phenomenality consists in an abstraction from affectivity. Affectivity cannot preserve itself as the result of its own alienation. And, thus deprived from any possibility of affection, the world is not explained in its sensibility either. Sensibility cannot be generated from life's objectification.

## The Affective World: The Cosmos

In order to understand what Henry means by an "affective world,"[9] one needs to think of another form of generation. The world is not doomed, in Henry, to designate the objectifying structure of phenomenality or to designate that which differs from life. The world reappears, instead, from within life, as its own interiority.

Every phenomenon, the world included, can give itself interiorly, says Henry in *Seeing the Invisible*, referring to the theoretical writings of Kandinsky. And by depriving the world of any objectifying reference, abstract painting would reveal the world's very interiority, its elements of pure affectivity. The interiority of the world then consists in these sensible qualities, these forms and colors which, once deprived of any reference to the utilitarian meanings of the objects that they constitute, reveal themselves as pure affectivity. These qualities are not exterior characters of things, but sensations that are interiorly constituted by life's self-affection, just as a pain or a sensation of warmth, a color, says Henry, is an inner sensation or, as Descartes puts it, a "quality of the soul."[10]

The first objection that can be addressed to this conception is that it reintroduces the relevance of secondary qualities, relative and subjective, whose relations to the things themselves can be thought only in terms of an objectification—even though it is thought here as a non-alienating projection, inner to life. "If there is a color that is spread on things, it is only the projection in the outside of what finds its primordial site in us" [Il y a bien une couleur étalée sur les choses mais elle n'est que la projection au-dehors de ce qui trouve son site originel en nous].[11] This first objection seems to be refuted, though, by Henry's extension of these sensible qualities to the very forms of the world—whereas forms traditionally belong to the things as their primary qualities. According to Henry, the form is, indeed, inhabited by this very same force that inhabits us. Hence the possibility of understanding a point or a line as the invulnerable force of a self-affection. These secondary qualities are not opposed to primary qualities, then, and every reality resolves itself into these elements' self-affection. From these elements Henry deduces therefore the world's affectivity:

> Because each cosmic element has its own tone—its experience of itself in an impression that is its life—the whole cosmos is alive [. . .] As such, there can be no world without an affection and without the sensations that are the Whole of our sensibility and that continually make it vibrate like the flesh of the universe. [Parce que chaque élément cosmique a sa sonorité propre—l'épreuve qu'il fait de lui-même dans une impression qui est sa vie—, le cosmos tout entier est vivant [. . .] Ainsi n'y a-t-il pas de monde sans une affection, sans l'ensemble des sensations qui sont le Tout de notre sensibilité et ne cessent de la faire vibrer comme la chair même de l'univers].[12]

This leads us to a second objection, this time condemning the atomism of such a conception of sensibility. The world would be constituted by these atoms of sensations and would consist in their totality. The world's generation would not consist in life's alienation anymore, nor in a mere projection, but, rather, in the synthesis of these atoms of self-affection, which fails in the first place to account for the priority of the world's givenness over its elements. The world cannot be generated from a point and, as Henry himself argued in *The Essence of Manifestation*, its self-affection is not secondary with respect to its elements. But this also fails to account for the dimension of otherness of a self-affecting world. If the world affects itself, opening the possibility of any affection, it precisely does not affect itself as a point—as the concentric and invulnerable force of that which remains absolutely close to itself. This explains the systematic reintroduction of a split in these descriptions between the elements of the world that affect themselves absolutely and their necessary loss. Henry's thesis of the superiority of abstract painting over figuration relies, in fact, upon this split.

We have at first tried to answer the question "From where does the world get its sensibility?" negatively: the world's sensibility cannot be deduced from life's absolute originality. From the autonomy of life, thus conceived by Henry, nothing can result but a sensibility which is itself thought as autonomous—conceived as a power of opposition, a power of projection, or a power of synthesis. The sensible becomes the production of a world from which it cannot be affected in return, that is, the production of a world that does not affect itself.

## From Sensible Life to Absolute Life

We will now try to present the opposing phenomenological thesis of life's primordial fragility. According to this thesis, only this fragility could explain sensibility and enable life to be thought as the world's very mode of phenomenality.

### Fragility and Sensibility

Life's fragility is thought by Henry in *La barbarie* as life's inner generation of the world through its practical development. Self-affection gains here a threefold dimension: (1) as a desire—life's desire to feel itself more intensely; (2) as an effort—life's effort to feel itself more intensely through a self-affected praxis or action; (3) as a bodily self-affection—because "this praxis . . . is our Body" [cette praxis . . . c'est notre Corps].[13] In its always increasing effort of coming to itself, this praxis generates the cultural world in which life feels itself always more intensely. And the world not only results from this practical power of production. It is thought, from the very beginning of this process, as being inherent to the body's self-affected movement. Life's desire is the desire of "a sensibility to feel more" [une sensibilité qui veut sentir davantage].[14] And life desires the world itself, a world that is already there, immanent to the action's self-affection, as that which first resists this action. The world resists this self-affected action, from "the inside," says Henry. First, the body can affect itself only in an effort, as overcoming the resistance of the organic body. Between the body that affects itself and the body that is being affected by itself, a resistance already lies. And this resistance then becomes the earth's itself—a resistance that cannot be overcome anymore. The earth's insurmountable resistance, says Henry, is experienced "from within the corporeal and subjective movement" [à l'intérieur du mouvement corporel subjectif][15]—a movement that therefore becomes the world's itself. According to this text, the earth's insurmountable otherness would be inherent to life's self-affection. Self-affection would experience the earth interiorly as the otherness of an inner resistance. Henry does not stop here, though, and ends up overcoming the insurmountable in a "corpspropriation."[16] However, this primordial breach of otherness at the heart of self-affection negates life's absolute autonomy and can explain its sensibility—the bond that attaches life to itself becoming more tenuous. Thus only can the world be thought from this primordial mode of phenomenality as that which experiences itself through otherness—an otherness that incessantly threatens its identity. Yet, in this exposure, life opened itself to its own loss, as if this tiny fissure at the core of its self-affection forbade life from remaining close to itself. Sensibility and fragility thus come to designate one and the same mode of phenomenality.

However, after having recognized life's primordial fragility, Henry in *La barbarie* ends up redoubling its absoluteness. He then divides life into this fragile life, on the one hand, and an absolute Life, on the other hand, whose coming to itself is prior to any praxis and does not risk any loss. Yet, sensibility cannot be thought as resulting from an absolute life, which will become God Himself in Henry's later texts. Rather, the idea of an absolute life reveals sensibility as life's repressed primordial fragility, as that which, in it, is being negated. Far from resulting from an absolute and autonomous life that could produce it, sensibility is supposed by an Absolute Life that represses it. In this text, therefore, there appears the exact reversed movement than the one that is explicitly described by Henry—not the movement that leads from life's absoluteness to its sensibility, but the movement that leads from life's primordial fragility to the thesis of its absoluteness. If Life ends up preceding itself, it is in order to escape the experience of its own fragility. Life's ultimate "absolutization" at the place of its greatest exposition is proportional to the threat hanging over it. And, as we eventually want to show, this movement does not depend solely on Henry's obsession with absoluteness. It is, rather, inscribed in the very essence of life's fragility, of a fragility that, by its very definition, contains the possibility of its own negation.

## Fragility and Insensitivity

Life's fragility is also thought by Henry as a "self-negation," a self-negation that, once radicalized, applies to Henry's very concept of Life. If absolute life is not subjected to life's self-negation, it is because it already results from such a negation.

Life's self-negation consists, according to Henry, in the "*self*-pathetic" dimension of self-affection. Life experiences itself as suffering, as that which afflicts itself and cannot get rid of itself. This suffering essentially contains the will not to be itself. Hence self-affection's essential tendency to self-negation. This negation is not, says Henry, an abstract hypothesis, but, rather, a true phenomenon[17]—the phenomenon of its own loss or abstraction. Except that, short of reducing suffering to sheer complacency, life's absolute autonomy forbids its pathetic dimension instead of explaining it. Life's suffering would not consist in an experience that we go through—since there is no otherness through which one could go. Life's suffering would consist here only in the impossibility of ridding itself of itself—hence the comforting necessity of this suffering becoming a *jouissance*. Life's weakness does not consist in its fragility, according to Henry, but, instead, in its invulnerability. Hence the possibility of deducing, from this "weakness," the superpower of an infinite force.

Conversely, to think life's genuine fragility would imply thinking the possibility of this bond coming undone in sensibility. Self-affection is pathetic, phenomenologically speaking, because it is always already a sensible experience of otherness. And life's self-negation here would bear on its very sensible dimension in such a way that the phenomenon that results from this negation is this Absolute Life thought by Henry as primordial. Henryan life suffers the very same sickness as the one it condemns. If life's foreclosed affectivity is a mode of phenomenality, it is a non-primordial mode that is grounded upon the negation, by life, of its own sensibility. If this remains a phenomenon, it is a phenomenon that experiences itself in its absolute autonomy only, and that is, as such, deprived of any other content that would constitute its reality: It is the phenomenon of its own loss or abstraction. Henryan Absolute Life would therefore find its literary counterpart in the character of the neighbor in Rilke's *Notebooks of Malte Laurids Brigge*. This character, who cannot bear feeling amid the earth's motions the passage of time and the reality of death, can only live his life lying down on his bed with his eyes closed, thus persevering in the illusion of his own indestructibility and losing life itself while trying to preserve it from its very fragility.

More than the insensibility of life, it is the correlative possibility of the insensibility of the world that explains such fragility. An absolute life that only feels itself can only posit an objective world that precisely does not feel itself. Whereas life and the world are confused in this primordial sensibility, they become opposed to each other as soon as life splits off its inner otherness to reject it entirely on the side of objectivity. These two modes of phenomenality—wrongly thought by Henry as "fundamental"—thus result from one and the same negation. And the world's insensibility—a world whose manifestation is essentially objective and non-affective—is phenomenologically grounded, as rooted in the very *fragility of its sensibility*. Life's newfound fragility explains not only the primordial sensibility of all phenomenality but also the inverse possibility of its own loss.

## Conclusion

To think the world's sensibility as a fragility is to think its indigence. In *Incarnation*, Henry does speak about the "ontological indigence of the world's manifestation" [l'indigence ontologique de l'apparaître du monde].[18] But the indigence at stake here is very different from the one that is thought by Henry. If the world is indigent, according to Henry, it is because it depends in its manifestation on a prior mode of manifestation—because it cannot explain by itself its own mode of phenomenality thus conceived as transcendence or objectivity. But, as soon as one stops presuming the relevance of objectivity as the world's mode of phenomenality—as soon as one stops accepting the world's dependence upon an objectifying power—the world is freed from such an indigence, appearing at its own beginning. The world is infinitely solid in this sense. And the sensible, said Merleau-Ponty, can be explained only by itself. The sensible experiences itself incessantly, its phenomenality being understood as a self-affection. The sensible world's indigence is not synonymous with dependence, and one could say that the sensible is being absolutized instead of life—as Henry argues against Merleau-Ponty.[19] But sensibility appeared here as a fragility. And what would an *absolute fragility* be but precisely nothing absolute? The world's ontological indigence is sensibility's very precarity, self-affection's pathetic exposure to otherness and its resulting possibility of negating itself. From this possibility arise both an Absolute Life that affects only itself and the non-affective otherness of an objective world that cannot affect itself anymore. Against such an essential possibility of life's and the world's autonomy, the recognition of their shared and primordial fragility certainly puts responsibility on the line. Ethics would not result from life's absoluteness but from its very fragility, awakening the responsibility to preserve the world's essential sensibility, from the possibility, just as essential, of its destruction.[20]

## Notes

1 See §52 of *The Essence of Manifestation*: "*As such, affectivity is never sensible*" [*L'affectivité comme telle n'est jamais sensible*]. Michel Henry, *L'essence de la manifestation* (Paris: PUF, 1963), 580; *The Essence of Manifestation*, trans. Girard Etzkorn (The Hague: Martinus Nijhoff, 1973), 464.
2 It reappears, for instance, in *Incarnation*.
3 This is clarified especially by Henry's preparatory notes to *The Essence of Manifestation*, ed. Grégori Jean and Jean Leclercq. See Michel Henry, *Notes préparatoires à L'essence de la manifestation: la subjectivité*, Revue internationale Michel Henry, Presses universitaires de Louvain, n°3–2012.
4 See Martin Heidegger, *Kant und das Problem der Metaphysik*, GA. III (Frankfurt am Main: Vittorio Klostermann GmbH, 1991), §21.
5 Henry, *L'essence de la manifestation*, 575; *The Essence of Manifestation*, 460.
6 Ibid., 601, 481: "*The tonality of the act of sensing is its self-feeling itself, it is its affectivity*. Affectivity and affectivity alone permits sensibility to be what it is, an existence, the thickness of a life gathered about itself and experiencing itself as affected, suffering and supporting that which affects it, and not the cold grasp of the thing or its indifferent contemplation" [*La tonalité de l'acte de sentir est son se sentir soi-même, est son affectivité. L'affectivité, elle seule, permet que la sensibilité soit ce qu'elle est, une existence, l'épaisseur d'une vie ramassée en elle-même et s'éprouvant elle-même tandis qu'elle est affectée, souffrant et supportant ce qui l'affecte, non la froide saisie de celui-ci ou sa contemplation indifférente*].
7 Ibid., 598, 479: "Affectivity is not the condition of sensing in the sense of a condition dislodged by reflexive analysis, a logical condition; rather, it constitutes the effectiveness of the act of sensing considered in itself, its own irrefutable and concrete phenomenality, it constitutes the experience of sensing identical to it and constitutive of its reality" [*L'affectivité n'est pas la condition du sentir au sens d'une condition dégagée par l'analyse réflexive, d'une condition logique, elle constitue bien plutôt l'effectivité de l'acte de sentir considéré en lui-même, sa phénoménalité propre, irrécusable et concrète, l'expérience du sentir, identique à celui-ci et constitutive de sa réalité*].
8 Ibid., 293, 237.

9 Ibid., 608–9, 487: "It is the world itself, this external and 'real' world of things and objects which is affective and must be understood as such" [C'est le monde lui-même, ce monde extérieur et "réel," le monde des choses et des objets, qui est affectif et doit être compris comme tel].

10 Kandinsky would thus reveal "the sensible and carnal stratum of the dawning universe, this flow of pure impressions in which it gives itself to us by merging with our life" [la strate sensible et charnelle de l'univers à l'état naissant, ce flux d'impressions pures en lesquelles il se donne à nous en se fondant en notre vie]. Michel Henry, *Phénoménologie de la vie, Tome III, De l'art et du politique* (Paris: PUF, 2004, 234), our translation. And the world thus appears as a cosmos, through the interiority of its sensible qualities. See Michel Henry, *Voir l'invisible. Sur Kandinsky* (Paris: PUF, 2005), 234; *Seeing the Invisible: On Kandinsky*, trans. Scott Davidson (London: Continuum, 2009), 136: "It follows that the reality of the world is the same as the reality of art, exhausting the division between the visible and the invisible. That is why everything given in the light of the world also belongs to art, which possesses its inner essence" [Il s'ensuit que la réalité du monde est la même que celle de l'art, s'épuisant ici et là dans le clivage du visible et de l'invisible. Voilà pourquoi tout ce qui se donne dans la lumière du premier appartient également au second, possède son essence intérieure].

11 Henry, *Phénoménologie de la vie, Tome III, De l'art et du politique*, 236 (our translation).

12 Henry, *Voir l'invisible*, 234; *Seeing the Invisible*, 139.

13 Michel Henry, *La barbarie*, 2nd ed. (Paris: PUF, 2004), 80; *Barbarism*, trans. Scott Davidson (London: Continuum, 2012), 44. Translation our own.

14 Ibid., 3; xiv. Translation our own.

15 Ibid., 81, 45. Translation our own.

16 This "corpspropriation" is described by Henry as being more original than any possible objectification: "Body and Earth are bound by a Corpspropriation so original that nothing ever occurs in the 'in front of' of a pure Outside, as an ob-ject" [Corps et Terre sont liés par une Corpspropriation si originelle que rien n'advient jamais dans l'en-face d'un pur Dehors, à titre d'ob-jet]. (Ibid., 82, 45). Translation our own.

17 Ibid., 5, xvii.

18 Michel Henry, *Incarnation. Une philosophie de la chair* (Paris: Seuil, 2000), 138; *Incarnation: A Philosophy of Flesh*, trans. Karl Hefty (Evanston, IL: Northwestern University Press, 2015), 95: "what we have recognized to be a general and decisive characteristic of the appearing of the world: its ontological indigence, its inability to posit on its own the content that it makes appear without being able, for all that, to confer existence on it (without being able to 'create' it)" [ce que nous avons reconnu être un trait général et décisif de l'apparaître du monde : son indigence ontologique, son incapacité de poser par lui-même le contenu auquel il donne d'apparaître sans pouvoir le 'créer'].

19 See §21 of *Incarnation*, entitled "The Attempt to Overcome the Opposition between the Sensing Body and the Sensed Body: The Issue Facing the Later Merleau-Ponty and the Absolutization of the Sensible," 113–15.
20 This paper is the English translation of a communication entitled, "Le monde ou la vie fragile. Une nouvelle lecture critique de la phénoménologie de la vie," which was given at the Université catholique de Louvain for an International Conference organized by the Fonds Michel Henry (October 2018). The French version has been published in *Considérations phénoménologiques sur le monde. Entre théories et pratiques,* ed. J. Leclercq and P. Lorelle (Presses Universitaires de Louvain, 2020).

# Part II

# Applications

# 8

# The Liberal Subject

## The Politics of Life in Michel Henry

J. Rivera

## Introduction: Political Anthropology

The topics interrogated over the course of Michel Henry's career are as diverse as they are opportune to the moment. Whether in the form of an analysis of phenomenology during its ascent in France in the 1950s and 1960s (*Essence of Manifestation*) or an inventive exploration of Christianity in the midst of the theological turn in phenomenology in the 1990s (the Trilogy that began with *I am the Truth*), Henry's publications typically reflect the spirit of the era in which they were written. His political philosophy proves to be no exception. Writing *From Communism to Capitalism*[1] soon after the fall of communism in Eastern Europe, Henry asks in what way such a swing from fascism to unbridled consumerism can distort the human condition at its most basic existential level. Politics, taken as the public affair of humans consciously interacting with each other, does not consist of a sphere that overlays a pure state of nature but one imbued from the start with the living subjectivity of individuals.

Hence political theory as a discipline need not contrast with the philosophical study of the structure of selfhood. For Henry, the two remain intertwined, for "the question of the essence of the political is tied to human nature" (CC 93). And yet, as readers of Henry well know, the visible manifestation of the political, properly conceived, must acknowledge that it emerges out from the source of all concrete praxis and public activity, life's fundamental origin: the primitive invisible domain of selfhood known as the irrepressible wellspring of auto-affection. In this auto-affection I feel myself inside myself in that I inhabit myself inwardly at every turn. Irreducible to anything outside of itself, the essence of my subjectivity endows itself only with itself, so much so that it crushes against itself and "succumbs under the weight of its own pathos." I am inescapably me in this auto-affective, nonreflective feeling. Offered only in the trace of the visible world in the form of universal affects, the domain of life is evocative of expressions associated with hunger, pain, suffering the effort to carry a heavy item or wield a hammer; even the "irresistible happiness of existing" reflects a trace of life.

This dynamic domain of self-affection is necessarily invisible to the world of sensibility. It eludes our grasp because it draws resources only from its own pathos. Due to its origin in a self-pathos, Life never attaches to an object constituted by the mind's eye. How is Life visible or detectable at all? Henry addresses this question in part by recourse to the embodied effort and praxis that undergirds labor, public activity, and political endeavors.

As the essence of who I am, then, Life functions as the underlying power of the public, embodied mind. Life consists in the force of my embodied effort employed out of habit, in my every action and movement, even while Life cannot be grasped in any reflective idea or mental concept (CC 28). Akin to my "I-Can," Life expresses itself in the form of the spontaneity of instinct and thus establishes a correlation between my inward force (subjectivity) and embodied outward movement (objectivity).[2] While there may not be a clear distinction between the political and the anthropological, there is nevertheless a clear moral imperative that motivates Henry to make an unwavering distinction between the visible world of political power, technology and capitalism, on the one hand, and the invisible world of the subjective pathos of life, the transcendental site of genuine affective solidarity to which all citizens belong, on the other.

What makes Henry's work prophetic in the current context is the following thesis: that the former (the visible) attempts to conquer and thereby vanquish the latter (the invisible identity of subjective life we share) through technology and an economic calculus. Henry outlines the dramatic battle between them only to intervene with a call to a renewed commitment to the simple art of living we can enjoy if we should only open our hearts to it: the life lived apart from technology, science, economics, politics—all late-modern ideologies that transform us into objects to be conquered and exploited. No doubt parallels could be invoked here about Henry's unacknowledged debt to the Frankfurt school of critical theory embodied in the work of Adorno, Horkeimer, and Marcuse. For example, one need only to read the *One-Dimensional Man* to notice resonances between Marcuse's critique of capitalism's excesses and Henry's claim that technology and capitalism have reduced Western culture to barbarism.

In light of the contrast between the visible and invisible, whereby Henry urges the liberation of the latter from the chains of the former, the concept of the liberal subject comes into view. What I mean by what I call the "liberal subject" (not a term he employs) may well go beyond the letter of Henry's argument, but my position should keep close to the spirit of Henry's double critique of fascist socialism (the devaluation of the individual) and capitalism (the hyper-individualism of consumerism).

In what follows, I trace out Henry's practical philosophy of the "liberal subject" in his *From Communism to Capitalism*, in order to explore how a liberal democracy may survive if, and only if, its policies can hem in its inclination to exploit and impoverish the individual rights it legally protects and exalts.[3] What of a social democracy? Social democracies are what we see on display in much of the European Union and what Bernie Sanders often praises as the ideal model of liberalism's economic strategy—higher taxes on the top 1 percent used to fund strong social entitlement programs such as affordable healthcare, university education, pensions, paid sick leave, unemployment benefits, and the protection of worker's rights. Senator Sanders singles out Denmark as the exemplar of the balanced application of social democracy.[4] Whatever the concrete case study (France, Denmark, etc.), the point remains that Henry's work here can be harnessed in favor of a more humane and economically equal society that also relies on regular input from the citizenry with recourse to democratic elections. That is, in what way we can take up our individual self-expression while avoiding the excesses and dangers of socialist policies that stunt individualism.[5] We should first give pause to take notice of Henry's strong claim that we must first avoid the collective identity of radical socialism of the Soviet kind: the fascist death of all forms of subjectivity.

## The Death of the Subject: Fascism

Fascism, for Henry, is an object of precise historical analysis. It reigned across the Soviet Union, Eastern Europe, and much of Asia for decades in the twentieth century. That is, this catastrophe has spanned several states and areas, from Moscow to Phnom Penh to Baku and to Budapest or Bucharest. In all these unfortunate countries, whether for the Khmers or the Laotians, the Hungarians or the Polish, the Azerbaijanis or the Armenians, their struggles inevitably gave rise to the same disastrous consequences. Marxist fascism yielded a cohesive group of theories that led to the economic catastrophe and political upheavals, which in turn, caused widespread suffering among ordinary citizens: families, children, farmers, teachers, bankers, and so on. The damage economically and socially we barely can fathom.

Ultimately, Henry asks a basic question on behalf of those afflicted citizens: "What is the point of working for nothing—for a wage that gives one the right to stand in endless waiting lines for a little bit of bread or some frozen potatoes?" (CC 108). Unsurprisingly, desperation of this kind gives rise to violence. In circumstances like these, you to take what you need, do you not? From shelter and clothing to food and drink, you must survive, right? Pillaging, trafficking of goods, and general brutal behavior no doubt is built on the foundation of endless waiting lines produced by fascist socialism's management of the population at every level, not simply its abolition of private property. In this concrete way, precisely, Marxism negates the individual.

But for Henry this must be clear not only for how such a negation serves to throw into relief his countertheme of Life, but also for the general reader. Given the grave consequences of Marxist fascism, I wish to unveil here as clearly as I can the grammar of the "devaluation of the individual" that funds Marxist fascism—its very definition is the eradication of the individual. Why does it ignore, or worse, exterminate the individual? Marx's goals seem pure and noble, do they not? He wants to end class warfare and install a fair and economically equitable society. Certainly, Marx himself is distinct from Marxism—Henry labors this point in his widely read two-volume work on Marx from the 1970s.[6] In *The German Ideology*, Marx, with a snarky tone, refutes the claim (made by Max Stirner) that the society in his system has grown up to be a person or subject in its own right, as if society signified a holy incarnation of the collective self, a superego who displaces the individual ego.[7] But this displacement of the individual by the society-as-subject appears to take place in Marxism as a fascist ideology. For Henry, the logic of Marxism (not Marx) nonetheless results in a classless society where individuals relinquish their individuality, their subjective genius. The reason this form of socialism cannot function properly as the redemption of society is precisely because "society" or "class" becomes a surrogate for the individual.

The abstractions of the terms "society," "history," "social class," the "proletariat," the "people's party," taken collectively, seem to replace the individual subjective experience that is valid for me to the degree it is experienced as "mine," in a way unique to me, just as you experience yourself as uniquely and irreplaceably "you." Society or history cannot exist without individuals, but, ironically, fascist regimes, for Henry, often resort to violence and partial genocides and "liquidations" of individuals in order to achieve the goal of a peaceful and equitable society. Whether it is the bourgeoisie, the holders of privilege like education, or even the owner of a house or a few cows, these "classes" of privilege are vulnerable to elimination. In other manifestations of fascism, whole racial groups could be targeted, their elimination and murder justified on the grounds of social cohesion. Religious belief, along with priests and ministers, becomes a principal target; no more extreme an example can be adduced here than destruction of mosques and churches carried out by Enver Hoxha's fascist regime installed in Albania just after the Second World War, or Pol Pot's brutal policies against religion of every kind in 1970s Cambodia.

How can violence against the individual occur with no protest from the people? Henry asserts that the passivity of the individual agent is manifest as the sole way of interacting with the State. Freedoms are so brutally curtailed that the only logical reflex is the following:

> the inhabitants of socialist countries have a passive attitude that leads them to expect everything from society. To them, society is the only reality and the sole principle of effective realization. It was thus up to society, in the end, to do everything: to subsidize the various needs in every domain—food, clothing, shelter, health, education, work leisure, even the truth and everything that one must believe. (CC 31)

It is as if the citizenry has swallowed a "magic pill" that has captivated their minds, making them serene, passive, and ultimately, docile in the face of State violence.[8] The fascist leaders, without legal restraint, tend to turn citizens into dispensable objects in the name of Marxist elevation of society or class equality (CC 21). That is, on Henry's interpretation, "Society is the Whole and the individual is the part, a part which is a function of the Whole. The individual is defined and determined by it" (CC 27). No doubt, argues Henry, the materialism of Marx discloses a dissymmetry between illusory subjective lives and real, concrete material societies. Here, the subjective experience of the individual is an antithesis to the representation of all citizens known as society. *The denial of the subjective individual in favor of objective society constitutes the fascist heart of fascist-like communist countries.*

The existential cost is high, as one could imagine. The subjective reality each of us possesses should formulate a bulwark against fascism. But it has not. Is there hope for a liberal subject? For Henry, it was not only the long lines for bread and soup that constituted the "face" of the fascist grievance experienced by the everyday Eastern European. The chief principle of Marxism, expressed concretely in Lenin, Trotsky, Stalin, Mao, and others, shall not escape us: it is the devaluation of the individual [*L'abaissement de l'individu*] as such. The communist empire, reduced here to fascism, consists of a direct assault on the living genius of "me" as this particular individual whose self-expression trades on particular skills, gifts, and narratives. Bureaucratic secrecy, a hallmark of fascist regimes, denudes me of my gifts; for I know not why I am in this profession rather than that. Even though I have done nothing wrong, once I was an artist and now a bellboy at a hotel. If I am a professor, at any moment I could be sent to the fields, separated from family, to move dirt or to care for pigs. Prejudice against the individual penalizes and attenuates one's very sense of self and professional identity. The horror of clandestine bureaucracy, much like that found on display in Kafka's incisive and dark story *The Trial*, involves misdirection, miscommunication, and the arbitrary and neurotic violation of my rights as a person. I may be arrested by a secret and unspecified authority, only to be told nothing of the crime for which I am found guilty or the sentence I am given; and yet, everyone in the regime but me will naturally agree that what has befallen me is deserved.[9]

In what way, one may legitimately ask, does this reveal a naked materialism at work? How does materialism of the Marxist kind result in a systematic and violent campaign against the living subjectivity of Life? It should be noted once more that, to answer this query, one can define Life as an irrepressible impulse, the instinct of "I-Can" that marks and shapes and even nourishes the natural world as we experience it. This, above all, is what makes some versions of communism a fascist theory: it privileges the inert object over the living subject.

Life, as in all of Henry's works, consists of two aspects. First, Life is a subjective experience involving pure self-experience, so that my subjectivity unfolds without a gap between itself and the experience of itself. This is one's "metaphysical or ontological condition": I am myself insofar as I undergo and suffer myself as this particular self glued to myself in auto-affection. Because it remains a transcendental domain, and as an *a priori* domain, I cannot escape its reach. Hence, nor can I therefore escape from myself. No narrative can subsume within its logic the transcendental foundation of Life. For example, society, culture, race, gender or religious identity are expressions or products of Life, so they do not exercise the authority to divest me of the transcendental condition of life that already underlies all cultural, moral and religious accomplishments (CC 15). Ultimately, fascism cannot touch or violate this fundamental, transcendental dimension of my life.

The second chief dynamic of the living subject lies in the practical power that emanates out of this subjective core: visible force. It affects the world around us. The many objects, communities, technologies, and public goods that make up important components of our public identity rest on the invisible subjective dimension of Life's force. Without Life, such cultural productions suffer the ignoble death of purposelessness. Labor and production of any sort, if it consists of living labor, must be embraced by the subjective genius of individuals. Objects of all kinds would cease should living labor cease. After Life removes itself, the visible work can no longer sustain itself. Without life, metal rusts. The port fills with sand, the barge rots and slowly sinks into the canal that stagnates. The channels or aqueducts, from which the water dumps into the fields where fertile soil turns into pestilent marshland, crack (CC 67). The function and utility of society depends on individual prowess, genius, and living labor, invisible though it is. This is the individual depth that was reclaimed by the liberal democracy of the postwar period of the second half of the twentieth century. Its political arrangement, of course, has problems of its own making, as Henry shall highlight for us.

## Reclaiming the Individual

Critics of liberal democracy are consistent in tone and content. They suggest that its chief theoretical indiscretion lies in the following error: unreflective optimism about self-reliance of an isolated subject. Liberalism's anthropology may suffer the ignominy of certain unkind labels forced on it, such as "atomism" or "possessive individualism," or in overt moral vocabulary, "selfishness." Any social and political project, it goes without saying, that relies on the vice of selfishness or pride is destined to fail. Patrick Deneen's volume, *Why Liberalism Failed*, judges its anthropology in a manner consonant with this failed moral trajectory. The fundamental "anthropological assumption" of modern liberalism consists in the enlargement of "the realm of individual freedom," which necessarily invites modern citizens to overcome and transcend widespread social and religious norms, cultural practices, and the arbitrary accidents of birth.[10]

Indeed, he labels the liberal framework of individualism an "ideology of selfishness," in order to depict in plain language the divide between ancient virtue and modern vice. The modern ego, since Descartes and Hobbes, and later refined by the collective composition of the social contract, has credulously denied the embeddedness of culture in favor of a descent into the discourse of "anticulture." The violence of anticulture, for Deneen, is manifest in a vocal prejudice against parochial expressions of community. It should be obvious to Deneen that liberalism's chief protocol, that of the State's division of citizen from community, should aim to detach citizens from their local and particular cultural identities, lest a greater violence of "identity politics" break loose.

The citizenry, formed according to the logic of anticulture, articulates its desires and explores its identity-formation according to a strategy of liberal agency. According to the logic of this style of anthropology, public virtue consists of a group of utility-maximizing individual actors who make decisions in isolation from the larger cultural norms passed on from generation to generation. For Deneen, communitarianism is the antidote: for its political ethic nourishes local, grassroots social capital and cultural know-how, whose content is rich in religious tradition, linguistic inheritance, and familial alliances and bonds (that is the very definition of communitarianism).

After liberalism, however, we are freed from the encumbrances of tradition and inheritance. So what bonds us now? Unfortunately, claims Deneen, nothing binds us but the liberal market. Our most visible national holidays, in America and elsewhere, are shopping holidays (think of Black Friday) or holidays that embody the national liberal State. Even interpersonal dynamics, for Deneen, do not escape the subtle prescriptions for utility and atomism imposed on us by liberalism's anticulture: even friendships resemble more an association between individuals, a mere conjunction of moods, rather than a union of love and trust. Now the tie of friendship is lived in a mode governed by the evanescence of fashion, based on the fungible and fluctuating needs of the particular time and place. Hence the "loose connections" cultivated by liberalism correspond to the social fact that many of us submit our sense of identity and place to constant redefinition. From the neighbourhood, to nation, to family, and to religion, we reconfigure (argues Deneen) who we are in the face of the fluid and variable elements of identity.[11] No doubt the following quote from Robert Nozick's self-conscious adoption of libertarianism would represent one natural mood of anticulture:

> But there is no social entity with a good that undergoes some sacrifice for its own good. There are only individual people, different individual people, with their own individual lives. Using one of these people for the benefit of others, uses him and benefits the others. Nothing more. What happens is that something is done to him for the sake of others. Talk of an overall social good covers this up. (Intentionally?). He does not get some overbalancing good from his sacrifice, and no one is entitled to force this upon him—least of all a state or government

that claims his allegiance (as other individuals do not) and that therefore scrupulously must be neutral between its citizens.[12]

Western culture, on the basis of social contract theory, decides that its political obligation is to protect citizens, at a minimum, from tyranny and theocracy. Yet, the radical individualism formulated in Nozick's aforementioned statement can arouse in liberal-minded and communitarian-minded readers alike a complete suspicion of the conceivability of an "overall social good." I do not mean to translate the concept of "overall social good" into the language of the common good, as if social goods like universal healthcare and affordable university education constitute political categories of the entitlements born of welfare state that only make sense in light of the particular virtues of Judeo-Christianity (i.e., the Christian common good that communitarians prize).

The practice of philosophical scrutiny I wish to undertake here (with Henry) against Deneen and Nozick must work to allay the violence of totality bound up with (i) communitarian fascism *and* (ii) unregulated liberal individualism. The prospect of a liberal subject, who wields his/her agency to decide many things about his/her personal identity, if it is to avoid the assimilation into either totalizing economy, need not use his/her agency to construct an identity that contradicts a larger social good. Can we posit a social democracy in which the citizenry as a whole participates in a fairly distributed economic context, and which makes more available social and educational opportunities for all? The virtue of Nozick's violent reflex against the liberal State's penchant for oppressive oversight, not least its layered attempts to engineer an image of a paternalistic guardian who knows best, is that his position preserves in part the genius of individuality. In the process of invoking of libertarian critique, Nozick opens up a relationality within the medium of a necessary political context, namely, liberal democracy (even if it is the most minimal kind of libertarian, laissez-faire political liberalism for Nozick).

Deneen and other strong communitarians, on the other hand, would reject individualism (of any kind) out of hand because it is tantamount to capitulation to a selfish "anticulture." That is, for Deneen, citizens cannot be truly themselves if they exist outside the moral vocabulary and social norms of traditional political virtue. The withdrawal of the individual from civic duty would be justified for Deneen only on the basis of the individual's legitimate anxiety about imminent tyranny. Yet, can an individual not also withdraw for other reasons? What of personal preference or temperament? Am I selfish if I enjoy my family and friends without recourse to civic duty? I would argue against Deneen that the ostensible "need" for order and collective unity, embodied in a culture of a community, grows too powerful in its tendency toward a totalizing violence against forms of individual particularity that breaks from communitarian norms.

I would tend to agree with Deneen that some "communitarianism" is unavoidable; I can appreciate, to be more precise, his worry that liberalism's anthropology, if left unchecked, cannot escape a violence of its own, the abstract and amoral individualism, an anthropology ultimately dislocated from time.[13] This critical proposition (i.e., dislocation from time), upon careful consideration, must be understood as a straw man or contrived by Deneen. His own critique of the violence of liberalism descends into an opposite form of violence, that of the straightforward communitarian counternarrative, a blunt and hasty demonization of liberal democracy as such. Does the liberal order manufacture certain anticultural merchandise, such as "weaponized timelessness" (his term), a commodity that enforces a progressive worldview? If so, how? Where do I purchase such a weapon? Is the past, as a horizon of time, wiped away from public consciousness? Is the past and its richly cultural achievements understood by liberalism to represent products as redundant as they are unenlightened? Is the past not just surrendered but also victimized by liberalism?[14] A subtler language and more balanced point of departure for thinking about liberalism's anthropology is found in Henry's political philosophy.

Henry does not deny liberalism's disposition toward an anthropology of the "timeless individual." Timelessness in this very particular "Henryian" sense can empower each of us with liberty, however. The subjectivity of the liberal subject, as an individual whose sense of "me" matters at an essential level, necessarily entails a metaphysical critique of fascism and tyranny. Liberalism, and its economic expression in capitalism, was not mistaken in its original impulse, for it "put its finger on what matters, on the only force that exists in the world which is the force of life, the force of living labor" (CC 69).[15] Henry's recuperation of the inward essence of the dignity of the human condition endows political anthropology with a genuine sense of caution in the face of Deneen's desire to impose communitarian norms.

But capitalism is in possession of its own problems. Henry's discovery of the living ground of labor follows from his discovery of the living domain of subjectivity, auto-affection. This original domain, though it is invisible, infuses the practical and embodied action of labor, work, and ultimately, economic production. Objects, things, and goods, they all are mere inert objects, void of value and purchase, unless the living domain of subjectivity confers on them force, productivity, and meaning:

by themselves, the objective factors would be no more than inert terms, left to die; they become elements of production only if, poured into the crucible of production and consumed by it, turned as if into liquid by the fire of living labor, they are, due to living labor alone, given a new form which restores them to being. (M 262)

Mutually sustaining each other, then, auto-affection and labor are co-involved. Working in conjunction with each other, their bond forms the phenomenon of "living labor." Capitalism, if unregulated, breaks this bond.

Capitalism, in the eyes of Henry, becomes a problem once it becomes "techno-capitalism" (CC 80).[16] It too eliminates the individual, no less than fascism. Just like fascism, the liberal order of capitalism invests all of its focus on efficiency. On the face of it capitalism appeals to the naïve celebration of liberty: we can use our unique genius to create products for sale. But a deeper analysis reveals that it exults in work for the sake of profit alone, which casts laborers into a cycle of long hours of aimless labor. Since the profit "bottom line" determines the work day and the quality of one's labor, it follows that capitalism will take whatever hours it deems necessary from living labor, so long as a profit is not only obtained, but also wholly secured for future growth. Here, living labor ceases to be identified with Life, and thus ceases to be living labor. The bond between Life and work dissolves in the face of the profit principle.

Many have observed that a chief internal contradiction of capitalism, at least since Daniel Bell's *The Cultural Contradictions of Capitalism,* is the chronic problem of the overproduction of goods for a class of underpaid workers, many of whom do not find employment at all. Capitalism's investment in technology tends to create a surplus of labor. The outcome is that "necessary labor" that used to be required for the production of goods is a relic of the past. Now, technology replaces workers in every industry, from coffee machines that make baristas redundant to automated assembly lines that transform technicians into mere quality-control observers. The surplus of labor means there is always unemployment (there are simply too many laborers for the amount of job openings). Many workers take whatever paid job they can acquire (or remain unemployed) and, as such, they frequently do not have enough cash to purchase the goods on offer in a capitalist market (think of the adjunct lecturer here!). Many goods, therefore, become subprime commodities. Why? The wages brought in by workers cause them to struggle mightily to purchase the goods; or they simply have a salary that does not equal the amount needed to purchase the commodity. Many commodities are unable to realize their exchange value on the market since they will find no buyer (CC 89). The technical-economic world of capitalism makes us undergo a "metaphysical transubstantiation" so that our human being no longer occurs within the pathos of subjectivity but "in things" (CC 113). Henry's metaphor of capitalism as a "vampire" that sucks the life out of living labor is appropriate to the present description.

Such rhetoric, of course, should be qualified as metaphor. Machines do not have agency, not least fangs. As Marcuse judges, science's and technology's breakthroughs in themselves can function as vehicles of liberation, so that many of us are freed from the painful sweat of the endless toil. That is, cars, televisions, coffee machines, do not repress us. Household gadgets are repressive only once they are understood to be "produced in accordance with the requirements of profitable exchange, they have become part and parcel of the people's own existence, own 'actualization.'"[17] Should we forget, as Henry sternly warns us, the emergence of technology is due to Life itself, to living labor, and this should not be forgotten. Once forgotten, techno-capitalism arises.

What, then, becomes the end or *telos* of techno-capitalism? It is production itself. Living labor, pressed in service only of bald consumerism, fails in the face of the production and profit principle. Each of us, should we cease to resist, become economic "playthings" whose subjectivity fades from view (CC 98). The death of living labor is the death of the subject: modern citizens ultimately fall prey to the status of objects subdued by technology.

## Conclusion: Social Democracy and the Liberal Subject

Where do we proceed from here? If neither communitarianism, in its fascist expression, nor liberalism, in its techno-capitalist inflection, shall serve the social good of the citizenry, then what option do we have? We can only sketch here a possibility, in bare outline: a social democracy that relies on the liberal subject for its anthropological foundation.

The liberal subject may never yield to the strict logic of auto-affection as Henry conceives it. And, yet, liberal democracy of any kind must ask each of us, as citizens and as responsible adults who coexist with others in a polis, to bracket or at least minimize our identity politics. For the sake of establishing a social contract between various groups (or between all individual subjects), we must learn first to listen to the other and consider the other in his/her genuine individuality. This does not mean that I divest myself or abandon my own communitarian identity, say as a French Catholic or a Moroccan Muslim or as a gay-rights activist; it does demand, however, that I do grant the other the same courtesy to exercise his/her own unique, irreplaceable mode of personal identity, whatever language, culture, religion, or gender that he/she may traffic in. Even someone like Mark Lilla, champion of liberal politics though he remains, asks his liberal-minded American readership to implement a broader, more sober-minded approach, and so, to temper the passion emanating out from a single cause of a particular political platform, however progressive and urgent it may be, and however marginal the group may be (and whose injustice is in need of redress).[18]

In the mood of restraint, we can work with each other, as well as grant to citizens of other political persuasions a basic sense of dignity. True, liberal democracies are not neutral in all matters of morality and religion: language, architecture, school curricula, and so on are all representative of a particular worldview. Identity lies within the fabric of democracy.[19] Certainly, too, democracies licence groups to discriminate without the State sanctioning that discrimination; and yet, as soon as discrimination disrupts civil equality, it must be regulated by State intervention.[20] Democracy should not strive to fulfill the demands of identity politics per se, yet, public life is too diverse in its commitments for the State to eliminate all identity politics.

We are, as citizens of democracy, embedded subjects. We have thick identities. We are, also, citizens who can exercise self-restraint in a concerted effort to listen liberally. I have outlined elsewhere the pragmatics of this kind of liberal listening or charitable public dialogue.[21] The formidable problem, then, is not communitarianism, since its full-fledged platform has no real place in democracy. Strict communitarianism would promote the state-sanctioned, legal imposition of one identity on a citizenry that adopts a plurality of identities. This would amount to a withdrawal of liberal democracy in favor of a dictatorship of identity. For Henry, the result here is no different than fascism.

For Henry, and those who promote liberal democracy, the real problem is techno-capitalism. While liberal democracy is here to stay, it can still threaten the subject with extinction, if its capitalist impulse to extract profit from every member of the citizenry does not undergo precise regulation. How do we protect each of us from the fangs of the profit principle and the expansion of technology? The answer begins with economic regulation, and thus, taxation and redistribution that is attentive to income gaps between the poor, the middle class, and the upper 1 percent. This style of economic regulation is called social democracy.

A liberal subject, then, not only occupies a particular time and place, and recognizes that others do as well, but it also expresses its liberal spirit in another way: redistribution. We are the citizenry, together, a whole will, even while each individual's right to self-expression is protected. In order to nourish the art of Life, as Henry would propound it, we need ample opportunity to do so. While the State can only minimize crime and consumerism, as well as selfishness, it can offer profound economic opportunities to those who might otherwise languish in poverty and disadvantage; this lays the groundwork for the enaction of the liberal subject. Enaction of each self, therefore, is made possible by economic opportunities that arise from redistribution and entitlement programs. I am free, that is, to be a liberal subject due to the economic opportunities I now can utilize that once were available only for certain socioeconomic classes.

Techno-capitalism, without proper regulation, tends to increase the gap between rich and poor. Profit is the point of departure for globalized, multinational companies (many of them based in the United States), and for this reason, the individual worker remains an afterthought. The middle class continues to shrink. Its earnings suffer, its debts grow. As of 2018, Forbes reported, on the basis of findings from the Institute for College Access and Success, that there is collectively over $1.5 trillion in student debt. Much of that prevents citizens in their twenties, thirties, or even forties from saving to purchase a home or save for retirement.[22] Elsewhere, studies have shown that in America between 1979 and 2007 the income gap between the very rich and the middle class has tripled. In the course of those three decades, the average after-tax incomes for the top 1 percent rose by 281 percent (after adjusting for inflation), an increase of $973,100 per household. This is compared to an increase of 25 percent for the middle-fifth of households, an increase of $11,200.[23] Economic stress originating from debt, healthcare costs, and rising tuition costs leads to existential stress for the large band of the population known as the middle class. A recent study finds that Americans are among the most stressed individuals in the world.[24]

We are confronted here with the demand to produce a concrete alternative, and one executed by a liberal State whose economic redistribution makes possible a social democracy. But to ask for a blueprint, with particular policies implemented by specific institutions, is meaningless for a new social democracy. Such demands cannot be addressed *a priori*, but only in piecemeal fashion, over time, and in relationship with the particular liberal cultural context.

The enaction of the liberal subject shall thrive in the context of economic opportunity and job protection afforded by a social democracy. There are a set of entitlements that, generally drawn, could be applied to any liberal State: the redistribution of the millionaire's and billionaire's profits to the benefit of the whole of society. Something as progressive and forward-thinking as Thomas

Piketty's "global tax" on global capital would not find a hearing yet.[25] Our world is not yet global enough. But that would be an ideal toward which the liberal subject would aspire: all billionaires would pay taxes at a globally set tax bracket. Funds here could be used to lower publicly funded university education, establish a pension fund for the middle class, and provide ample paid maternity and paternity leave for families struggling to enter or flourish in the workforce. Student debt in the United States, while a problem chiefly unique to the North American context, could be paid off or forgiven by strong, State-sponsored, internal (i.e., not global) legislation that privileges education over the expansion of the military industrial complex. Healthcare, as is the case in many European contexts, could be viewed not as a commodity but as a basic need to be met by the State (like fire departments, primary school education, etc.). Indeed, social democracies, as some political theorists have tried to show in detail, has led to an increase in happiness of the populace, whether it is in Denmark, France, or Scotland.[26] State involvement can be, and often is, a force for good, and it has been active in this way for the last century or more as Piketty has shown in sufficient detail.[27]

The enactment of the liberal subject, in conclusion, takes its bearings from the living subjectivity each of us possesses. But this subjectivity is simultaneously an intersubjectivity, since I realize myself and my praxis only in the context of community. It is in the political economy of public life, with regulation and entitlement reform, that we can see the liberal State as a means of empowerment and protection. While either fascism or techno-capitalism as forms of government may resist public accountability and abuse the individual, it is a social-liberal democracy, glimpsed by Henry's political philosophy, that may chart the middle path between fascist communitarianism and selfish capitalism.

## Notes

1 Henry, *Du communisme au capitalisme: théorie d'une catastrophe* (Paris: Odile Jacob, 1990.) Translation: *From Communism to Capitalism: Theory of A Catastrophe*, trans. Scott Davidson (London: Bloomsbury, 2014). I refer to the English translation throughout.

2 For more on the anthropology of the "I-Can," see IAT p. 135ff; also see Husserl, *Ideas Pertaining to a Pure Phenomenology and to a Phenomenological Philosophy: Second Book, Studies in the Phenomenology of Constitution*, trans. R. Rojcewicz and A. Schuwer (Dordrecht: Kluwer Academic, 1989.), 266ff.

3   For a helpful introduction to Henry's practical philosophy, which is not limited only to his political philosophy, see Michael Staudigl, "From the 'Metaphysics of the Individual' to the Critique of Society: On the Practical Significance of Michel Henry's Phenomenology of Life," *Continental Philosophy Review* 45, no. 3 (2012): 339–61.

4   For more on Bernie Sanders' discussion of the prosperous ideal of Denmark, see https://edition.cnn.com/2016/02/17/politics/bernie-sanders-2016-denmark-democratic-socialism/index.html.

5   Herbert Marcuse, *An Essay on Liberation* (Boston: Beacon Press, 1969), 90.

6   See his original, Henry, *Marx, Tome I: une philosophie de la réalité; Tome II: une philosophie de l'economie* (Paris: Gallimard, 1976).

7   See Karl Marx with Friedrich Engels, *The German Ideology* (New York: Prometheus Books, 1998), 50 and 221.

8   This is a passing reference to Milosz's "Murti-Bing pill" in *The Captive Mind*, trans. Jane Zielonko (New York: Vintage Books, 1955), chapter 1.

9   See Franz Kafka's not so thinly veiled critique of fascism to come, *The Trial*, trans. David Wyllie (New York: Dover, 2003).

10  Patrick Deneen, *Why Liberalism Failed* (New Haven: Yale University Press, 2018), 23–6.

11  Deneen, *Why Liberalism Failed*, 34. For more on anticulture, see chapter 3, "Liberalism as Anticulture."

12  Robert Nozick, *Anarchy, State, and Utopia* (Oxford: Blackwell, 1974), 32–3.

13  Pierre Manent states, rightly I think, that some communitarianism is needed in any liberal democracy, especially as Western culture finds balanced political means to welcome Islam (his own immediate concern is the interplay between Islam and Catholicism in France). See his *Beyond Radical Secularism: How France and the Christian West should Respond to the Islamic Challenge*, trans. Ralph C. Hancock (South Bend, IN: St. Augustine's Press, 2015), 109 ff.

14  Deneen, *Why Liberalism Failed*, 73–4.

15  Henry, *From Communism to Capitalism*, 69.

16  Ibid., 80.

17  Marcuse, *An Essay on Liberation*, 12.

18  Mark Lilla, *The Once and Future Liberal: After Identity Politics* (New York: Harper, 2017), chapter 3, "Politics."

19  Amy Gutmann, *Identity in Democracy* (Princeton, NJ: Princeton University Press, 2004), 39ff.

20  Ibid., 209.

21  Joseph Rivera, *Political Theology and Pluralism: Renewing Public Dialogue* (New York: Palgrave Macmillan, 2018), chapter 4, "Strategies for Dialogue in a Pluralist Age."

22 https://www.forbes.com/sites/zackfriedman/2018/06/13/student-loan-debt-statistics-2018/#70cf70007310 (accessed April 25, 2019).
23 https://www.cbpp.org/research/income-gaps-between-very-rich-and-everyone-else-more-than-tripled-in-last-three-decades-new (accessed April 25, 2019).
24 https://www.nytimes.com/2019/04/25/us/americans-tressful.html?action=click&module=Latest&pgtype=Homepage (accessed April 25, 2019).
25 Thomas Piketty, *Capital in the Twenty-First Century,* trans. Arthur Goldhammer (Cambridge, MA: Harvard University Press, 2014), 444ff.
26 See the excellent work by Benjamin Radcliff, *The Political Economy of Human Happiness: How Voters' Choices Determine the Quality of Life* (Cambridge: Cambridge University Press, 2013).
27 Piketty, *Capital,* 474–7.

# 9

# Michel Henry's *Barbarism* and the Practices of Education

B. Harding

Philosophers and phenomenologists rarely read Michel Henry as contributing much to education theory or to the philosophy of education; our focus is usually on his account of subjectivity and affectivity, and his theological speculations. On the other hand, a number of educational theorists have turned to Henry's work for inspiration.[1] Henry, while not developing the theme at length, occasionally makes remarks relevant to educators and educational theorists. For example, at the end of *I am the Truth*, Henry claims that if people today have forgotten the truth of life, it is because they were *trained* to forget it in school; we are, he says, "trained in school to despise ourselves, to count for nothing—just particles and molecules."[2] Contemporary education, this passage suggests, teaches students to reduce themselves to mere biology, ignoring or degrading everything noble about humanity. The effect of this education is to alienate humanity from life, creating "men given over to the insensible ... whose eyes are as empty as a fish's" (IATT, 275). With these words Henry recapitulates an argument he made about a decade earlier in *Barbarism*. There Henry claimed that educational institutions that once passed on culture from generation to generation have succumbed to Galilean techno-science, abandoning that mission in favor of mere technical and professional training.

In *Barbarism*, Henry mentions two questions that, he claims, are essential for reflections on education, "What knowledge is to be transmitted? And how is it to be transmitted?" (B, 122). The first is concerned with curricular, the second with pedagogical, methods. Taking this advice, the chapter will first focus on inclusions and exclusions in curricula, and later attend to teaching methods; both sections will attend to historical developments that have contributed to barbarization.

## Curricular Debates

Debates about curricula are, and perhaps always have been, contentious. The decision about what should be taught presupposes a number of substantive views about knowledge, politics, the aims of education, and even metaphysics or ontology.[3] As such, my treatment of curriculum is bound to be partial and limited. Nevertheless, I think there is some value in even a limited reflection on curriculum in light of Henry's work. In fact, Henry circumspectly addresses questions about what a university curriculum is and should be in the final chapter of *Barbarism*. The chapter laments changes in the university that have, in Henry's eyes, betrayed its mission and given it over to barbarism. By looking closely at that lament, and exposing it to some criticisms, we can get a clearer idea of what Henry thinks a non-barbaric curriculum would look like.

Henry points to two changes that introduced barbarism to the university. First, there is the "abolition of the borderline that ... had separated the University and society up till now": universities are expected to be a part of society, serving its needs and comporting themselves according to societal standards, rather than expected to be a place set apart for special pursuits (B, 120). These needs are primarily understood in a commercial sense, such that even the production of, for example, citizens equipped for living in a multicultural democracy is subordinated to the demands of commerce, creating employees of the future. The choice to cultivate employees rather than citizens brings us to the second change: a focus on technology and science overwhelms the university, excluding the university's traditional concern with culture (B, 120–1). The prestige programs are in STEM, not the liberal arts. In sum, these changes lead universities to reproduce within themselves the "very same presuppositions of the techno-scientific world" (B, 122) that are the target of vituperative criticism throughout the rest of Henry's book. Henry's complaints illuminate, in a backhanded way, his ideal university as (a) devoted to the development of culture and (b) not answerable to the immediate commercial or political needs of the society in which such a university is housed. To be sure, such a university would *indirectly* benefit such a society by producing cultured students, but it would not understand itself as primarily offering job training. Henry admits that teaching has a dual vocation and that one of them is precisely to help students become employable (B, 121). However, his claim is that the vocational element of education should appear *only* as a part of a larger whole devoted to cultural transmission rather than as the sole end of education. Henry's point, it seems to me, is that even those whose circumstances require careful thought about employment prospects following graduation should be taught *more* than what is needed for employment. This separates him from theorists who would endorse a mixture of contemplation and aristocracy as an ideal for education (in the tradition of Matthew Arnold) and puts him a bit closer to those educational reformers that attempted to bring liberal education to a wider population.[4]

All that said, there is a tension between the aims Henry endorses, and the kind of university structure he endorses. Henry pays little attention to the material conditions of the university in his considerations of curricula; however, the "organizational chart" of the university, the way it divides areas of inquiry into departments and programs, always affects curricula. There are a few pages devoted to the history of the university in *Barbarism* and we can get a better view of this tension by looking there.

According to Henry, the university began in the Middle Ages, and was founded on a principle of marginality. To study at a university was to become something strange: members of a medieval university were considered clerics (and could not be tried in secular courts) but were not necessarily ordained. Neither fish nor fowl, the university and its scholars existed at the blurry margins of throne and altar. This marginality created the space, Henry maintains, "to transmit knowledge in teaching and increase it in research" (B, 118). Henry also claims that the major faculties in the medieval university were philosophy and theology (B, 127). Both of these claims are worth examining more closely. Beginning with the first, while it *seems* true enough, (since medieval scholars produced volumes of commentaries and *Summa*) it misleadingly presupposes a distinction between teaching and research that is foreign to the medieval mind. Indeed, it is questionable whether a scholastic (formed by Augustine's critique of *curiositas* and Aristotle's ideal of a demonstrative science terminating in knowledge of first principles) could approve of the quest for *infinite* increase in knowledge that animates the modern research university. This is not to say that medieval schoolmen did no research but—as José Ortega y Gasset stresses[5]— that "increasing it [knowledge] in research" was *not* part of the medieval university's official mission or self-understanding. This is a conception one finds in Humboldt's nineteenth-century vision, wherein teachers and students exist *solely* for the purpose of pursuing research and where teaching is justified in terms of its benefits for research, but it is anachronistic and ahistorical to read this into the medieval university.[6]

Henry's second claim is not correct: there was not a philosophy faculty in medieval universities but, rather, an arts faculty.[7] Moreover, in limiting the faculties to philosophy and theology, Henry suggests a parity between them when, in fact, the arts faculty was *always* subordinate to the theology faculty. If the first point showed that Henry anachronistically projects the spirit of the research university back into the Middle Ages, in the second we see the structure of the nineteenth-century research university, where the philosophy faculty was increasingly important and had gained autonomy vis-à-vis theology, also projected back onto the Middle Ages. In sum, Henry's description of the medieval university interpolates elements of the Germanic reforms of the eighteenth and nineteenth centuries into it. My point is not to score cheap points by criticizing him as a historian but to highlight his attachment to, and implicit endorsement of, that model—despite his relative silence about it. The projection of the modern university into the medieval university prevents him from seeing the role that nineteenth-century university reform played in the spread of the educational barbarism he laments.

## Barbarism and the Research University

While an exhaustive study of the nineteenth-century transformation of higher education goes beyond the scope of this chapter, a few points will suffice to show that despite Henry's preference for the research university model, it is not resistant to barbarism—quite the opposite, in fact. I am not claiming that the early reformers were barbarians, but only that the transformation of the university into the modern research university created the conditions for the formation of a barbaric curriculum. For our purposes, l will stipulate that the pre-reformed university was not barbaric and, on that assumption, focus our attention on what changed to create the predisposition toward barbarism. I believe this stipulation can be justified in our context insofar as Henry himself seems to think that the barbarization of the universities happened at a fairly late date (B, 123). While Henry suggests some time around the late 1950s, I think it happened earlier.

My claim that nineteenth-century university reform led to barbarism is not as idiotic, or idiosyncratic, as it may sound. I am only echoing José Ortega y Gasset's argument in his 1930 text, *The Mission of the University*. Anticipating the spirit of Henry's complaints about the late twentieth-century university, Ortega complained that the reformed university has abandoned "the teaching or transmission of culture" in favor of professional training and highly specialized research programs where professors seek only to reproduce themselves: researchers training researchers.[8] Ortega argues that the "unpredicted barbarity" of the early twentieth century was closely linked to "the pretentious nineteenth century university of all countries."[9] Russian literature also suggests this point: I don't think it accidental that Turgenev's Barazov (a quintessential barbarian), Dostoyevsky's Raskolnikov, and like-minded university students appear in literature at this point. Historians of education have long noted that the Humboldtian reforms introduced radical changes to the university, such that it is plausible to maintain that a modern yet unreformed university (e.g., Harvard prior to its reformation) had more in common with a medieval one than one reformed on Humboldtian lines.

There were, at least, two important elements of nineteenth-century reforms that planted the seeds of barbarism in the modern university. The first change is the exclusion of *schöne Wissenshaft;* the second is the focus on research. These two changes are, in different guises, the same two changes (mentioned earlier) that Henry points to and laments in his day. In what follows, I am going to argue that these changes are contained in ovo in the university structure Henry implicitly endorses, rather than due to external pressures as Henry argues (B, 120–1).

Beginning with the first, according to historian Bas van Bommel, pre-reform universities did not exclude what Henry calls "culture" from study; indeed, well into the eighteenth century, university *Bildung* introduced students to art, literature, politics, and ethics under the rubric of *shöne Wissenshaften*.[10] It is important to note at the outset that the *shöne Wissenshaften* cannot be identified with narrowly aesthetic reflections on the beautiful but, rather, denoted something like Cicero's claim in On Duties that *decorum* is inseparable from moral virtue and that acting with a sense of *decorum* is inevitably to act according to virtue.[11] The development and disciplining of sensibility through the study (and imitation) of classical art and literature was thought to entail, or at least encourage, moral growth as well. To put it in Henry's terms, this kind of study was meant to deepen and enrich life, transforming the student morally and spiritually.[12] Moreover, it was, and claimed to be, a *Wissenshaft* and to have a rightful place in a university curriculum. Nevertheless, changing conceptions of science pushed it out of the curriculum in the early nineteenth century. The *schöne Wissenshaften* seemed too imprecise to meet the standards of a proper science. Under the influence of Kant's third critique, *Schönheit* was increasingly seen as the product of genius or the expression of an incommunicable subjectivity, and *not* as something that could be taught.[13] Intentionally or not, denying that *shöne Wissenshaft* is, in fact, a *Wissenshaft* had profound effects on the curricula of reformed universities. Humboldt, for example, held that the task of the university is to pursue *Wissenshaft*; if one denies that *schöne Wissenshaft* is, in fact, a *Wissenshaft*, then it is hard to see what place it has in the reformed university. Though not immediately, it was excised slowly but surely from the curriculum to make way for more scientific approaches—even the study of classical Latin and Greek was transformed (as van Bommel documents extensively) to meet the standards of science. No longer did one study the classics as a source of moral examples, stylistic elegance, and overall spiritual development. The discipline was reconceptualized as *Alterumwissenshaft* and what once was a means—textual criticism, grammar, and so on—became the end. For F. A. Wolf (1759-1824), classical studies had to be reconstituted as a pure science, studying the ancient world in excruciating detail while specifically excluding the appreciation of classical texts for their exemplary qualities, literary or otherwise.[14] The transformation of classics into *Alterumwissenshaft* provides a case study in what Henry calls "the ideology of barbarism"—the importation of Galilean ideals of rigor into the human science with the inevitable effect of expelling humanity from the humanities (B, 81-4). But—note this well—it happened at least a century earlier than Henry thinks it did.

This is not to say that *Bildung* was immediately abandoned. To complete the mission of *Bildung* in the absence of the *schöne Wissenshaften*, the natural sciences initially took on the burden of humanistic education; the argument was that a scientific understanding of, for example, mathematics, geology, or astronomy would cultivate humane values as well, even if those values were not strictly speaking scientific. This would compensate for the lack of any explicit study of art, ethics, or religion. One still *hoped* for something like spiritual development from study, but not as an end of study but, rather, as a kind of halo or glow that accompanies a unified vision of *true Wissenshaft*. *Bildung* becomes a side effect of study, but not the goal.

To the extent that the natural sciences hoped for a kind of spiritual halo effect, the rejection of *schöne Wissenshaft* does not represent the immediate barbarization of the university: the university still hoped to have a spiritually transformative effect on the student by different means. However, another element of the university reforms worked against this goal. As I already mentioned, nineteenth-century reforms envisioned unity of teaching and research—and as we noticed earlier, Henry seems to endorse this view. The institutional expression of this ideal is the seminar, where a professor and advanced students work together on research projects, synthesizing all that they know, analyzing new problems as they appear, and, in the end, contributing to the march of science. If a unified vision of true *Wissenshaft* was to appear, it had to appear in these seminars! However, this model was a victim of its own success and its virtues became vices: the rapid increase in knowledge and the growing tendency for fields to divide and subdivide into increasingly incommunicable specialities soon made that kind of unified vision increasingly implausible. Slowly but surely, the sciences abandoned or forgot their humanistic claims and developed alternative, mainly instrumental, justifications.[15] This has led, finally, to a hyper-specialized university without either "culture" or cultural pretensions. This has had two effects. First, there is now a proliferation of investigative projects having little or nothing to do with each other—a point Henry complains about in *Barbarism* (B, 77), although not in reference to the modern research university. Second, the emphasis on research and knowledge production is an emphasis on transcendent or external products, rather than the transformation of life (B, 125). The point is publications, not interior transformation. Which is to say that (alas!) the emphasis on research, if history is to be our guide, tends to fragment the university as each teacher and researcher dives deeper and deeper into specialities that are increasingly opaque to outsiders, and research (rather than spiritual growth) becomes the sole end.

This incipient barbarism spread to the French university system that Henry is predominantly concerned with; reforms of the French system were carried out in the 1860s through the 1890s to model the German system.[16] Indeed, the German system was adopted in the United States and in the "new" colleges of the United Kingdom in roughly the same time period—although the ancient universities of Oxford and Cambridge largely resisted. In sum, the exclusion of culture from the university began much earlier than Henry suggests, and is (ironically) rooted in the confluence of (a) the abandonment of *schöne Wissenshaft* and (b) the increasing specialization that accompanied the transformation of colleges into research universities. So much for the curriculum; let us now turn to teaching.

## How Is It to Be Transmitted?

Despite his failure to acknowledge the significant differences between reformed and unreformed university curricula, Henry is quite right, I think, to maintain that barbarism in the university is not merely a matter of *what* is taught, but also of *how* it is taught. According to Henry, in barbaric universities, the transmission of knowledge is understood simply as the sharing of information; there is no recognition of the subjective cultivation of the love of knowledge or one's own development as a person (B, 125).[17] On the other hand, true teaching and learning, Henry argues, occur when "the acquisition and transmission of knowledge are identical to its concrete actualization in repetition" (B, 125, italics removed). The student ought to repeat what is to be learned, not in a mechanical way but insofar as the student repeats the initial discovery, appropriating for himself/herself the lesson, rather than merely the words of the lesson. Repetition in this sense makes the student "contemporary" with the truth; indeed, he or she is transformed by it: "he or she becomes this truth" (B, 125). To become contemporary with the truth means, according to Henry, that the student enters "into the process that leads towards what one wants to be contemporary with and the contemporaneity which one reaches at the end of the process" (B, 125). In seeking after the truth, one rethinks or rediscovers the truth; rather than memorizing a list of, for example, valid argument forms in logic, one (re)proves their validity. This is why I would reject any attempt to describe the Humboldtian model as a barbaric simpliciter. While its exclusion of *schöne Wissenshaft* is a first step toward barbarism, the research seminar does, it seems to me, engage the student actively in learning in precisely the way Henry recommends (even as it contributes to the fragmentation of the university).

Henry compares learning with "the acquisition of bodily movements, apprenticeship in all forms, the phenomena of imitation and intropathy" (B, 124).[18] Henry's choice of examples is worth dwelling on, since the bulk of them (to me anyway) suggest that he views learning kinesthetically or at least as analogous to kinesthetic learning. This suggests a different paradigm for teaching than that of the college lecture: when I am coaching soccer, and wish to teach the kids that the center-forward should run toward the goal when the left- or right-forward is advancing toward the goal with the ball, I do not talk about it for an hour. Instead, I briefly introduce the concept, demonstrate the technique, and then have the players practice the play, offering tips and corrections as they go on. I want them to learn kinesthetically how it *feels* to run the play correctly, to feel how and why it works, and for this affective knowledge to transform how they relate to strategy and the game. I do not lecture for an hour about the benefits of splitting the goalie by having multiple players approach the goal while crossing the ball from, for example, left to right: they feel the benefits when the play works. This kinesthetic-affective pedagogy does not preclude theoretical knowledge of soccer strategy but provides the only basis on which that knowledge could be meaningful to the players.

Henry believes that the contemporary university has given up on this sort of pedagogy, preferring to reduce teaching to information transfer. In general, Henry sees barbaric educational methods as reducing the complex phenomena of learning to a simplistic repetition of the "right answers." This is, essentially, what educational theorist Paulo Freire called and criticized as the "banking" or storage model of education; describing it he writes,

> [The teacher's] task is to "fill" the students with the content of his narration— contents that are detached from reality, disconnected from the totality that engendered them and could give them significance. Words are emptied of their concreteness and become a hollow, alienated and alienating verbosity.[19]

I think Henry is on the trail of something like this point in his critical discussion of contemporary university life, but doesn't develop the point as much as he could have. In any case, Henry's concern is to defend professional qualifications against various attempts to reduce the credentialing requirements for teaching staff (B, 123). Freire's claim is quite different; while he agrees with Henry regarding the importance of phenomenology for the analysis of teaching and learning (compare *Pedagogy* 79–86), he is more concerned with developing ways for students to take a more active role in their education.[20] I take his point to be that the "banking model" is itself a problem, regardless of the credentials of the banker. One should point out immediately— to ward off suggestions that I am being too irenic—that Freire would probably disagree sharply with Henry's dismissive attitude toward teacher-training. While the situation Henry describes is certainly regrettable (instructors with teaching credentials but no knowledge of the subject matter), an in-depth knowledge of the subject matter with no idea of how to motivate students to engage the subject matter is equally regrettable. That said, despite the difference in emphasis, I think there is a fair bit of common ground and Freire can be used to extend some of Henry's points. The model of education Henry endorses in *Barbarism* bears more than a passing resemblance to what Friere calls "problem-posing"—that is, where students are presented with carefully crafted problems or questions, the working through of which allows them to discover for themselves that which the teacher hopes for them to learn.[21] In problem-posing pedagogy, the student (ideally) not only learns the content but also internalizes it, becoming, as Henry puts it, contemporary with it.

Earlier in *Barbarism*, Henry identified various practices that he associates with the spread and reinforcement of barbarism. It is here that one finds his trenchant criticisms of the media and what is now called "screen time." These practices of barbarism turn life's attention away from itself and toward some external thing—most problematically from Henry's view, the two-dimensional lights flashing across the screens that adorn our rooms. These screens are the *dii familiares* of barbarism—jealous household gods that demand hours of time each day reducing their supplicants to voyeurism (B, 113). Henry's use of the term is, I think, more than merely salacious: the voyeur does not engage in any act, but simply watches; the watching takes the place of the doing. The sports fan does not play sports, he or she watches it; the romantic does not engage in romance, but watches romantic movies on TV. Being a sports fan demands familiarity with something external such as win/loss records, statistics, and so on, rather than playing the game.[22] But this critique of media, it seems to me, is readily transferable to a critique of the banking model of education insofar as both reduce one to being a mere spectator. And just as the sports fan is expected to be able to recite the statistics of his/her preferred teams and players, the good student is expected to return the deposits of the teacher upon command. The media, according to Henry, stifles the life within us; the banking model does the same. According to Friere, the banking model of education teaches the student that he or she has nothing to offer and doesn't really matter; he or she is simply a repository for information or a beast to be trained,[23] or as Henry puts it, an "automaton" (IAT, 275). In the banking model, the content is more important than the student; or perhaps better, the student is only important insofar as he or she can recall the content. In this environment, the student is trained to think of himself or herself as material to be directed and formed by some authority figure; for the students, doing well in the course and doing what the professor tells them to do are coextensive.[24] And how does the student know if he or she is doing well? By getting good grades.

The banking model of education, combined with the Galilean drive for quantification, lends itself to the imposition of a particularly insidious and widespread practice of barbarism. I mean, of course, grades. It may seem strange to identify grades as a form of barbarism, but they are a primary and enduring habituation to the reduction of a complex subjective experience (i.e., learning) to external quantification stripped of *pathos*. Henry doesn't explicitly discuss grades, but his argument suggests that the multifaceted phenomenon of learning—he notes that it has practical, theoretical, affective, and cognitive elements (B, 124–6)—cannot be reduced to a number or a letter without being severely distorted.[25] Indeed, doing so is the essence of barbarism: it voids or obscures the mysterious life of the learner and replaces it with an abstraction that purports to specify exactly how much one has learned. David Carr has argued, correctly in my view, that the behaviorist learning theories of Watson and Skinner (criticized by Henry in B, 130–1) had more influence on twentieth-century education than any philosophical theory one cares to name.[26] For the behaviorist, one measures learning by measuring behavioral output. We say that a rat has learned its way through the maze when it runs through it faster with fewer wrong turns; this can be expressed numerically. We say that the student has learned history when he/she can name the first few American presidents quickly with few or no mistakes; this too can be expressed numerically, as a grade.

Or course, once there were no grades; student evaluation was either through face-to-face discussions or through written essays or short notes. There is some debate as to who invented grades. Sometimes, Yale president Ezra Stiles (1785) is credited for it. His 'grades' are short Latin comparative phrases used to compare students, not letters or numbers, and they are, I think, better understood as proto-grades rather than grades in the modern sense. If not Stiles, the next likely originator is the Cambridge chemistry tutor William Farish, in 1792. Neil Postman's comments on Farish and his importance are worth quoting at length:

> No one knows much about Farish; not more than a handful of people have ever heard of him. And yet his idea that a quantitative value should be assigned to human thought was a major step towards constructing a mathematical concept of reality. If a number can be given to the quality of a thought, then a number can be given to the qualities of mercy, love, hate, beauty, creativity, intelligence, even sanity itself.[27]

The practice of grading didn't really take off until a few generations later: the University of Michigan—famously inspired by the German university system[28]—experimented with various quantitative grading methods in the 1850s.[29] The A–F system Americans know and love began in 1897 at Mount Holyoke College and spread from there. Via number and letter grades, students can be ranked, compared, and categorized almost like things. But, interestingly, not exactly like things: Herbert Mumford, a professor of agriculture at the University of Illinois, worked hard to persuade the meat-packing industry to adopt the same grading scheme for beef as used in schools—A through F. While the meat-packing industry eventually did adopt this way of grading beef, they insisted (in marked contrast to academic transcripts) that written comments be attached to each grade insofar as the quality of something as complex as beef could not be readily reduced to a letter. Apparently, universities had no such worries about student learning.[30] Once it spread through the universities and teacher-training colleges, grading soon entered K-12; educational historians have shown that grading originally functioned as a means of communicating students' progress to the scholars themselves and their parents; scales and methods were idiosyncratic and varied from place to place. Grading gradually became an end in itself, functioning not as a pedagogical tool facilitating communication between teachers, scholars, and parents, but as part of bureaucratic system-building enterprise facilitating communication between educators and administrators.[31] On a more Henrian note, this transformation functions to eliminate, or rather, obscure, the subjective elements of learning, ensuring that even at the tender age of five or six, children learn that learning is indicated by an externalized quantity rather than a deepening or enrichment of their life. Learning, Henry maintains, is the act of entering into a relationship with a truth, having a profoundly affective element to it; representing this as a letter or number is precisely the kind of thing *Barbarism* warns against. If we return to the lament that closes *I am the Truth*, we find Henry writing a sentence that could serve as a summary for the preceding paragraph: "Men treated mathematically, digitally, statistically, counted like animals and counting for much less" (IAT, 275).

## Conclusion: Toward a Henrian Practice of Education

I don't want to be read as suggesting a straight line from the modern research university to modern barbarism; there are, as readers of Henry know, a constellation of factors at play. Moreover, while agreeing with Friere's critique of the banking model of pedagogy, I am not claiming that it is necessary and sufficient for barbarism. I am, however, claiming that the confluence of the exclusion of *schöne Wissenshaft* and the banking model contributes greatly to the spread of barbarism. The spread of barbarism is, if I am correct, much more closely tied to the history and theory of higher education in the last two centuries than *Barbarism* suggests. Since the most likely readers of this chapter are students or employees of higher education institutions, it suggests that we are better positioned to respond to the spread of barbarism than focusing our critiques on politicians, the media, and technology alone might imply.

In closing, I will offer three points in a sketch of what a pedagogical practice built on Henry's critique of barbarism would look like. First, it would aim at the elevation rather than the degradation of the student. If modern education trains students to despise themselves (IAT, 275), then the alternative is to enable them to see themselves, and human beings more generally, as noble beings. In Henry's case, this would mean reminding the student of the truth of life and the unfathomable depths thereof. Second, and more concretely, educators ought to focus on the transmission of culture—not in the sense of this or that culture, but the works and deeds that deepen and enrich life—rather than mere technical or professional training.[32] This would require an unwinding of the research university model to allow for the return, albeit in a new twenty-first-century guise, of the exiled tradition of *schöne Wissenshaft*. Likewise, teaching would have to take precedence over research. The "techno-scientific" emphasis on production—in a university context, of articles, essays, books, and grants—would have to give place to an emphasis on the unquantifiable and unpredictable effects a good teacher can have on a good student. In this, the university would return to its earlier position of marginality although, rather than the medieval marginality between throne and altar (B,116), the university would be marginalized vis-à-vis technology and industry. Third, the methods of teaching would have to be altered to allow for more active learning on the part of the student—he or she should not be a voyeur of culture but a vigorous participant. Relatedly, it seems to me that a pedagogy inspired by Henry's work would, while not sacrificing rigor, move away as much as possible from an accent on grades. Instead, individual evaluation and communication with students about their learning should be emphasized. Much of this, alas, requires smaller class sizes; it is impossible to give individual evaluations to a class with hundreds of students. But there are strategies for dealing with large class sizes (e.g., peer evaluation, team learning) that the pedagogical training Henry is so dismissive of explores.[33]

# Notes

1 See, for example, S. J. Smith, "Phenomenology of Movement and Place," in *Encyclopedia of Educational Philosophy and Theory*, ed. M. A. Peters (Dordrecht: Springer, 2016.) and W. -M. Roth, "Hermeneutic Phenomenology and Cognition," in *Hermeneutic Phenomenology in Education*, ed. N. Friesen, C. Henriksson, and T. Saevi (Leiden: Brill, 2012), 79–103.

2 Michel Henry, *I am the Truth: Towards a Philosophy of Christianity*, trans. Susan Emanuel (Palo Alto: Stanford UP, 2003), 275. Henceforth cited in the text as IAT.

3 See David Carr, "Curriculum and the Value of Knowledge," in *The Oxford Handbook of the Philosophy of Education*, ed. H. Siegel (New York: Oxford UP, 2009), 280–99), 280–1.

4 See Carr, "Curriculum and the Value of Knowledge," 284–5 for a discussion of these views.

5 See the discussion in José Ortega y Gasset, *Mission of the University*, trans. H. L. Nostrand (Princeton: Princeton University Press, 1944), 36–7. Reading this text in light of Henry's comments on the university is very illuminating.

6  See Louis Menand, Paul Reitter, and Chad Wellmon (eds), *Rise of the Research University* (Chicago: University of Chicago Press, 2017), 109 and 113.

7  Generally speaking, there were four major faculties in the medieval university: the "undergraduate" arts faculty and the "graduate" faculties of law, medicine, and theology. Henry's elision of law and medicine is, I think, not entirely innocent, for this allows him to present "professional" training in the universities as a modern and barbaric innovation and identify the medieval university entirely with the contemplative life (B, 121). Even in the golden age of scholasticism, many people went to school to qualify for high-paying jobs. Indeed, at least half the faculties (i.e., law and medicine) were devoted to professional training.

8  Gasset, *Mission of the University*, 38.

9  Ibid., 39. The reader might wonder if I have overemphasized Ortega's distance from Humboldt's model. For example, C.A. Lemke Duque, "Limites de innovacion': La *Misión de la Universidad* y el concepto ortegiano de ciencia (1922–1936)," *Estudios Sobra Educación* 35 (2018): 391–408 argues that even when distancing himself from it, Ortega's entire argument of *Mission of the University* takes place within a broadly Humboldtian view of things. To be sure, Ortega borrows some ideas from his experiences in German universities, but it seems to me that his criticisms of (a) research and (b) specialization create an intense separation. Moreover, as his practice of giving public lectures to all comers, rather than restricting himself to graduate seminars, testifies, he did not see the aim of education as the production of researchers.

10 Bas van Bommel, *Classical Humanism and the Challenge of Modernity: Debates on Classical Education in 19th Century Germany* (Berlin and Boston: De Gruyter, 2015), 70–1; my reason for focusing on German universities, if the reader doesn't already know it, will be clear soon.

11 Cicero, *On Duties*, I.27 ff.

12 Although referencing neither Henry nor *schöne Wissenshaft*, I believe that Graham Oddie's words can be applied to the project: "values education would be, in part, a matter of cultivating appropriate experiential responses to various values; in part, a matter of refining and honing such responses; and in part, a matter of providing a framework that supports those responses and that can be challenged and revised in the light of further value experiences. Further, if experiences of value are a matter of emotion, feeling or desire, values education would need to take seriously the training of folk in having, interpreting, and refining appropriate emotions, feelings and desires. This would not in any way diminish the crucial role of logic, critical thinking and rational constraints like universalizability. But it would open up the educational domain to cultivation and refinement of affective and conative states" (Graham Oddie, "Values Education," in *The Oxford Handbook of the Philosophy of Education*, ed. H. Siegel (New York: Oxford University Press, 2009), 260–77), 269. This, it seems to me, is precisely what a Henrian view of education would endorse.

13  Bas van Bommel, *Classical Humanism and the Challenge of Modernity*, 73–5.
14  Ibid., 79.
15  Van Bommel, "Between Bildung and Wissenshaft," 44; in American universities, the project of *shöne Wissenshaft* (although obviously under different names) lasted longer; we can find it as late as 1871, in Noah Porter's Inaugural Address as president of Yale University (in RRU, 248–64). Nevertheless, it too died out in the States for similar reasons: the rise of research and increasing specialization (RRU, 334–5). Arguably, the various proposals for a general education or core curriculum for undergraduates can be taken as evidence that (in the United States at least) the project continued into the twentieth century. But it isn't as clear as it might seem: to take the one that started it all—Columbia's—the core was designed not so much for ethical as for ideological goals (an early version was taught in 1918 as "War Aims"); see Louis Menand, *The Marketplace of Ideas: Reform and Resistance in the American University* (New York: Norton, 2010), 32–6. Even the argument advanced by Robert Maynard Hutchins (in the mid-1930s) that his proposed general education program at the University of Chicago would serve to cultivate intellectual virtue (Menand et al., *Rise of the Research University*, 347) specifically disclaims teaching moral virtue; the development of practical wisdom is left for the student after graduation; general education can only provide the intellectual tools that are required for prudence. To be fair, Aristotle, who guided much of Hutchins' discussion, held that the young are too inexperienced to have practical wisdom. But the exclusion of "character building" from the aims of the curriculum shows the distance from the ideals of *shöne Wissenshaft*. For a discussion of the philosophical issues raised by values education (in contrast to supposedly value-neutral scientific education), see the discussion in Oddie, "Values Education."
16  See Walter Rüegg (ed), *A History of the University in Europe, Volume Three: Universities in the Nineteenth and Early Twentieth Centuries* (Cambridge: Cambridge University Press, 2004), 55–7.
17  Interestingly, one aspect of the transformation of the ante-bellum American college into the research university that was controversial at the time but largely taken for granted now is the abandonment of the idea that colleges had a duty to act in the place of parents and ensure the moral development of the student. Indeed, Charles William Elliot, largely considered the leading figure in the growth of American research universities specifically rejected the claim that a university has any role to play in providing for the moral development of students. On this, see Menand et al., *Rise of the Research University*, 279. Also, in a way that might seem weird or paradoxical, the current trend on campuses to develop, for example, strict rules regarding active consent for students engaging in sexual relationships or to enforce guidelines that seek to control a student's off-campus (including online) behavior can be read as a return to the old ways—although representing a style of parenting far from that of the nineteenth century.

18  There is a short, but informative discussion of *Barbarism*'s account of learning in Michael O'Sullivan, *Academic Barbarism: Universities and Inequality* (London: Palgrave 2016), 25–6.
19  Paulo Friere, *Pedagogy of the Oppressed*. 50th Anniversary Edition, trans. M. B. Ramos (London: Bloomsbury, 2018), 71. One need not, it seems to me embrace the entirety of Friere's pedagogical-political program to draw from his insights regarding pedagogical methods; indeed, one can find other theorists, for example, John Dewey, making similar points. I focus on Friere because of his explicit dependence on phenomenology for the formulation of his theories (see note 20). Moreover, there are, at least, affinities between the Frierian criticisms of neoliberalism and Henry's warnings in *From Communism to Capitalism*, although exploring them at any length would be a separate task. David Carr, "Curriculum and the Value of Knowledge" describes Friere's criticisms as holding that "the key purpose of curriculum theorizing is the radical reform of educational institutions and practices for the empowerment of the traditionally marginalized and disenfranchised" (293). I believe that this is close to Henry's view, provided that one agrees that, due to the spread of barbarism, Life itself has been marginalized and disenfranchised.
20  Indeed, it is fair to say that Freire's proposal for "problem-posing" education, wherein students should be taught by posing problems, the teacher only coaching them along the way, is rooted quite clearly in phenomenology, although not that of Henry. While introducing it, Friere specifies that intentionality is the essence of consciousness (OP, 79) and he goes on to cite Jaspers, Husserl, and Sartre. Indeed, the fundamental insight of Freire's method is that if consciousness is, indeed, intentional, then the educator should allow consciousness to "go out" into the world and solve problems rather than, as if it were a bag, box, or bank, simply stuffing it with information: "an empty mind passively open to receptive deposits from the reality of a world outside me" (OP, 75). For a lengthier discussion of Freire and Husserl in particular, see Eduardo Duarte, "Thinking Together as One: Freire's Rewriting of Husserl" (in *Philosophy of Education 2000*, ed. Stone, Lynda (Champaign: University of Illinois, 2001), 180–8). Nevertheless, I think the kinesthetic-affective pedagogy I attributed to Henry comports perfectly with Freire's program.
21  One could just as easily argue for affinities between Dewey and Henry on this score, in part because of the similarity between Dewey's idea for project-based learning and Friere's problem-posing method. I focus on Friere because of his proximity to phenomenology, but for a discussion of Dewey's method, see Carr, "Curriculum and the Value of Knowledge," 288–9.
22  Am I a soccer fan? I don't follow any teams, nor could I name any but the most famous players. But I have coached soccer for the last five or six years and kicked a ball around the field by my house innumerable times. I believe Henry would say that I am, but most self-identified sports fans would say that I am not.

23 Friere, *Pedagogy of the Oppressed*, 73.
24 Ibid., 78.
25 As teachers, many are concerned with grade inflation. But few have noticed that grades are able to inflate precisely because they mean very little, despite their apparent precision. First, they don't measure learning, understood as a subjective state, but, rather, some set of outputs or behaviors that the professor hopes will be indicative of learning in his or her class. (I would wager that all those reading this have experienced the student who learns everything in the course, but ends it with a bad grade because of a missed assignment; no doubt the reader has experienced the inverse: the student who seems to have learned nothing, but ends the course with a good grade.). Second, the uniformity of the system masks a jungle of variety. An "A" from Professor Jones and an "A" from Professor Smith in Philosophy 101 may correlate with vastly different behaviors or outputs, standards of evaluation, as well as topics and authors studied. The fact that Student X received an "A" from Professor Jones tells one slightly more than nothing.
26 Carr, "Curriculum and the Value of Knowledge," 289.
27 Neil Postman, *Technopoly: The Surrender of Culture of Technology* (New York: Vintage, 1993), 13–14.
28 In 1850 Michigan amended its constitution to develop a "Prussian"-style educational system; this included the reorganization of the University of Michigan in 1852 along Humboldtian lines. Prior to this time, most American universities were modeled on the English system of tutorials; the German system began to influence American education more strongly following the founding of Johns Hopkins along German lines in 1876.
29 William Durm, "An A Is Not an A Is Not an A: A History of Grading," *The Educational Forum* 57 (1993): 294–7.
30 Nancy Davidson, *The New Education* (New York: Basic Books, 2017), 204–5.
31 Jack Schneider and Ethan Hutt, "Making the Grade: A History of the A–F Marking Scheme," *Journal of Curriculum Studies* (2013), doi:10.1080/00220272.2013.790480.
32 It is worth noting that nothing in Henry's comments entails what could be called a "conservative" view of curriculum a la Alan Bloom in opposition to a more "multicultural" curriculum: Henry's main concern is that universities pass on a culture of life to students, but not a *particular* culture such that the poetry of, for example, Sor Juana de la Cruz would be just as acceptable to Henry as that of Dryden or Shelley. I put "multicultural" in quotations to acknowledge the difficulties associated with the concept, as described by M. Levinson, "Mapping Multicultural Education," in *The Oxford Handbook of the Philosophy of Education*, ed. H. Siegel (New York: Oxford University Press, 2009), 428–50.
33 Earlier versions of this paper were read at conferences in Mexico City and San Diego in the fall of 2018; I am grateful to the participants at both conferences for their comments.

# 10

# Abstract Color and Esthetic Experience
## Michel Henry Reading Kandinsky

I. Podoroga

When, in the 1950s, Henri Matisse argues that every art is abstract and that the distinction between figurative and nonfigurative art is no more relevant, he means that art naturally proceeds via abstraction, by preserving only the essential in the object and leaving aside all the secondary and fortuitous aspects. He seems thus to repeat what has already been claimed by Wassily Kandinsky in his book *Concerning the Spiritual in Art* some forty years earlier, at the very dawn of abstraction. In his influential interpretation of Kandinsky's theoretical writing, *Seeing the Invisible: On Kandinsky* (1988), Michel Henry would generalize this remark and endow it with ontological value: abstract art is crucial to the extent to which it helps to elucidate the essence of art as such. The focus of artistic interest switches from the sensible objects (to be re-presented on canvas) to what had been considered as subsidiary and pertaining rather to a technical dimension of art (*how* to paint the object that is to be re-presented): command of colors and forms. It means that colors and forms come to occupy the place of the sensible object. Thus, Henry attributes to abstraction a well-determined heuristic function, that of disclosing art's essential properties, of the fundamental (spiritual) meaning that colors and forms are able to manifest. From now on the spectator must accept to engage in a different kind of relationship with art, one based on a radically new visual experience. No more mediated by the objects of the sensible world, this experience is governed by different principles, principles which Henry's book on Kandinsky will attempt to account for.

Let us put a preliminary question, at the risk of sounding naive: How can one, a spectator more or less initiated to abstract art, be conscious of such an artistic disclosure? What kind of intellectual insight combined, undoubtedly, with an emotional arousal, should this artwork provoke in her or him, in order to confirm its high artistic value? Is it something immediately graspable—this truth about art and its abstract nature—or should one accept to enter into its logic in order to apprehend it? If we go back to Michel Henry's book and his philosophical exploration of the artistic field, we may get a contradictory response. Indeed, one is supposed to be subject to a powerful emotion: when looking at Kandinsky's paintings, one ought to be already artistically conquered by it. But, at the same time, this art needs some philosophical explanation, one that Henry himself tries to formulate throughout his rich and passionate book. The question thus boils down once again to the same eternal problematics posed by contemporary art: What is the share of the sensible in it and what is the share of the intellectual, rational? Does philosophy have to be involved in our understanding of abstract art, and how insightful it can be? And, conversely, doesn't the new kind of aesthetic experience that abstract painting offers shake some of our philosophical presumptions, on the nature of subjectivity, for instance? In this chapter I would like to investigate in detail, how Henry copes with this difficulty by considering only one, but a decisive, element of his analysis of Kandinsky—the issue of color and its ideal (philosophical or phenomenological) and emotional perception.

## The Essence of Red (Husserl-Kandinsky-Henry)

Let us start at the point where abstract art and philosophy seem most naturally to meet. It is common to suggest proximity between abstract/nonfigurative art and phenomenology if one presumes that both put forward a similar methodological procedure: a reduction of the sensible reality as it is habitually perceived in order to establish the way it originates in our perception. In this perspective, Kandinsky's art offers a kind of eidetic reduction close to the one performed by Edmund Husserl. Henry doesn't hesitate to use this analogy: "Kandinsky's analysis operates in the same way as does Husserl's eidetic analysis. It proscribes the foreign properties from the essence of art in order to perceive art in its purity. With the elimination of objective representation, the pure essence of painting is laid bare."[1] He pursues the analogy a little further in order to specify the meaning of those foreign or nonessential properties: "The non-essential characteristics are the objective meanings constituted intentionally by consciousness; they are external, 'transcendent' in the Husserlian sense. The essential characteristics, the pictorial and graphic forms, belong to sensibility, that is to say, as will be shown, to absolute subjectivity and its Night."[2] Abstract art, as the result of an operation of abstraction, retains from the sensible reality only two—but fundamental—properties: colors and forms. Art and philosophy share, then, the same starting point, but the question is to understand exactly what the difference between philosophical and artistic reductions is, given that both try to resolve a purely gnoseological problem.

Husserl introduces for the first time his newly discovered method in the lectures of 1907, later published under the title *Die Idee der Phänomenologie*. He calls it a "phenomenological" or "epistemological" reduction and he puts it into effect as a solution to the problem of knowledge that he has been working on since the *Logical Investigations* (1900–1). In the passage that follows, of a special interest to us as it takes an example of color, Husserl tackles an intricate problem of the self-givenness of general essences. Do those essences transcend our knowledge or can they be immanently grasped at the outcome of the process of reduction?

> Let us consider cases where the universal is given, that is, cases where a purely immanent consciousness of universality constitutes itself on the basis of a seen and self-given particularity. I have a particular intuition of red, or several particular intuitions of red; I attend to pure immanence alone; I perform phenomenological reduction. I separate off anything that red might signify that might lead one to apperceive it as transcendent, as, say, the red of a piece of blotting paper on my desk, and the like. And now I actualize in pure seeing the sense of the thought red, red *in specie*, the *identical universal* that is seen in this or that; now the particularity as such is no longer meant, but rather red in general.[3]

The color "red" is transcendent when it is a red spread over a certain object (blotting paper), when it seems to belong to this *particular* object. But we can reach the essence—the redness of the color in the immanent way—after implementing what Husserl calls the "eidetic reduction." The essence of red lies simply in its universality, which we do not have to deduce from a series of different red objects. We do not have to generalize, but we grasp its meaning in the process of "ideating abstraction," as an *a priori* truth of our perception of red. Of course, it is the immediate grasping of the general idea that interests Husserl here, and not the material or sensible nature of the color as such. The important term is "pure seeing," which is not seeing "with our eyes" but a kind of intuitive immanent seeing.[4]

In an analogous manner, if the task of abstract art in Kandinsky, according to Henry, is "to perceive art in its purity," it must first aim at separating colors and forms from all particular objects in the sensible world to which they are commonly attached. In *Concerning the Spiritual in Art*, he attempts to establish, in a somewhat Goethean spirit, a vocabulary of colors and forms each of them being invested with a definite spiritual value. Each color, regardless of the objects it can refer to (red as blood, or fire, or even the Bolshevik revolution, etc.), has its inner tonality, which constitutes its spiritual meaning. If we take the color "red," we see that it occupies a particular place in Kandinsky's grammar of colors. He says, among other things, that red's capacity is that of provoking excitation. But there is no causal determination between the red of the fire or the blood and the way we perceive redness as such. We can associate the red color and the effect it produces on us with those phenomena, but we cannot deduce this effect based on our experience of getting burnt by fire or of being hurt and bleeding, for example.[5] But most importantly, when Kandinsky speaks about the materialization of the color red in the real artistic practice, where each color is combined with a form, he sets forth the same differentiation as Husserl: between pure seeing (that of the mind) and empirical seeing:

> Form can stand alone as representing an object (either real or otherwise) or as purely abstract limit to a space or a surface.... Colour cannot stand alone; it cannot dispense with boundaries of some kind. A never-ending extent of red can only be seen in the mind; when the word red is heard, the colour is evoked without definite boundaries. If such are necessary they have deliberately to be imagined. But such red, as is seen by the mind and not by the eye, exercises at once a definite and an indefinite impression on the soul, and produces spiritual harmony. I say "indefinite," because in itself it has no suggestion of warmth or cold, such attributes having to be imagined for it afterwards, as modifications of the original "redness." I say "definite," because the spiritual harmony exists without any need for such subsequent attributes of warmth or cold.[6]

The experiment of pronouncing a word is essential for Kandinsky's theory, as he maintains that the sound is a privileged way in attaining abstraction. He borrows this procedure from poetry, and especially from Maurice Maeterlinck.[7] When we say "red" (or any other word) and repeat it, the tonality of the word is likely to emancipate itself from its meaning. Red is no more related to any particular object but develops an existence of its own. By repeating it several times we lose our capacity to understand its common meaning. That is why, if we place ourselves in the sphere of the spiritual, we grasp immediately the sense of red—"original redness"—and this impression is quite definite. On the contrary, it is indefinite from the point of view of the empirical act of seeing, because we assume that it needs to materialize on the actual canvas, and end up "possess[ing] some definite shade of the many shades of red that exist." Yet, the operation of reduction related to vision seems much harder to accomplish than that related to hearing. That is why Kandinsky continues with the same analogy, but this time evoking a musical instrument. When we pronounce the word "trumpet," we get the same impression as with the word "red": without actually hearing the sound, we nonetheless "hear" the trumpet quite distinctly in our mind. No one will object, argues Kandinsky, that such a general representation of the sound really exists. We are dealing here with a sort of experimental enactment of Husserl's ideation, one that seems to function quite well but mostly as regards our sense of hearing. Can't we, then, imagine the same when it comes to the sense of vision and its relation to the essence of "red," its redness? Wouldn't, then, the objective of abstract art be a visual representation of pure redness?

In his book on Kandinsky, Henry does not elude this passage, and comments on it extensively. First of all, he congratulates Kandinsky on his "profound philosophical instinct," his "ingenious idea" that consists in saying the word "red," while putting aside any image of this color, and any actual perception of it. This philosophical gesture is further again compared to that of Husserl:

> Philosophically speaking, it can be said that what Kandinsky seeks to define is the essence of red, the ideal type of red as well as the impression of this red that is conceived by the mind but not sensed. The following observation establishes that this tonality of red does exist, and likewise, that there is a tonality belonging to the triangle, the circle, and the point. (SIK, 88–9)

This passage on color in Kandinsky is quite crucial for Henry's argumentation. Kandinsky distinguishes clearly between the ideal "red," redness, and empirical red that is always chromatically determined, more or less "warm," more or less "cool," or "deep," or "sharp" (p. 86–8). The essence of the color bears its fundamental tonality, the redness of the red, in our case. And this essence, reminds Henry, is not sensed or visually perceived but only "conceived by the mind." This does not prevent, of course, the tonality or element from receiving, eventually, numerous modifications, as long as it is combined with other colors and forms on the canvas. Henry singles out three principal characteristics that "protect the internal-being of the element from its absorption by the environment" (SIK, 89): the first, which we can call a linguistic identification of a tonality, marks an automatic correspondence between the tonality and the sign that designates it ("red"); the second one is more philosophical, as it ascribes tonality "to an ideal type, which also exists and can be conceived as such"; the third one ensures the temporal perpetuation of the tonality or its "permanence throughout all subsequent transformations" (SIK, 89).

In the interview, "Art and the Phenomenology of Life" (1996), Henry explains precisely how Kandinsky becomes aware of the ideal dimension of color that exists beneath each particular and limited application of material color or paint.

> Kandinsky shows how a painting is organized around a colour. In the woods around Munich, for example, he sees a colour and paints what is around it. He paints a canvas that is composed starting with red, with a red note, etc. But when he reflects on his subject, he realizes that this colour seems to be a fragment of exteriority. There is a kind of red spot, even if he no longer considers this red as the red of a blotting paper or the red lips of a woman or her scarf: it is however something that unfurls in a kind of first world, even if it isn't the utilitarian world. Actually, he adds, the reality of this colour is an impression, a radically subjective impression.[8]

The operation of preliminary reduction that dissociates the color red from red objects is not sufficient. It occurs to Kandinsky, according to Henry, that it is finally much harder to get rid of the exterior environment of the color ("red spot") and grasp it in its purity. The artist needs to switch from one register to an entirely other. The reality of the color does not belong to the phenomenality of the world but happens to be "radically subjective." This is what Husserl names "noematic color," adds Henry just after that. Exploration of the nature of colors gets Kandinsky very close to philosophy, indeed. And Henry concludes his comment by declaring the double nature of the color in art:

> That is how colour is double, it is first a red that I see on the palette, but at the same time I am fooled by an illusion in believing that the red is limited to this spot that I see on the palette. Actually the reality of the red is the impression that this red spread upon the palette created within me. And it is this impression that is the true essence of the colour.[9]

Paradoxically, we trust the data of our vision so much that we continue to deduce the redness from different red objects, and even when the red appears only as a formless touch of paint, an indefinite spot, we recognize it as such only thanks to its material presence. The essence of red is not *this (or that)* red, whatever abstract its figuration might be, but the *impression* it exercises. And this impression hiding behind each color provides—as we will see further—the real reason why the artist should call upon this or that color in his painting.

## The Experience of the Color

We can admire the precision of Kandinsky's analysis, but the domain of the general, of the ideal, remains only "philosophical" and does not put us in touch with the particular with which art normally deals. Henry is very attentive to this would-be drawback in Kandinsky's argumentation. He makes two points: (1) "if it is possible to display the discrete, autonomous nature of the element and to recognize it as the true element of an analysis, this possibility only holds for its external aspect (for example, what is perceived by the mind as pure red when I say the word 'red'[. . .]) but does not hold for its internal relation"; (2) "the discreteness of the external element is only identifiable within the domain of ideality, which is the domain of the genus red and geometrical forms. This domain is precisely not the domain of painting."[10] What then constitutes the domain of painting? It is what Kandinsky calls composition, where distinct colors and forms, each endowed with its fundamental tonality, enter into a profound, internal relation. Kandinsky never concentrates, claims Henry, on just one element, but always reflects in terms of the whole, of the future combination of different tonalities with which a picture must deal.

But let us put aside these subsequent elaborations of Henry, who follows exactly the structure of *Concerning the Spiritual*, and focus on the aesthetic experiences of Kandinsky that will put us directly in touch with the "domain of painting," as opposed to that of philosophy. Most of those experiences come from the autobiographical book *Rückblick* ("a look into the past"), translated to English as *Reminiscences* or *Retrospects*.[11] This book, written in 1913, embraces some seminal aesthetic and artistic (pictorial) experiences of Kandinsky that punctuate his itinerary in becoming a painter. Kandinsky announces from the start what will be the object of his memoirs: "The first colors that made a strong impression on me were light, juicy green, white, crimson red, black and yellow ochre. These memories go back to the third year of my life. I saw these colors on various objects which are not as clear in my mind today as the colors themselves."[12] By claiming to remember only colors and not the phenomena to which they were attached, he sets a clear-cut anchoring point to what will follow: the book will present a history of his artistic life exclusively as a series of various encounters with colors. The experiences that unfold before our eyes mingle different kinds of biographical episodes, visual "chocs," ecstatic upsurges, and so on. Most of them concern the vision, but some come from music. Philippe Sers in his seminal book on Kandinsky and philosophy reconstitutes the logic of these experiences and offers a very persuasive genealogy.[13] Henry doesn't analyze those experiences systematically and as such, but he evokes them one by one at the different moments of his demonstration. I propose to enter into our problematics by examining how Henry makes use of certain passages of *Retrospects* to support his argument. Here, again, Henry starts by evoking Husserl, but this time in order to draw a dividing line between art and philosophy. He opposes the object of philosophy, given through eidetic reduction, to the traditional object of art accentuated with the arrival of the impressionism:

> Husserl says that the object is an ideal pole of identity over and above the multiplicity of its sensible appearances. That is why the painter does not really want to paint this ideal pole, this concept or entity which is always one and the same—*the* cathedral of Rouen or *the* haystack. Instead, the painter seeks these "sensible appearances" in their singularity and changes: this form with ungraspable contours and with faint lights that twinkle in the dazzling night, a bedazzlement where reality breaks down into pure bursts of blinding light, slips into the unknown, loses all consistency, and ultimately disappears. (SIK, 15)

At first glance, this passage seems confusing. Haven't we been talking lately about the essence of red which is more or less the same in art and in philosophy? And yet, we have never mentioned up to now the *act* of painting the red, or using red paints on canvas. Does the fact that Kandinsky is interested in the fundamental tonality of each painterly element or means he uses (colors and forms) imply that surrounding objects or things are able to attract him in exactly the same manner—solely by their essence or fundamental property? Undoubtedly, and that is what this early experience, in a certain respect, prefigures.

We have a feeling, drawing on what has already been said, that impressionism is not an option for Kandinsky and can't serve as a guiding light in our approach to abstraction. Indeed, the dissipation of the object, the dissolution of its material reality that it proclaims, lies at the heart of Kandinsky's experience. However—and this is the nodal point of Henry's demonstration—we must not interpret this experience as an experience that pertains to the object. Kandinsky recalls his shock in front of the *Haystack* of Monet at the French Impressionistic exhibition held in Moscow in 1896. His first encounter with the impressionism is insightful not because he finds here an exemplary implementation of the style of painting he himself would like to adopt. The impressionism of Monet exercises on him, and this is not a vain wordplay, an "indelible *impression*":

> At the same time I experienced two things which placed a stamp on my entire life and which at that time stirred me to the bottom of my soul. They were the French Impressionistic exhibition in Moscow—particularly the "hay

stack" by Claude Monet—and a Wagner presentation at the Hof Theater—Lohengrin.

> Before that I knew realistic art only [...] And suddenly, for the first time, I saw a painting. The catalogue explained to me that it was a hay stack. I could not recognize it. I felt embarrassed at this lack of recognition. I also felt that the painter had no right to paint so indistinctly. I had a dull feeling that the object was missing in this painting. And I noticed with surprise and consternation that the picture does not only draw you, but indelibly impresses itself upon your brain and unexpectedly, to its minutest detail, constantly floats before your mind's eye. All this was unclear to me, and I could not draw the simple consequences of this experience. The thing, however, that was completely clear—was the unexpected power of the palette, until now unknown to me, which surpassed all my dreams. [...] Unconsciously, however, the object as the unavoidable element of a painting, was discredited.[14]

It is quite striking that a painting so "unclear" and vague, with poorly delineated forms, can produce such a persistent impression. Kandinsky sounds quite disconcerted. Indeed, what do the mind and the eyes of the observer attach to if it is not to the object? What does he mean by "impression"? Actually, that was said above: it reveals something that survives notwithstanding the temporal changing qualities of the object depicted, bathing in blurred light, enveloped in fuzzy shades, and so on. At the same time, what Kandinsky is aware of discovering, above all, is the "power of the palette," the freedom that he can suddenly enjoy as a painter to arrange colors as he sees fit. In other words, Kandinsky sees colors and forms as already completely emancipated from the initial object of the painting, a haystack.

When he comments on this passage, Henry takes necessary precautions in order to dismantle all causal links between the visual and aesthetic experience remarkably exposed by Kandinsky in *Retrospects* and the historical event of abstract art. It is not *because* Kandinsky was strongly affected by the view of Monet's haystacks, and by major scientific discoveries of his time, like the division of the atom, that he converted to abstraction. He did not deliberate if he had to abandon the object because it was for some reason no more valid. In fact, art history believes then it can explain convincingly the artistic trajectory of Kandinsky: if the artist calls into question the idea of representation in painting, that would be conditioned by the historical shift in perception, by a skeptical attitude toward the object, expanding on the wave of reaction against positivism and materialism. But Henry goes against the current. He separates vigorously philosophical and artistic (experiential) understanding of art from art history and claims his own phenomenological interpretation to be ontological and not historical: "Just as Kandinsky's abstraction does not come from a reworking of perceptual representation, it does not come from a sudden failure of the object, and its inability to define the content of the work any longer"[15] (SIK, 16). In this perspective, the emotional response to Monet's painting is not primarily that of a shock before the disappearing of its thematic object, but a coming to life of a certain new emotion related to the use of colors. Abstraction is linked to this emotion. This is exactly the kind of answer that Henry tries to provide. It is not surprising, nor unexpected:

> This abstraction, this content—the "abstract content"—is invisible life in its ceaseless arrival into itself. This continual emergence of life, its eternally living essence, provides the content of painting and at the same time imposes a project on the artist, namely, that of expressing this content and this pathetic profusion of Being. (SIK, 16)

Indeed, we have already encountered the term "Life" at the very beginning of Henry's study, when he announces his objective: "we are proposing a study of his [Kandinsky's] theoretical writings as a privileged means of access to the understanding of the essence of painting—or better—as a way to enter into the expanded life of aesthetic experience" (SIK 2). But now we can better see a sort of hesitation, in this formula, between two definitions: the first one pertains solely to philosophical ontology, and implies an effort of *understanding*, the second one opens up into the domain of art as aesthetic experience and conceives of it as an immediate, sensible *participation* in "the expanded life."

If we refer directly to Kandinsky's writings, we will be able to place *Concerning the Spiritual . . .* in a more theoretical, metaphysical perspective, whereas *Retrospects* puts us in touch with more intimate episodes from his artistic life. In other words, if the aim of the first book is to formulate the spiritual meaning of colors, the second one is a demonstration of how the theoretical interest in colors is rooted in the personal, and therefore, unique experience of the artist—the universal as opposed to the particular. Along with an intellectual, ideal color, obtained in the process of "eidetic" reduction, there is an emotional color intimately linked to the personal experience of Kandinsky as a painter.

Henry's concept of Life seems to relate to the concrete experiences similar to those lived by Kandinsky. We will consider two of them. The first one revolves around an almost physical sensation of colors squeezed from the tubes, and the second one describes the perception of colors, which emanate from the surrounding objects but do not belong to them—ungraspable undefinable transient colors that fleet around and expand. In both cases we deal with what Henry will call *"invisible* Life" of the color. Before getting to this focal point of Henry's demonstration, let us specify the differences between those two modes of existence of the color that Henry comments on in his study on Kandinsky.

The first one is related to the passage where Kandinsky recalls the purchase of his first paint box, at the age of fourteen or fifteen. Henry quotes the whole passage and comments extensively on it. Already in the first sentence Kandinsky, as if to be sure to express exactly and precisely what he means, substitutes the word "sensation" (*vpechatlenie*) with the word "experience" (*perezhivanie*—lived experience): "I can still feel today the sensation I experienced then—or, to put it better, the experience I underwent then—of the paints emerging from the tube." He attributes to colors different qualities, as if they were human beings, moved by the same desires and ambitions: "One squeeze of the fingers, and out came these strange beings, one after the other, which one calls colours— exultant, solemn, brooding, dreamy, self-absorbed, deeply serious, with roguish exuberance, with a sigh of release, with a deep sound of mourning, with defiant power and resistance, with submissive suppleness and devotion, with obstinate self-control, with sensitive, precarious balance." And then goes the sentence that puts in play the idea of Henry (with my emphasis): *"Living an independent life of their own*, with all the necessary qualities for further, autonomous existence, prepared to make way readily, in an instant, for new combinations, to mingle with one another and create an infinite succession of new worlds" (quoted from SIK, 29). Henry interprets this "independent life" literally, and claims that those "fresh, young forces" of colors that Kandinsky describes lead us "beyond every image," "back to our real life as the place in which every force is rooted" (SIK, 29). This is also how we can understand, according to Henry, this remark of Kandinsky, when he claims to "remember colours better than objects":

> In his work, his attention focused on the pure colours spread across the palette, affirming that his regard of them should replace the regard given to nature up to then. An important pictorial principle follows from his bedazzlement with this strange and autonomous world: the non-realist use of colours. (SIK, 30)

The second mode of existence of colors refers less to the sensation of their texture and body, when the sense of vision is impregnated with the sense of touch, than to a purely visual perception of the color. The major need to paint, to express an emotion on canvas, comes to Kandinsky from his early impressions of Moscow, the city that becomes a significant challenge for his painterly art, almost an obsession. He tells us, for instance, how he came to realize that almost all of his early pictures and studies painted in Munich and its suburbs bore this indelible imprint of Moscow. This imprint comes from a particular color impression, a color symphony, which starts with the red color of the sunlight. In a long passage of *Retrospects* Kandinsky confesses his unquenchable desire to paint a certain evening hour in Moscow, just before the sun goes down. Henry takes up the totality of this long description in his book. It would, indeed, be difficult to shorten it, as it is not only a magnificent inspired piece of Kandinsky's literary art, but a precious testimony of an extraordinary visionary, almost mystical, artistic experience:

> The sun is already getting low and has attained its full intensity which it has been seeking all day, for which it has striven all day. This image does not last long: a few minutes, and the sunlight grows red with effort, redder and redder, cold at first, and then increasing in warmth. The sun dissolves the whole of Moscow into a single spot, which, like a wild tuba, sets all one's soul vibrating. No, this red fusion is not the most beautiful hour! It is only the final chord of the symphony, which brings every colour vividly to life, which allows and forces the whole of Moscow to resound like the $_{ff}$ of a giant orchestra. Pink, lilac, yellow, white, blue, pistachio green, flame red houses, churches, each an independent song—the garish green of the grass, the deeper tremolo of the trees, the singing snow with its thousand voices, or the allegretto of the bare branches, the red, stiff, silent ring of the Kremlin walls, and above, towering over everything, like a shout of triumph, like a self-oblivious hallelujah, the long, white, graceful, serious line of the Bell Tower of Ivan the Great. And upon its tall, tense neck, stretched up towards heaven in eternal yearning, the golden head of the cupola, which among the golden and coloured stars of the other cupolas, is Moscow's sun. (quoted from SIK, 17 )

It is amazing how in order to convey a visual impression Kandinsky feels the need to express it in musical terms. The music is capable, we know it from the veneration Kandinsky displays toward the most abstract of all the arts, of producing and fueling the most powerful emotions. The visual dimension of art is quite poor in order to give access to this intense emotion. We start with colors and more exactly with this fundamental for Kandinsky color which is red, and end up in the realm of the sound. The intense red is a trigger moment, which opens up a celebration of all the spectrum of colors. The redness of the sun, its warmth, makes all the colors converge into one symphony, every color still conserving its fundamental tonality (its "independent song"). The number of words and images borrowed from the field of music is remarkable: "tuba," "chord," "$f\!f\!.$" (fortissimo) "orchestra," "symphony," "song," "tremolo," "sing," "allegretto," "shout," "hallelujah." A close reading of this passage leads to another important observation: Kandinsky does not speak of an empirical phenomenon as of something really existing and immediately accessible to anyone, as long as she or he takes the trouble to look attentively. This disclosure of colors does not belong to a certain period of the year either, it can be perceived whatever the season—and Kandinsky mentions at least three of them ("green of the grass," "singing snow," "bare branches"). In the end, we don't even have to do with a "particular hour"—because the impression, as Kandinsky states, repeats "on each sunny day"—but with an ideal, transcendental hour, an originary perception that makes possible the existence of every sunny day in any part of the world. That is why this specific light "must be for an artist the most impossible" to paint (SIK, 18). The artist does not attempt to depict a winter or summer day in Moscow, but a sort of quintessence of all the days with such a sunlight that he had already experienced or might still experience in the future.

In the vein of the analysis conducted by Henry, we should now get back to the mode of existence of those colors. The experience of emancipated living colors, of their material existence, and that of "sounding" colors "brought to life" have something in common—they partake in this ascent toward abstraction that Kandinsky tries to reflect on in his memoirs, but differently. On one hand, perception of colors as of living beings invests them necessarily with a form of subjectivity—impenetrable for the painter. This subjectivity requires, then, a real effort of artistic disclosure from the painter. That is how the relation to colors as a means of painting comes to supersede the relation to objects that are to be painted. On the other hand, Kandinsky provides us with the thematic object of all his paintings: Moscow.[16] The *impression* of Moscow is a founding experience of his art, and all particular paintings, whatever their subject might be, are intended to deliver a sort of immanent verification of this first pictorial intuition of Moscow.[17] Both experiences—of colors as material means of painting and as intuitive impressions—are complementary in what they reveal: the essence of art. And yet, it is not the abstract *idea* of Moscow that moves Kandinsky and makes him paint what he paints. The essence revealed by means of abstraction is not obtained through philosophical reduction, but only through a repeated aesthetical experience. But this experiential dimension does not exclude the need, also quite present in Kandinsky, to define that which he aims to paint. And this definition is necessarily linked with the operation of abstraction. This operation is different in our two examples. The first one illustrates how Kandinsky switches from the visually perceived objective color (paints) to its spiritual evaluation (living beings). The second one deals directly with spiritual colors: even though we can name those colors, describe them, their "symphony" cannot be identified from the chromatic point of view. This is where we can observe a subtle passage from the visible toward the invisible.

The ecstatic reaction of the painter to colors does not call upon imitation. There is nothing to copy from nature, because what he explains of the Moscow hour, for instance, can hardly be visually represented by the reader. What he depicts is a sheer emotion that operates in the domain of the "invisible." And this is probably one of the most complicated things to comprehend about abstract art, at least in Henry's reading of it. Henry repeats several times throughout his book that art's function is that of reinforcing our feeling of Life, strengthen our commitment to it through art. By negating all exterior determinations of artistic creation, Henry comes up with the fundamental concept of his philosophy, an ultimate explanatory principle, which acts like a transcendental argument of his philosophy—the concept of Life. The way of defining it resembles much of what Bergson does with his concept of duration. Just like Bergson he invites us to take a leap and plunge directly into it: "we said that no path leads to life except for life itself. One must stand within life in order to gain access to it; one must begin from life."[18] Life as such is ungraspable, and in this sense invisible: "no one has ever seen life," says Henry elsewhere.[19] Life defies any characterization which would objectify or spatialize it—and we read here the same fear before this rational appropriation of life that existed in Bergson regarding his *durée*. However, unlike Bergson, Henry doesn't leave this domain without positive determination; neither does he use images or metaphors in order to suggest something that is not rationalizable in any other way. Rather, he accumulates some paradoxical determinations or figures that allow a relative materialization or incarnation of life, while preserving its non-visibility. Abstract art offers one of those figures.

## Art of the Invisible

We come, in conclusion, to one of Henry's most provocative and controversial theses: that art does not obey the logic of the visible, of the objective world, but only the one imposed by inner experience, invisible life. I believe, unlike other commentators of Henry on this point,[20] that this thesis is incontestable inasmuch as we accept the rules of the game and remain in the context of Henry's philosophy. My purpose is not to invalidate this highly original idea or to show its shortcomings but to explore its further implications for our understanding of abstract art and our sensibility toward it. Does it help us, as it purports, to grasp the nature of this art? Or does it help us to feel it—this art or Life or both— more deeply? The question of vision and visibility is central in this sense, as it allows articulating together both components of abstract art—intellectual comprehension and sensible perception.

From where does the problem of visibility originate in Henry's philosophy? Henry dislocates the problematics of phenomenology inherited from Husserl, by pushing further its phenomenological reduction. Whereas Husserl discovers intentionality as an ultimate structure of our relation to the world, Henry questions further the way that intentionality itself is given to us: this dyadic mode of object-awareness is grounded more deeply in something else, something that makes possible its appearing to our consciousness. But this mode of givenness that precedes intentionality is no more related to it and consequently happens to be of no interest to a phenomenology solely preoccupied with the idea of the phenomenon (embracing all that appears *before* our eyes). Abandoning the primacy of transcendence as such, Henry claims that pure and irrevocable immanence determines our position in the world (or, better, Life); we cannot refer to an object, feel an emotion, even communicate with each other, unless we are already self-affected by (our own) Life—this original affection receives in Henry the name of *pathos*. This ambitious move and unprecedented philosophical challenge of Henry's consists thus in overcoming intentionality toward a non-intentional, non-relation to the world through the *immanence of invisible Life*.

He exemplifies this gesture with the help of Descartes and conceptualizes the grammatical form the latter uses in order to ascribe a limit to the hyperbolic doubt—the act of v*ideor* ("I am seen" or "I see"—the first-person passive form of *videre*, "to see"):

> Seeing that would only see, is a phenomenological nothing; it would see nothing. There is only seeing if, in an unperceived way, seeing is more than itself. There always acts within it a power other than its own, a power in which it is auto-affected so that it feels its seeing and feels itself seeing. In this way, we should not say that "we see" (*videmus*) but, like Descartes, "we feel our seeing" (*sentimus nos videre*). This auto-affection is the original phenomenality, the original givenness as a self-givenness, for example, the self-givenness of seeing to itself. (MP, 81)

Seeing of an intentional kind must be conditioned by something else, for Henry, otherwise it is not essentially motivated (but only pragmatically) and, consequently, "sees nothing." Thus, for Henry, v*ideor* must be interpreted as a form of a non-intentional affection: I sense myself seeing or before seeing something in particular, I have an inner feeling of the act of seeing as such, a non-intentional self-givenness in which the act of intentional seeing is grounded. In another work, though, Henry specifies what he means by this immanence or self-affection by introducing the transcendental condition of seeing—its opposite, "the non-seeing":

> *Sentimus non videre* says Descartes against hyperbolic doubt. But this can only be understood, sight being notoriously doubtful, if there is, in the originary feeling through which sight senses itself seeing and experiences itself, no seeing. Sight is— appears—only under the condition of a non-seeing.[21]

The non-seeing does not mean blindness in the sense of deprivation of sight, but emphasizes once again the rootedness of the intentional act of seeing in affectivity that precedes every single act of seeing. We can also call it intrinsic seeing, seeing inside ourselves, so to speak. In other words, Henry finds it necessary to detach the act of seeing from exterior objects, given to our sight, and to link it tightly with our own subjectivity. It is *me* who sees first of all, and my subjectivity is indebted to nothing else but myself in Life, which means that the act of seeing is never determined by what is seen but exclusively by what is not to be seen (by itself), namely, Life itself. This reduction of visibility will lead Henry to formulate a new regime of non-objective or immanent "vision." Since the vision, being naturally directed toward an exterior object, cannot, by definition, be immanent, Henry is brought to introduce this paradoxical expression: vision of the invisible.

> since there is no separation, there is no ek-static deployment as Heidegger understands it, no seeing is possible. In order to see, there must be some kind of distance. But there is no distance, revelation occurs solely in the flesh of affectivity, it occurs without any distance.[22]

Seeing without any distance—what a challenge for art! But that is exactly what abstract art is supposed to demonstrate. The ban on visibility is a consequence of the ban on representation on the whole and comes from the iconoclasm, one of the most frequent characteristics of abstract art. But the interdiction of the visible doesn't automatically involve the relapse into the intellectual (if we use the ordinary opposition image—text, common for the contemporary art, for instance). Quite on the contrary. Henry maintains that in order to see differently, the act of seeing must originate in sensibility. Otherwise, the sense of the sight can never lead to something other than itself and would not be able to procure us an emotion. We cannot be affected by something completely exterior to us.

Here lies the major difference between the French phenomenology of art and that of Henry, as it is clearly formulated by Carole Talon-Hugon:

> For its theorists, phenomenology enjoys a secret affinity with art. For Heidegger, Mikel Dufrenne, Merleau-Ponty, or Henri Maldiney, this affinity is due to the fact that artworks are exceptional phenomena that put the being of beings into view. For Michel Henry, the proximity between art and phenomenology is otherwise: the disclosure performed by art is not one of the horizon outside of ourselves but of the life within us.[23]

This life is "mystical" in the sense of its lack of transparency, its opaque mode of existence, since it can never be brought to light (=visibility).

> The painting does not show what one has never before seen, like the surface of the moon as one finds in illustrated magazines for childish adults. It shows by leading vision to itself. It increases vision's ability to see in and through the intensification of its pathos. Through the experience and exaltation of its power, vision takes hold of itself and can see. (SIK, 122)

It is frequently said that abstract art is an art of immediacy, but Henry, rather than stating this feature of abstract art, shows exactly how this immediacy works. An abstract picture is not to be seen (observed, contemplated, etc.) as it does not include any observer, nor a point of view or a perspective making possible the viewing. This is where the idea of "invisible," unseen colors, stems from. We do not see or contemplate colors, but colors directly affect us and we can only accept to submit ourselves to this experience. In this sense, abstraction would be a founding *experience* of art as such, experience of its essence. The principle of the invisible announced by Henry should be directly put into practice, experimented in our relation to art. Abstraction makes possible the return to a "primitive" contact with a painting—as if all paintings, all pieces of art we have seen so far, were to find their real value in this virginal experience.[24]

Let us now return to our initial question: What kind of relationship then exists between art and philosophy? As we were able to see, the vision founded in the invisible allows to bring together the philosophical (phenomenological) dimension and the pictorial one in what goes beyond and underlies them: the pathos of Life. To this end, phenomenology must overcome intentionality and art must abandon figuration. Phenomenological reduction and artistic abstraction are two indispensable intellectual procedures that lead, each in its respective field, to the discovery of the same reality: the invisible Life. One can say, then, that art is not considered for itself in Henry's philosophy, because it participates in something more fundamental: it is valuable because of its relationship to life. Does this verdict mean, consequently, that we can hardly draw anything from Henry's analysis for our understanding of abstract art, since, at the end, it is not the essence of abstract art that appears to us through Henry's concept of Life? On the contrary, art (and especially abstract art) reveals our belonging to Life by instilling powerful emotions. Is his reading of Kandinsky that biased by his conception of Life and thus somewhat limited for us? Does it really sacrifice art to his peculiar quasi-theological conception of Life and its sensible materiality to the extreme spirituality?[25] Indeed, the elucidation of the concept of Life determines Henry's aesthetics and his reading of Kandinsky. The specificity of Henry's system of thought is that we cannot separate one from the other. We must try to understand art from Life and conversely Life from art. They are mutually dependent and can only be elucidated in this movement of coming and going.

That is why the ultimate objective of Henry's aesthetics is to find a way of speaking about abstract paintings *in terms of Life*. His vocabulary revolves around the ideas of tension, energy, force, that is, everything that suggests vitality—physical, sensual, affective impact that the images as immediate expressions of Life produce upon us. If our initiation to abstract art should, then, pass by philosophy and philosophical understanding of the painting, we must also readjust the totality of art concepts destined to describe this experience. And Henry engages vividly in an almost complete review of these concepts (not only that of vision but also of imagination, of knowledge, of language, etc.). According to Henry, this unwavering connection between art and Life makes itself manifest not only in the way Kandinsky accounts for his own aesthetic experience or seeks for fundamental tonalities of colors and forms, but also, and above all, in his paintings. In fact, the evolution of Kandinsky's art through three periods is interpreted by Henry teleologically—as a progressive unveiling of Life. "Lyric abstraction" with its "bursts of colours," "a sumptuous proliferation of pure pictorial configurations with an intense Energy," "frenzied dynamism," transforms into "[a] new dynamism (. . .) with sharply cut out forms," "play of tensions," "advances confronted with subtle counter-attacks" during the Bauhaus period (46), and finally in the Parisian period, the geometrical figures become animated: the sphere turns into

> a transparent jellyfish with incandescent filaments caressed by the underwater currents. In this place without heaviness, where weight changes into lightness, forms wander about without their substance —bodies of light, glorious bodies,

bodies of life. They are organic forms with clear and cold colours, all kinds of protozoa, parts of insects, outlines of foliage—creatures from another world with another nature reveal the nature of all nature, every possible world, and consequently our own world. (SIK, 146)

It is thus in the paintings of the Parisian period that Henry finds an ultimate illustration for his conception of Life: progressive emancipation of forms losing their substance, their weight, becoming transparent, in order to give birth to the "bodies of light, glorious bodies"—bodies revealing finally their invisible nature, Life itself.

# Notes

1 Michel Henry, *Seeing the Invisible: On Kandinsky*, trans. Scott Davidson (London: Continuum, 2009), 40.
2 Ibid., 41.
3 Edmund Husserl, *The Idea of Phenomenology*, trans. L. Hardy (Boston: Kluwer, 1999), 42.
4 In the act of seeing one should distinguish between the object, which the act of seeing refers to, and the act of seeing itself. The latter may be considered as "pure seeing" insofar as it is not determined by the object (of seeing) it refers to. According to Husserl's terminology, this object remains "transcendent" in relation to the act of seeing or knowing, since it is not "self-given." The self-givenness seems only to characterize a singular experience, a *cogitatio* in a Cartesian sense: *this* particular act of seeing. But Husserl's eidetical reduction goes much further: his ambition is to prove the givenness (immanence) of universals, that is, of essences, as, in our example, the essence of red.
5 Henry comments on the danger of this association: "Once again, in spite of all appearances, the recourse to representation—to sickness, summer or autumn—does not point back to an external referent. The external referent is solely mentioned for its subjective value. The tonality of each one of these natural or human events is evoked in order to allow the reader to understand the tonality of the colour (e.g., yellow) through a comparison that operates on the level of these tonalities" (SIK9, 78).
6 Wassily Kandinsky, *Concerning the Spiritual in Art,* trans. M. T. H. Sadler (Auckland, New Zealand: The Floating Press, 2008), 64–5.
7 Cf. pages 44–7 in *Concerning the Spiritual in Art.*
8 Michel Henry, "Art and the Phenomenology of Life: An Interview with Michel Henry," trans. M. Tweed. Available online https://academia.edu/5595144/Art_and_ the_Phenomenology_of_Life_an_interview_with_Michel_Henry 1996 (accessed August 12, 2019).

9 Ibid.
10 Ibid.
11 We will refer to *Retrospects* (New York: Solomon R. Guggenheim Foundation, 1945). Available online https://archive.org/stream/kandinsky1945reba/kandinsky1945reba_djvu.txt.
12 Ibid., 22.
13 Philippe Sers, *Kandinsky, philosophie de l'art abstrait: peinture, poésie, scénographie* (Genève: Skira, 2003).
14 Kandinsky, *Retrospects*, 24.
15 English translation modified. It is quite instructive to point out that at this particular place of the text, the translator misunderstands Henry completely and delivers a translation exactly the opposite of what Henry tries to say: "It does not come from a reworking of perceptual representation, either. Kandinsky's abstraction came from a sudden failure of the object, its inability to define the content of the work any longer." It means only that we, readers, are not at ease with this rather Bergsonian interpretation: Henry does not give reasons why at some point abstraction emerges as an artistic movement, but chooses to show the unique and very personal path toward abstraction, the one opened up by Kandinsky.
16 Cf. Kandinsky, *Retrospects*, 32.
17 For the term "verification," see Sers, *Kandinsky, philosophie de l'art abstrait*.
18 Henry, *Seeing the Invisible*, 18.
19 Henry, "Qu'est-ce que cela que nous appelons la vie ?" in *Phénoménologie de la vie I: De la phénoménologie* (Presses Universitaires de France, 2003), 39–57, quote on page 48.
20 In France we can mention, for instance, L. van Einde, "L'essence lyrique de l'art abstrait. Contribution à l'esthétique de la Stimmung" in *La Voix des phénomènes: contributions à une phénoménologie du sens et des affect*, ed. R. Brisart and R. Célis (Bruxelles: Facultés Universitaires Saint-Louis, 1995), 147–90 or J. -F. Lavigne, "Transcendance du visible et immanence du pathos: le statut de la couleur dans l'esthétique de Michel Henry?" in *Michel Henry et l'affect de l'art. Recherches sur l'esthétique de la phénoménologie matérielle*, ed. Adnen Jdey et Rolf Kühn (Leiden and Boston: Brill, 2012), 97–112; both criticize Henry from a classical phenomenological point of view.
21 Michel Henry, "The Critique of the Subject," in *After the Subject*, ed. Eduardo Cadava, Peter Connor and Jean-Luc Nancy (New York and London: Routledge, 1991), 157–66.
22 Henry, "Art and the Phenomenology of Life."
23 Carole Talon-Hugon, "L'esthétique henryenne est-elle phénoménologique?" in *Michel Henry et l'affect de l'art. Recherches sur l'esthétique de la phénoménologie matérielle*, ed. Adnen Jdey et Rolf Kühn (Leiden and Boston: Brill, 2012), 3–22, 3.
24 Of course, our sight would never be able to recover its "innocence" and we know that the "innocent eye" is a blind eye, that is, would see nothing (see, for example, E.

Gombrich, *Art and Illusion* (Princeton: Princeton University Press, 1956), 298. Our sight is already highly educated, that is why, in order to be receptive to abstract art, we must conduct the operation of abstraction (of bracketing off the sensible world and its objects). But this bracketing does not signify the voluntary impoverishment of our perception: on the contrary, this operation adds an extra "layer" to our aesthetic experience, or, speaking Henry's language, we get access to "expanded life."

25 The idea of "sacrifice" appears, for instance, in the study of P. Rodrigo, "La vie à l'œuvre: le Kandinsky de Michel Henry" (ALTER, 15, 2007), 1–10.

# 11

# Affectivity and Its Effects

## Social Prospects for the Pathetic Community

J. A. Simmons and M. Wellborn

## Introduction

Let's begin with a passage from Michel Henry that will serve as something like a general guide for our thinking in this chapter: "Things differ entirely depending on whether they are immersed in the pathos of life in which they never see themselves, or whether they are held in front of a regard" (MP, 6). Broadly construed, phenomenology is a methodology that prioritizes affectivity as a mode of engagement. Phenomenology appreciates that we are constituted by a world that is already meaningful even while we are actively invested in the task of meaning-making. As such, affectivity has often been considered a property either of conscious life or of physical relationships. Yet, in light of the rise of scholarship associated with the "affective turn" since the early 2000s, it is important to ask how affectivity serves to condition *social* life. Getting clear on what is at stake in this question is important because even if affectivity structures existence, how we handle, conceive, and articulate that structure makes a striking difference in the way we exist in shared contexts of social meaning.

Although Michel Henry discusses affectivity throughout his writings, especially regarding the notion of auto-affectivity of Life itself, his work remains an untapped resource for social theory. Despite the fact that much of his authorship is devoted to a critical intervention into, and radicalization of, phenomenology, Henry offers occasional discussions of what we might view as the practical dimensions of sociocultural existence. In this chapter, we will explore just some of the possibilities for Henry's practical philosophy by specifically considering the prospect of seeing Henry's philosophy as a resource for praxis in light of the "affective turn." In particular, we will suggest that by drawing on Sara Ahmed's theory of affective economies, we can better understand how Henry's notions of "flesh" and the "pathetic community" serve as an invitation for sociocultural engagement.

Our thesis is that, far from being irrelevant to the concrete issues attending social theory and practice, Henry offers a model of what it means to be truly alive as beings touching, and touched by, others in the "real world" of affective meaning. Our hope in this chapter is to think with Henry and Ahmed about the *effects* of affectivity in order to resituate Henry's work in the context of contemporary social life and the ongoing theoretical consideration of it.

## Phenomenology and the Affective Turn

In his foreword to the volume *The Affective Turn*, Michael Hardt explains that the radicality of this "turn" resides in "the syntheses that it requires" between the mind and body.[1] Playing up the implicit connection between affecting and being-affected-by, Hardt's suggestion is that the "focus on the body" in feminism and the "exploration of emotions" occurring in queer theory have come together in order to reposition the relationship of mind and body such that thought and feeling are intertwined in ways that do not admit of an absolute priority of one to the other.[2] Drawing on Spinoza as "the philosopher who has advanced furthest the theory of the affects and whose thought is the source, either directly or indirectly, of most of the contemporary work in the field," Hardt concludes that "the perspective of the affects requires us constantly to pose as a problem the relation between actions and passions, between reason and the emotions. We do not know in advance what a body can do, what a mind can think—what affects they are capable of."[3] According to Hardt, Spinoza's account of affect offers "a new ontology of the human, or rather, an ontology of the human that is constantly open and renewed."[4] Resulting from such a new/renewed ontology are a variety of social transformations at the level of social expression, economic engagement, information transfer, and collective practice.[5]

Hardt's general account of the affective turn in social theory is echoed in other texts associated with the movement. For example, Patricia Ticineto Clough claims that affect theory "draws on the line of thought from Gilles Deleuze and Félix Guattari back through Baruch Spinoza and Henri Bergson."[6] She goes on to explain affect theory as a general social manifestation of a transformation in embodied existence:

> The increasing significance of affect as a focus of analysis across a number of disciplinary and interdisciplinary discourses is occurring at a time when critical theory is facing the analytic challenges of ongoing war, trauma, torture, massacre, and counter/terrorism.[7]

According to Clough, thinkers associated with the affective turn all see "affectivity as a substrate of potentially bodily responses, often autonomic responses, in excess of consciousness."[8] "For these scholars," Clough continues, "affect refers generally to bodily capacities to affect and be affected or the augmentation or diminution of a body's capacity to act, to engage, and to connect, such that autoaffection is linked to the self-feeling of being alive—that is aliveness or vitality."[9] It might seem then that affect is pre-social insofar as it is the background condition of social life, but with Massumi, Clough stringently rejects such a conception. Instead, even though never without an unconscious remainder, affect happens, as it were, as a social phenomenon of embodied psychic life. As such, "the affective turn throws thought back to the disavowals constitutive of Western industrial capitalist societies, bringing forth ghosted bodies and the traumatized remains of erased histories."[10]

In agreement with Clough's and Hardt's general framing of the affective turn, John Protevi also draws deeply on Deleuze and Guattari in order to challenge what he terms the "rational cognitive subject."[11] His basic thesis is that "to do philosophy of mind properly, we need to study the multiple ways in which subjects develop as a result of different social practices."[12] Distinguishing between emotions and affect as two forms of human feelings, Hoggett and Thompson suggest that "affect concerns the more embodied, unformed and less conscious dimension of human feeling, whereas emotion concerns the feelings which are more conscious since they are more anchored in language and meaning."[13] A key component of emotion is the object-orientation such that "focus and intentionality" are constitutive of the meaning of a particular felt emotion as discursively present.[14] Alternatively, affect is less object-oriented such that the "object is secondary to the feeling" and, as such, affect is a feeling more "detached" from discourse than an emotion.[15]

Of particular note in this emerging discourse is that the repeated philosophical lineage mentioned by those associated with the affective turn rarely features sustained engagement with phenomenology. With the possible exception of Merleau-Ponty, and occasional references to Scheler, few phenomenologists are prominent interlocutors in sustained ways. Instead of a Husserlian or Heideggerian inheritance, the vitalist genealogy tends to move from Spinoza, Bergson, and Nietzsche, to Deleuze and Guattari.

There are a variety of explanations that one could offer for why these thinkers do not draw more heavily on phenomenology in their work on affect. In particular, (1) phenomenology is often weak when it comes to a consideration of social and political existence, (2) phenomenology is often concerned more about the conditions that attend the givenness of the world than about the embodied experience of such givenness as a social reality, and (3) the impact of Deleuze and Guattari brings with it a particular retelling of the history of continental philosophy that tends to downplay the existential and phenomenological trajectories in relation to the critical theoretical and psychoanalytic trends.

Although we should resist trying to make phenomenology relevant to everything, we see the lack of sustained engagement between affect theory and phenomenology to be a missed opportunity on two levels that run in alternate directions. First, developing such connections enables us to develop possible lines of phenomenological social theory. Second, and alternatively, pursuing such a conversation facilitates a more robust account of the phenomenological conditions that make possible the social focus of affect theory. In this way, these two discourses supplement each other because they are both devoted to overcoming any reductive theory of mind, selfhood, society, culture, and life itself. Accordingly, Hardt's synthetic approach to the relation of mind and body, Protevi's rejection of the rationalist conception of selfhood, and Clough's notion of traumatic memory are all moments where phenomenological sensibilities are on display in affect theory.

It makes sense, then, that a concern for affective embodiment would motivate an interest in mining phenomenology for possible resources. Although there are a variety of places in phenomenological philosophy to which one might turn to find fecund interlocutors, Henry's work is of particular relevance given his abiding, and largely unwavering, concern with what he will present as the essence of Life itself: *affectivity*.

## Henry on Life, World, and Affect

One of the early works in what would eventually emerge as "new" or "radical" phenomenology,[16] Henry's expansive *Essence of Manifestation* pushes phenomenology forward in original ways precisely insofar as it attempts to mark out the movement's (or better, *methodology*'s) historical failures. Henry shifts from classical (or "hyletic") phenomenology to what he terms "material phenomenology" by asking about the conditions of phenomenality itself rather than simply about the specific modes of givenness of particular historical phenomena. In this way, Henry offers a "transcendental" approach to phenomenology in that he pursues the conditions of possibility for what historical phenomenology not only considers but also for what it often misconstrues, misunderstands, and covers over. Explaining this general strategy, Henry suggests that "material phenomenology is devoted to the discovery of the reign of a phenomenality that is constructed in such a surprising way that the thought that always thinks about the world never thinks about it" (MP, 2). "To the internal structure of this originary manifestation," Henry continues, "there belongs no Outside, no Separation, no Ek-stasis. Its phenomenological substance is not visibility. None of the categories that have been used by philosophy, since the Greeks at any rate, are appropriate for it" (MP, 2). Appealing back to the notion of the "essence of manifestation" as not itself manifest as a phenomenal object, here we see Henry gesture toward his much-discussed distinction between the "truth of the world" and the "truth of life."

In something of a radicalization, or perhaps better, *intensification*, of Husserl's distinction between the natural and phenomenological attitudes, and Heidegger's distinction between the ontic and ontological registers, Henry positions world and life as two different frameworks for phenomenality. Whereas "world" is necessarily a concern with externality—and the intentionality and horizons that attend to it—Life is absolutely immanent to itself. Although "world" names the domain of objectivity itself, Life is never an object, but, instead, the condition for being able to take oneself up as engaged with anything that could be intentionally perceived. As such, "world" is the horizon by which intentional correlates occur *as* some particular phenomenon that is made manifest, and Life rejects horizonal contexts and intentional consciousness in the name of the *essence* of manifestation. As Henry will sometimes say, Life admits of no "as-structure" because there is no separation or distance between Life and itself. So, whereas world is mediated by conscious appropriation, Life is immediate self-relation.

It is "world" that allows for things to become phenomena—as given to us in particular ways according to an as-structure. "The 'world's truth,'" Henry writes, "is nothing other than this: a self-production of 'outsideness' as the horizon of visibility in and through which every thing can become visible and thus become a 'phenomenon' for us" (IATT, 17). The problem with worldly truth is that, due to the process of externalization that is inherent to its mode of manifestation, it fails to allow things to be what they "really" are. Instead, everything that appears "as" something is subject to what Henry will term the process of "principled derealization" (IATT 20). Because every thing shows itself in the world only within the mode of distance/externalization/objectification, every worldly object is always already in a "state of original unreality" (IATT 20). Alternatively, it is "life" that "designates a pure manifestation, always irreducible to that of the world, an original revelation that is not the revelation of another thing and does not depend on anything other, but is, rather, a revelation of self, that absolute self-revelation that is Life itself" (IATT, 34). In this way, reality is possible only as *Life*. Or, said a bit more provocatively, only Life is truly *real*.

We admit that the frequency with which Henry retraces the distinction between world and Life is likely due, in part, to the conceptual difficulties that attend a non-intentional, non-object, that would underwrite the seeming contradictory idea of a "phenomenology of the invisible" (MP, 3). However, rather than seeing Henry as problematically repetitive on this front, we view him as a good teacher: he continues to try to explain something to his readers/students in as many ways and using as many examples as he can in the hopes that one of these attempts might click.

In all of his discussions of the Life/world distinction, Henry does three things. First, he presents classical phenomenology as not going far enough to move from world to Life (and thus despite its important contributions to the history of philosophy, it remains trapped in philosophy's self-enclosed framework). Second, he situates world as a matter of external appropriation and Life as affective self-relation that stands as the condition of all worldly manifestation. Third, he attempts to avoid misunderstanding by clarifying that Life is not to be confused with the focal content of biological study. As just one example of these repeated moves, consider the following from *Barbarism*:

> The life we are speaking about cannot be confused with the object of scientific knowledge, an object for which knowledge would be reserved to those who are in possession of it and who had to acquire it. Instead, it is something that everyone knows, as part of what we are. . . . Life feels and experiences itself in such a way that there is nothing in it that would be experienced or felt. This is because the fact of feeling oneself is really what makes one alive. . . . This is life not in the biological sense but in the true sense—*the absolute phenomenological life whose essence consists in the very fact of sensing or experiencing oneself and nothing else*—of what we will call subjectivity. (B, 6, emphasis in original)

In this passage, and many others (e.g., see MP, 2–3; IATT, 38), Henry's point is that only by going beyond the limits of modern science and traditional phenomenology can we hit upon the condition of truth, culture, and subjectivity: Life's auto-affectivity.

It is this persistent emphasis on the immanence of lived affect that truly distinguishes Henry's focus from other new phenomenological thinkers who also attempt to explore phenomenological limits by inquiring into that which exceeds, overflows, or saturates phenomenal experience. So, despite his rightful location as part of the new phenomenological trajectory with thinkers such as Levinas, Derrida, Chrétien, and Marion, Henry does not focus on that which constitutes selfhood in some sort of interruptive way whereby alterity is the key to pathos/affect (e.g., the other, the call, *différance*, etc.), but on that which constitutes selfhood in a maximally immanent way such that affect is always auto-affective and pathos is a self-relation of Life to Life.

At this point, given Henry's almost mystical-seeming account of the phenomenology of the invisible, it might seem quite sensible that the social theorists associated with the affective turn have not more deeply engaged his authorship. However, Henry does not stop with simply an account of the affectivity of life, but he goes on to explain how it is life that allows for a distinction between "flesh" and "body" such that selfhood is about much more than the socio-historical identity markers so often discussed within contemporary social and political theory. Let us turn, then, to the way in which Henry develops a theory of flesh that will open onto a notion of community and culture that might find more practical traction in contemporary social theory.

## Enfleshed Selfhood, the Pathetic Community, and Barbarism

Henry fully develops his notion of "flesh" in the context of his attempt to offer a "phenomenology of incarnation." However, the distinction between flesh and body is a presiding interest throughout Henry's authorship. As Karl Hefty notes in the translator's preface to *Incarnation*:

> In treating the question of flesh, [*Incarnation*] also returns full circle to an issue raised at the end of [Henry's] first book, *Philosophy and Phenomenology of the Body* . . . where he poses for the first time "the problem of incarnation." There the problem of incarnation and the problem of flesh come together in the question of finitude, and it is this question, one might say, that *Incarnation* develops most fully.[17]

Appreciating his abiding interest in embodiment is important for understanding that Henry's consideration of incarnation should not be reduced simply to a concern emerging within his philosophy of religion (though there are certainly aspects of it that he takes to be accessed in their richness only within a specifically Christian conception). Instead, making sense of embodiment, finitude, and our relations with others is central to his broader project of material phenomenology itself. As he notes, "incarnation concerns all living beings on earth since these are all incarnate beings" (INC, 3). Depending on the distinctions between world and life, Henry explains that we should not confuse "incarnate" with simple objective materiality accessible to empiricist theories of knowledge. Instead, "an abyss separates forever the material bodies that fill the universe, on the one hand, and the body of an 'incarnate' being such as man, on the other" (INC, 3). In contrast to an "inert body," then, incarnate beings feel themselves in their own affective subjectivity. They are defined not only by the *fact* of existence but also by the *experience* of living. Accordingly, Henry suggests that there are two sorts of bodies: those, like "our own, which feels itself at the same time it senses what surrounds it" and, alternatively, "the inert body of the universe" (INC, 4). To the first sort of body, Henry gives the name "flesh" and reserves the term "body" for the second sort.

Flesh is fundamentally alive in that it "is nothing other than what *feels itself, suffers itself, undergoes itself and bears itself, and thus enjoys itself according to impressions that are always reborn*" (INC, 4, emphasis in original). Notice here the stress on the *affective* dimension of flesh. Indeed, flesh is distinguished from body due to its affective feeling rather than objective being. As with the repeated claim that Life is not available for biological study, Henry rejects any worldly analysis of flesh such that scientific inquiry would make possible our knowledge of feeling as, itself, an embodied phenomenon:

> *The analysis of body can never become an analysis of our flesh*, or eventually its explanatory principle; rather, the contrary is true: Our flesh alone allows us to know, within the limits prescribed by this inescapable presupposition, something like a "body." (INC, 5; emphasis in original)

Flesh is the affective experience that makes knowledge of bodies possible. This realization is a crucial component for attending to the practical implications of Henry's philosophy. In his account of enfleshed feeling as the condition for embodied knowing, Henry provides the phenomenological conditions for embodied cognition and its relationship to such discourses as feminism, queer theory, or race theory. As just a few examples, we might say that Michèle Le Dœuff's account of "the sex of knowing," Linda Martín Alcoff's political approach to coherentist epistemology, and Elizabeth Grosz's appreciation of the dynamic interplay between bodies and knowledge are all possible only if flesh is not reducible simply to body.[18] Implicitly anticipating all of these various philosophical developments, Henry announces a "strange inversion" such that our flesh conditions our embodiment, rather than bodies being distinguished as flesh.

How, though, would we actually "know" anything about flesh itself as conditioning and animating our conception of bodies? Henry provides a striking example of what such incarnate knowledge might involve:

> The man who knows nothing, nothing but the hardship of all the suffering in his bruised flesh—the poor, and the "little ones"—probably knows much more than an omniscient mind situated at the end of the ideal development of science. (INC, 5)

Here we see Henry flip epistemic privilege on its head. In so doing, his account resonates with the contemporary idea in standpoint theory of approaching the world from the perspective of those "on the margins," the Hebraic idea that it is in relation to the "widow, the orphan, and the stranger" that God appears, and also the Christian conception that service to God happens in service to "the least of these." Accordingly, there is no graduate course that can replace the lived experience of one's own fleshed, that is, affective, body. As Henry profoundly states, we do not "first think in order then to live," but, instead, we live (and feel ourselves as flesh) in order then to think (INC, 93).

Underwriting the mistaken epistemic priorities of the modern world, Henry suggests, is the "pretension that a new technology that itself is scientific and material, and in itself foreign to the human, can furnish the true approach to humanity, and find man in the depth of his being, even in his pleasure, in the heart of his suffering or distress—of his life or death" (INC, 97). Modern science, and much of modern/post-modern philosophy, begins by understanding human existence as an externalized abstraction—a category of comparison, rather than a singularized experience of oneself. For Henry, to be flesh is to be affected first and foremost by one's own status as flesh. Only on the basis of the auto-affection of enfleshed living do we then bear witness to the "birth" of selfhood. Henry attempts to clarify this complicated move by explaining that "the flesh is thus not added to the self as a contingent and incomprehensible attribute," but, rather, "because the flesh is nothing other than the most interior possibility of our Self, it is a unitary Self" (INC, 124). We might say that, in something of a radicalization of Heidegger's notion of *Jemeinigkeit*, Henry locates flesh as what occasions subjectivity as the *principium individuationis* according to which concrete embodiment can then be understood (see MP, 121).

At this point, it can again seem like Henry has provided a robust theory of transcendental conditions at the cost of his account being detached from the realities of historical existence. Even if he is right that flesh is the condition of knowing bodies, it seems that somehow we need to translate that conditionality into instruction for how best then to live. Can affectivity stand as *a way of life*, rather than simply *a way of making sense* of the possibility of various ways of life? This question, and the worry it reflects, is not limited to Henry, but is a common critique of phenomenology. In the focus on "how" things appear, instead of on "what" appears, phenomenology can often seem to be so descriptively minded that it is of no normative good. And yet, almost anticipating this objection, Henry clarifies that "the Self thinks where it acts, where it desires, where it suffers, where it is a Self: in its flesh" (INC, 124). For Henry, the Self is always located, singularized, and we might even say, launched, into the world from its transcendental positionality as flesh. As affective, we are always already affected-by. We touch only insofar as we are also touched. Conditions and concrete reality are always two sides of the same lived coin.

One might object here that the idea of touching/being-touched is famously considered by Merleau-Ponty in ways that do not seem to require so many new phenomenological acrobatics. So, even if phenomenology is helpful for social theory, maybe Henry's phenomenology is just too far removed from embodied social existence. Although noting the important contributions made by Merleau-Ponty, Henry insists that unless we attend to the distinction between flesh and body, any consideration of touching/being-touched will occur at an inappropriate register. That is, it will run aground in what Henry terms a "naïve realism," rather than a robust appreciation of the literal invisibility of the most essential manifestation of lived affect. That I could even take myself up as a concrete "ego" and consider *my* hands as objects in the world, Henry contends, is always secondary to the auto-affection of Life that gives birth to my status as "self." In this way, I am touched before "I" could reflect on the phenomenon of touch as an historical occasion. Thus, Henry critically asks: "was Merleau-Ponty not duped by his prestigious writing to the point of replacing philosophical analysis with a system of metaphors?" (INC, 116).

Henry's view is that being flesh (i.e., an incarnate body) does not remove us from the world, but situates us within it as not determined by its logic, its significance, and its mode of knowing. In other words, even if Henry does not provide an instruction manual for how to live in the world, he offers something just as necessary, but significantly more basic: a defense of why our worldly existence matters. Embracing significance as an attribute of affective life, not of worldly objectivity, is a way of life with much to recommend it. To borrow from a biblical idea, Henry resituates concrete embodiment such that even though we are "in the world," as it were, "we are not of it" (see 1 Jn 2:15-17; see also Jn 17:14-16). Ultimately, Henry's concern with Life is not a speculative abstraction motivated by technical academic interests. Instead, his focus is a thoroughly *practical* investment grounded in the importance of resisting nihilism in the name of human cultural achievement.

The most thorough consideration that Henry gives of the consequences of not correctly understanding the world as always conditioned by living flesh occurs in his 1987 book, *Barbarism*. Therein, he offers both a sustained critique of the excesses of scientism due to its costs on human culture, and also an extended defense of the importance of concrete *humanistic* activity as culture preserving. Rather than ignoring culture as a merely "worldly" phenomenon, Henry suggests that culture simply *is* the "self-transformation of life, the movement by which it continually changes itself in order to arrive at higher forms of realization and completeness, in order to grow" (B, 5). This is an important admission because with this claim Henry forestalls any interpretation of his work as abstract or mystical. Life is not a concept, flesh is not merely a transcendental idea. Rather, living flesh expresses itself in culture. Culture is where Life happens in the world, but without thereby becoming simply a worldly object.

Henry's worry is that modern scientism has created a reductive notion of knowledge that not only forgets subjectivity but also erases it. In so doing, all flesh gets reduced to *mere* bodies. Interestingly, though, it is not just that the enfleshed self is eliminated, but also that the very condition for our being-touched-by (i.e., affected by) objects, rather than just comprehending them. Henry offers the example of a biology student to illustrate this point. In order for this student to be able to gain scientific knowledge, he/she must already possess the "knowledge that made possible the movements of the hands and the eyes, the act of getting up, climbing the stairs, drinking and eating, and resting," namely, the "knowledge of life" (B, 11). Far from science being the highest point of human knowing, if all knowledge is scientific, then humans (as mere bodies) would be unable to do science.

What remains for humanity in a world that is not conditioned by life, but defined by its erasure? Henry's answer is simple: "nothing" (B, 77). The result is what Henry terms "barbarism." This is a key realization in order to unpack the relevance of Henry's phenomenology for social praxis. Rather than culture being merely a distorting worldly overlay on enfleshed life, culture is what grows from living flesh. In this sense, then, there is no living except in a cultural framework. Henry does not ignore sociocultural realities, but, instead, offers a plea for how they are able to be maintained as life-giving. His description of phenomenological conditions thereby functions as a normative claim about human social action. Ethics, religion, and art are not merely possible activities for human bodies; rather, they are encouraged precisely due to their status as embodied manifestations of affective flesh.

Henry does not hesitate to extend his analysis to other domains of human cultural life, such as history, economics, and politics (see B, chapter 5; and especially CC); the distribution of media, technology, and information (see B, chapter 6); and even the university (see B, chapter 7).[19] But in every case, Henry fights hard against the assumptions of (post)modern society as informed by latent commitments to neoliberalism and late-market capitalism. Of particular note is the way that he challenges the notion that universities should be oriented toward getting students jobs (see B, 121–2). Always rejecting any reductive instrumentalism at the level of cultural production, Henry celebrates the fact that human embodiment in a social world matters because we are more than data for scientific or economic analysis. Because we are flesh, we are not simply biological organisms. Because we are affective, we are not simply workers. Instead, we study and work because the cultural "world" is already meaningful.

Crucially, Henry not only offers a theoretical account of the possibility of practical philosophy, but his philosophy also invites particular modes of human practice. His critique of capitalism and socialism, for example, is offered in the name of the human dignity and freedom that he sees as inherent in living (see CC). Specifically, his frustration with socialism and capitalism is that it replaces human flesh with conceptual abstractions. "Capitalism is thus," he writes, "eaten away by the same evil that led socialism to its ultimate demise: the elimination of subjective life and the living individual" (CC 10). Henry's consistent recommendation for human praxis is that we maintain the *humanity* opened by incarnation.

Humanity is never able to sustain itself in separation, however. Remember, the truth of the world is ek-static distance, but the truth of Life is radical relationship: to touch and be touched by. Despite being radically singularized in one's own living, singularity occurs in what Henry terms "community." In *Material Phenomenology*, Henry develops this line of thought by suggesting that in its essence, *pathos is always pathos-with*. "To the extent that the subjectivity of life constitutes the essence of the community," Henry explains, "the subjectivity of life is precisely a community, not only of life but also a potential group of the living" (MP, 121). The "pathetic community" of living individuals is never a space where individuals are erased into some larger collective, but, instead, where they are able to continuously signify as singular, affective, enfleshed beings. Communities are defined by something shared in common. For Henry, the shared commonality of the pathetic community is the affectivity of life itself.

Nonetheless, this notion of a pathetic community is likely still too abstract to be of much interest to the social theoretic focus of contemporary affect theory. Henry himself worries about such abstraction: "One will say that our example, as hackneyed as it may be today, is an extreme case. We have sought to conceive the human community outside of the world, as if it were not a community of human beings in the world" (MP, 128). In conceiving the community in this way, "do we not place ourselves on the level of an abstraction?" Henry asks (MP, 128). In short, Henry worries that he may be guilty of the very thing with which he charged socialism and capitalism. In response, though, Henry claims that the world that gets rejected by the idea of the pathetic community is simply the "world" that is already defined by abstraction, by representation, by objectivist reductionism, and by scientific totalization. It is not an abstraction to reject a mistaken conception of the real world. As he has already argued, "reality" is possible only in relation to life, and so if we are genuinely interested in real lived communal praxis, we must refuse the temptation to replace *being affected* with the *study of affect*, and the *lived participation* in community with a sociological *theory of groups*. As he explains:

> This pathetic community does not exclude the world but only the abstract world, which is to say, the world that does not exist and has put subjectivity out of play. But community does include the real world—the cosmos—for which every element—form, color, and so forth—exists ultimately as auto-affective. That is to say, it exists in and through this pathetic community. (MP, 134)

In the end, of course, we should engage in sociological, psychological, biological, and philosophical studies, but such practice is possible only if we are not simply bodies. The ultimate goal is, then, not to *know* about affect, but to *live affectively*; not just to *understand* communities, but to *be-in-community*; not simply to *criticize* culture, but to be *culture creators*. Existing as flesh is not just a phenomenological postulate, but a cultural mode of existing. With his notion of the pathetic community, Henry suggests that *affectivity is not just a reminder to live fully, but actually stands as a particular way of life.*

Given our account of the relevance of Henry's philosophy to practical concerns, it might seem even stranger that his work has not been engaged by contemporary social theory in light of the affective turn. In the next section, we will offer just one possible example of how such engagement might be fostered. By looking at Sara Ahmed's account of affective economies, we will contend that profound spaces can be opened for understanding how we might begin to fill in the affective way of life that Henry recommends.

## Sara Ahmed, Affective Economies, and Embodied Engagement

If affectivity is, as Henry suggests, the mode in which life immediately and unceasingly experiences itself as interpolated, and thus embodied, in the world, then a pressing *social* concern arises: even if Life is what matters to flesh, we live out our enfleshed status as bodies *in* the world. The world, as manifest in the pathetic ipseity Henry describes, is a world of embodied intersubjectivity where selfhood is never fully exhausted in the descriptions adequate to subject-object categories. Although Henry's focus on phenomenal excess is rightly located as consistent with the general trends of new phenomenology,[20] the disruption of rationalistic and psychologizing logics on display in his account again speaks to the proximity between his thought and contemporary affect studies.[21] In particular, as we have seen, Henry's theory of enfleshed auto-affection demonstrates that social life can be radicalized such that the pathetic community announces a sociality built upon the "commonality" of permeable individuals—selves are thus in relation because they are *un*contained.

Yet, despite the potential of Henry's theory, it is not immediately clear how we should go about offering phenomenological accounts of sociality without the traditionally distinct boundaries, whether phenomenological or empirical, between subjects and the objects toward which they are oriented. It is here that we find Sara Ahmed's work on affectivity, specifically her project in *The Cultural Politics of Emotion*, to stand as an important resource for thinking through Henry's practical philosophy. In order to explore what an engagement between the two might yield, we will give just a brief summary of Ahmed's philosophical project, which positions us to consider its promise not simply for Henry's *theory* of life, but also for *living* in light of Henry's theory.

First, it is useful to highlight where Ahmed's phenomenological projects intersect with Henry's. For both thinkers, a crucial aspect of phenomenology's method of reflective analysis involves the critical awareness that reflection itself can cover over the production of its own phenomenality—the "how" of the appearance of the transcendental structures that classical phenomenology attempts to elucidate. In similar fashion, both Henry and Ahmed appropriate critical perspectives within their phenomenological frameworks. In fact, it is Ahmed's critical attention toward truth's emergence as socio-historically produced that has situated readings of her work within the emerging field of critical phenomenology, which, as Lisa Guenther explains, indicates an approach that "goes beyond classical phenomenology by reflecting on the quasi-transcendental structures that make our experience of the world possible and meaningful."[22] If classical phenomenology can be said to be a preoccupation with *a priori* structures of transcendental consciousness, then the "critical" signifies a "reflexivity" that attends to the "structural conditions of its own emergence" that reveal an "imperative to describe what it sees in order to see it anew."[23] So, critical phenomenology is essentially *practical* insofar as it takes up and describes contingent historical structures that shape embodied and differentiated experience so that these "quasi-transcendental" structures might be critically deconstructed, denaturalized, revised, and lived otherwise. It is simultaneously a revelatory reflex that illuminates normal structures that dominate subjective experience and also a "political practice"[24] for transforming them.

In general, scholars situate Ahmed's *Queer Phenomenology: Orientations, Objects, Others* (2006) within this critical phenomenological approach as an important resource for thinking through the production of racialized bodies, heteronormativity, queer orientations as effects of social nonconformity, and ontological expansiveness as a white, spatial privilege.[25] It makes sense to see her work in this way because Ahmed contends that embodied orientations are never neutral givens, but, instead, result from and reinforce certain normal ways of orientating toward others such that the possibility of queerness, for example, results from such normalization of "straight" orientations. In so doing, Ahmed questions the viability of embodied orientation, itself, as a phenomenological concept—whether an object becomes available for a subject is not merely a matter for a generic consciousness but can also reveal the material conditions that enable subjects to inhabit orientations as products of discursive histories.

Ahmed's specific project in *The Cultural Politics of Emotion* can be read within this context of a critical phenomenology—asking after the conditions of how *affectivity* resonates as a primary phenomenality of intersubjective life. In brief, Ahmed aims to "explore how emotions work *to shape the 'surfaces' of individual and collective bodies.*"[26] Displaying a marked difference with Henry's new phenomenological focus on transcendental phenomenality, Ahmed considers emotions and affects as forms of social and cultural practice. As such, she is critical of theories that would suggest models of emotions as psychological or transmittable states. Instead, Ahmed develops her own formal account of affectivity. She explicitly turns away from the substantial question regarding what affects[27] *are* and, instead, attempts to determine what they *do*—specifically insofar as they produce and reproduce subjective orientations that we might refer to as "affectively charged" or imbued with affective value.

Given this inherent emphasis on affective praxis, Ahmed develops what she terms "*affective economies*," or the structural circulation of affects in social life. The framework describes how different emotions involve "affective forms of reorientation"—for example, economies of love, pain, shame, hate, and fear all involve specific, affective transactions that materialize differentiated subject-positions.[28] Ultimately, Ahmed's claim is stronger than merely the suggestion that affects are the results of intersubjective social transactions. She argues that emotions and affective orientations reside in the contact between "surfaces" such that the very interactions themselves show up in affective relations/interactions. Revealing her own broadly (quasi)transcendental orientation, Ahmed identifies affect as a fundamental ontological condition of social experience—it makes surfaces/boundaries/bodies possible as recognizable within a frame of embodied meaning. As a result, the political saliencies of affective economies become an important theme and site of critical apprehension throughout *The Cultural Politics of Emotion*.

Ahmed develops her model as analogous to economic circulation of capital because it expresses the locomotion of affects contra a reifying theory of affectivity. Affects are never stable, but, instead, are affective, in the first place, insofar as they occur in relations that are inherently dynamic—socially and physically. Ahmed thus recognizes that affects work as a form of capital. They do not, however, "reside positively in the sign or commodity," but circulate as a result of the movement of cultural signs and objects.[29] Nonetheless, seemingly wary of a reductionism similar to that about which Henry worries, she denies that such emotions are objective "things" with property-like characteristics that originate from individuals. She stresses, instead, that emotions "create the very effect of the surfaces of boundaries that allow us to distinguish an inside and an outside in the first place."[30] Thus, although framed differently than Henry, Ahmed also seems to appreciate that historical reality consists in the enactment of affective flesh, not in the random contact between mere bodies.

Accordingly, the implications of Ahmed's account are particularly rich for a sustained phenomenological consideration of lived existence after Henry. In particular, Henry's enfleshed pathetic community that serves as the condition for shared embodied experience can be helpfully supplemented by Ahmed's treatment of impression and orientation as *auto-impression*. Ahmed posits that in our orientations to objects, we engage in an act of reading or recognition. That reading both impresses a meaning, judgment, or significance on the object, while simultaneously, it affectively "presses" upon us. Impression does the work of aligning significance to objects because those objects become experienced as *felt*. With Henry, Ahmed positions feeling prior to knowledge, but then thinks through the social implications of such priority. Affects produce bodies at the level of a social designation whereby the felt impressions of others and self work to reinforce the recognizable and usually invisible mechanisms of discursive formation—this *white* body, this *Black* body, this *queer* subject, and so on.

It is no wonder, then, that Ahmed notes that orientations do not occur in vacuums, but are, instead, the results of social evaluations that have already taken shape over time—sedimenting[31] different kinds of bodies with value that becomes fixed through social encounters. Not content merely to remain at the level of description, Ahmed unpacks the normative implications of such a structure:

> If bodies do not arrive in neutral, if we are always in some way or another moody, then what we will receive as an impression will depend on our affective situation ... how we arrive, how we enter this room or that room, will affect what impressions we receive. To receive is to act. To receive an impression is to make an impression.[32]

For Ahmed and Henry alike, being affectively situated is a matter of never being able to remove life from one's experience in the world. Jointly their work illustrates that to *experience*—to have an orientation as constitutive of embodied identity—is always and already to live in the world while still resisting its reductive logic.

Further, Ahmed allows us to see how embodied orientations are both the by-products of an exchange and also, and more importantly, the modes by which the exchange is first felt or experienced—in other words, *affectively known*. "Situations are affectively given," she suggests, "in the gap between the impressions we have of others *and the impressions we make on others, all of which are lively*."[33] To suffer an emotion—to be affected in some form or another *by* another is to be oriented in such a way that the orientation is already a matter of "how" others appear in, and experience, the social world. It is not the case, however, that orientations are naturalistic attitudes that are neutral in their intentions. Rather, orientation describes what "comes into view" only insofar as I am affectively invested in what becomes "reachable" for my gaze and my touch.[34]

The conflation of "seeing" and "feeling," in her account, is not accidental or ambiguous, but, rather, stands as the pivotal crux of what it means to privilege affectivity as situated in a social context (i.e., as an embodied experience). Indeed, Ahmed strikingly admits: "I begin . . . with the messiness of the experiential, the unfolding of bodies into worlds."[35] If Ahmed is correct to position affects in this way (starting from the truth of emotional *orientations* rather than selves that happen to externalize or internalize affects), then what follows is the possibility for a far more practical account of the pathetic community than is often acknowledged by Henry, but that remains, nonetheless, consistent with his account in important ways. Importantly, though, we should note that Ahmed would certainly not see the pathetic community as some sort of ideal toward which we should strive. Instead, it would be the political site in which we become better attuned toward the denaturalization of bodies as fixed in discursive categories of difference where some bodies are more dynamically empowered and others are more sedimented by becoming objects of hate and disgust. As such, she helps to remind us that the pathetic community can, itself, be responsible for negative circulations concerning the way in which bodies are oriented, affectively constituted, and then seek to navigate historically operative social structures. This caution notwithstanding, when we read Henry alongside Ahmed, we can better understand how Henry's theory of affect requires that affective bodies (i.e., flesh) show up *as social phenomena*. Accordingly, for both Ahmed and Henry, we should turn away from any understanding of affect and emotion as physiological or psychological "things" in order to return to a concern with *how* auto-impressions *do* us as embodied individuals. In this way, the distinction of Life and world is itself something that not only conditions selfhood but also makes possible *living* social selves who exist in, and are impressed by, affective economies.

## Conclusion: Affectivity and Social Practice

The way of life called for by Henry and filled in by Ahmed is one in which we turn away from all complacency. By attending to affective economies, we can better understand how the pathetic community is a call to action in light of social failures and phenomenological forgetfulness. For Ahmed and Henry, the first step in changing the "world" is being able to *see* it for what it is. This shift in perspective is not simply about appreciating the phenomenological method, but also about investing oneself in what we might term an *affective optics*. As Henry so rightly suggests in the passage we used at the beginning of this chapter, "things differ entirely depending on whether they are immersed in the pathos of life in which they never see themselves, or whether they are held in front of a regard" (MP, 6). When we begin to see others as not body-objects but as living flesh, we are better able to see culture as worthy of social protection and subjective energy. Here, Henry scholars can benefit from a deeper appreciation of the transformative impacts on social existence discussed by Ahmed, Hardt, Protevi, and Clough, on the one hand, and affective social theorists can enrich their account by better accounting for the phenomenological conditions that make such transformations occur at the level of human meaning, on the other hand.

Our aim in this chapter has not been to settle the existing debates in affect theory, but simply to demonstrate that the "affective turn" is well advised to draw on the resources available in new phenomenology—as specifically offered by Michel Henry. Despite the frequent difficulty of his authorship, Henry's work on the pathos of Life, when held up to our "regard," challenges us to see things differently and then to live accordingly. In the end, when read together, Henry and Ahmed demonstrate the ways that *lived affectivity* can *effect* social transformation.

## Notes

1 Michael Hardt, "Forward," in *The Affective Turn: Theorizing the Social*, ed. P. T. Clough with J. Halley (Durham: Duke University Press, 2007), ix–xiii, ix.
2 Ibid., ix.
3 Ibid., ix–x.
4 Ibid., x.
5 Ibid., xii.
6 Patricia T. Clough, "Introduction," in *The Affective Turn: Theorizing the Social*, ed. P. T. Clough with J. Halley, (Durham: Duke University Press, 2007), 1–33, 1.
7 Ibid., 1.
8 Ibid., 2.
9 Ibid., 2.
10 Ibid., 3.
11 J. Protevi, *Political Affect: Connecting the Social and the Somatic* (Minneapolis: University of Minnesota Press, 2009), xi.
12 Ibid, xii. Similarly, Paul Hoggett and Simon Thompson appeal to such thinkers as Nietzsche, Bergson, Scheler, Deleuze, and Guattari as offering the key philosophical

insights for the new developments in affect theory ("Introduction," in *Politics and the Emotions: The Affective Turn in Contemporary Political Studies*, ed. P. Hoggett and S. Thompson (London: Continuum, 2012), 1–20.

13  Ibid., 2–3.
14  Ibid., 3.
15  Ibid., 3.
16  See J. Aaron Simmons and Bruce Benson, *The New Phenomenology: A Philosophical Introduction* (London: Bloomsbury, 2013).
17  K. Hefty, "Translator's Preface," xiv in INC.
18  See M. La Doeuff, *The Sex of Knowing*, trans. Kathryn Hamer and Lorraine Code (London and New York: Routledge, 2003); L. M. Alcoff, *Real Knowing: New Versions of the Coherence Theory* (Ithaca: Cornell University Press, 1996); E. Groz, *Volatile Bodies: Towards a Corporeal Feminism* (Bloomington: Indiana University Press, 1994).
19  For more on Henry and the social implications of such notions, see J. Aaron Simmons and Brandon Inabinet, "Retooling the Discourse of Objectivity: Epistemic Postmodernism as Shared Public Life," *Public Culture* 30, no. 2 (2018): 221–43; J. Aaron Simmons and David Scott, "How to Recover from Barbarism: Michel Henry and the Future of the Humanities," *Pli: The Warwick Journal of Philosophy* 28 (2017): 1–31.
20  See Simmons and Benson, *The New Phenomenology*.
21  As just a few examples of such disruptive attempts within affect theory, see Grosz, *Volatile Bodies Toward a Corporeal Feminism*; Teresa Brennan, *The Transmission of Affect* (Ithaca: Cornell University Press, 2004), and Sara Ahmed, *The Cultural Politics of Emotion* (New York: Routledge, 2015).
22  Lisa Guenther, "Critical Phenomenology," in *50 Concepts for a Critical Phenomenology*, ed. Gail Weiss, Ann V. Murphy, and Gayle Salamon (Evanston, IL: Northwestern University Press, 2020), 11–16, 15.
23  Gayle Salamon, "What's Critical About Critical Phenomenology?" *Puncta: Journal of Critical Phenomenology* 1, no. 1 (2018): 12.
24  Guenther, "Critical Phenomenology," 15.
25  See for example, George Yancy, "Confiscated Bodies," in *50 Concepts for a Critical Phenomenology*, ed. Gail Weiss, Ann V. Murphy, and Gayle Salamon, (Evanston, IL: Northwestern University Press, 2020), 69–75; Megan Burke, "Heteronormativity," in *50 Concepts*, 161–7; Lauren Guilmette, "Queer Orientations," in *50 Concepts*, 275–81; Shannon Sullivan, "Ontological Expansiveness," in *50 Concepts*, 249–54.
26  Ahmed, *Cultural Politics of Emotion*, 1, emphasis added.
27  Ahmed's *Cultural Politics of Emotions* treats both concepts (viz., emotion and affect) as qualitatively indistinguishable in impressionable experience. Accordingly, she conflates the terms in order to avoid an arbitrary need to treat the phenomenological experience of each as categorically distinct.

28  Ahmed, *Cultural Politics of Emotions*, 8.
29  Ibid., 45.
30  Ibid., 10.
31  Importantly, Ahmed alludes to Husserl and also Merleau-Ponty's descriptions of *bodily* horizons as "sedimented histories" (Sara Ahmed, "Orientations Matter," in *New Materialisms: Ontology, Agency, and Politics*, ed. D. Coole and S. Frost (Durham and London: Duke University Press), 234–57, 246. Moreover, Ahmed discusses how repetitive bodily action materializes sedimented orientations toward objects. As such, it is worth considering how bodies undergo a palimpsest of experiences—*auto*-affection as an *auto*-pilot of impressionistic tendencies over time.
32  Ahmed, "Orientations Matter," 40.
33  Ibid., 241; emphasis added.
34  Ibid., 245.
35  Sara Ahmed, *The Promise of Happiness* (Durham: Duke University Press, 2010), 22.

# Index

Adler, Pierre   31
Ahmed, Sara   181, 193–9
Aristotle   13, 144
Arnold, Mathew   144

Bell, Daniel   135

Carr, David   151

de Biran, Main   88
Deenan, Patrick   6, 131–4
Descartes, Rene   94–6, 114, 131, 173–4

fascism/fascist   68, 125, 127–31, 133–9
Frase, Peter   27
Freud, Sigmund   45, 88–105
Friere, Paulo   150–1, 153

Hardt, Michael   27, 39, 181–3, 198
Hegel, G.W.F.   10–11, 15, 90, 97
Heidegger, Martin   3, 99–100, 112, 174–5, 184, 188
Hobbes, Thomas   131
Hochschild, Arlie Russell   27
Husserl, Edmund   9, 30, 46–51, 54–5, 59, 96, 102, 104, 160–5, 173, 184

Kandinsky, Wassily   45, 60, 81, 88, 110, 113, 159–77
Kierkegaard, Søren   98–100

Lacan, Jacques   90–2, 97–8, 100–1, 105
Lilla, Mark   137

Maeterlinck, Maurice   162
Marcuse, Herbert   6, 126, 136
Marx, Karl or Marxism   2, 4–5, 10–16, 21–3, 27–41, 45, 60, 66, 68–70, 73, 80–1, 88, 127–30

Nozick, Robert   6, 132–3

Ortega y Gasset, Jose   144–5

Plato   104
Postman, Neil   152

Ricoeur, Paul   5, 22, 27–41
Rilke, Rainer Maria   117

Sanders, Bernie   127
Sartre, Jean-Paul   91, 101
Skinner, B. F.   151
Spinoza   94, 181–2

von Bomml, Bas   146–7

Watson, John   151

Žižek, Slavoj   90